T0358133

Australian GEOGRAPHIC

YOUR LIFE
YOUR PLANET

WHAT YOU CAN DO RIGHT NOW!

GEOFF EBBS

WOODSLANE
PRESS

Woodslane Press Pty Ltd

10 Apollo Street

Warriewood, NSW 2102

Email: info@woodslane.com.au

Tel: 02 8445 2300 Website: www.woodslane.com.au

First published in Australia in 2021 by Woodslane Press

© 2021 Woodslane Press, text and images © 2021 Geoff Ebbs or as indicated

This work is copyright. All rights reserved. Apart from any fair dealing for the purposes of study, research or review, as permitted under Australian copyright law, no part of this publication may be reproduced, distributed, or transmitted in any other form or by any means, including photocopying, recording, or other electronic or mechanical methods, without the prior written permission of the publisher. For permission requests, write to the publisher, addressed "Attention: Permissions Coordinator", at the address above.

The information in this publication is based upon the current state of commercial and industry practice and the general circumstances as at the date of publication. Every effort has been made to obtain permissions relating to information reproduced in this publication. The publisher makes no representations as to the accuracy, reliability or completeness of the information contained in this publication. To the extent permitted by law, the publisher excludes all conditions, warranties and other obligations in relation to the supply of this publication and otherwise limits its liability to the recommended retail price. In no circumstances will the publisher be liable to any third party for any consequential loss or damage suffered by any person resulting in any way from the use or reliance on this publication or any part of it. Any opinions and advice contained in the publication are offered solely in pursuance of the author's and publisher's intention to provide information, and have not been specifically sought.

 A catalogue record for this book is available from the National Library of Australia

Cover design: Luke Harris

Book design: Christine Schiedel

Printed on sustainably sourced paper

Photo by Bill Oxford on Unsplash

Australian GEOGRAPHIC

YOUR LIFE
YOUR PLANET

WHAT YOU CAN DO RIGHT NOW!

CON

1 LIVING ROOM 6

1. An empty room does not need a light 10
2. Turn down the air-con 12

We need to talk about … 14

3. Those packaged drinks 16
4. The snacks I love 18
5. Paying it forward 20
6. Indoor plants 22
7. Our high-speed lives 24
8. Buy green power 26
9. Control the airflow 28
10. Ordering in food 30
11. A no-spend day 32
12. The nature of time 34
13. Our alcohol consumption 36

Plan ahead 38

14. Meet your heater 40
15. Get a better light 42
16. Insulate your home 44
17. Get active in your community 46
Enter the app watchers 48
18. Hire a human 50
19. That doggy in the window 52
20. Invest ethically 54

2 BATHROOM, TOILET & LAUNDRY 56

21. Take a shorter shower 60
22. Lighten the laundry load 62
23. Recycled toilet paper 64
24. If it's yellow let it mellow 65

We need to talk about … 66

25. Those dripping taps 68
26. Essential oils 70
27. Home spun hair care 72
28. Lotions and potions 74

Enter the industrial chemist 76
29. That toxic detergent 78
30. Oil and vinegar 80

Look ahead a little 82

31. Process greywater 84
32. Solar hot water 86

3 BEDROOM 88

33. Put down the phone 92
34. What the cat does each night 94
35. The standby lightshow 96
36. A stitch in time 97

We need to talk about … 98

37. Fast fashion 100
Enter the designers 102
38. Secondhand clothes 104
39. Quality and comfort 106
40. Hemp and bamboo 108
41. Make it. Don't buy it 110

4 KITCHEN 112

42. Half fill the kettle 116
43. Turn off the dishwasher 117
44. Pause before breakfast 118

We need to talk about … 120

45. What's on the label 122
46. Where the herbs grow 124
47. Mung beans and love 126
48. Things we eat for lunch 128
49. What's wrong with the supermarket 130
50. Eating better meat 132
51. The power of the bean 134
Enter the vegans 136
52. A vegan lifestyle 138

Photo by Simon Maisch on Unsplash

TENTS

53. Feeding friends 140
54. Baking bread 142
55. Energy efficient appliances 144
56. The packaging we purchase 146
57. Silicon and beyond 148

Plan ahead **150**
58. Salt and sugar 152
59. Smoke your own 154
Enter the fermentiers 156
60. Things that grow in the dark 158
61. Things that grow in bottles 160

5 GARAGE **162**
62. Shank's pony 166
63. Drive like a smoothie 168

We need to talk about … **170**
64. Zombie apocalypse kits 172
65. The problem with recycling 174
Enter the recyclers 176
66. Holding a garage sale 178
67. Shop locally 180
68. The hidden treasure 182
69. Borrow the power tools 184
Enter the librarians 186
70. Repair café 188
71. Use public transport 190
72. Buying a bicycle 192
73. Cycle to work 194
74. Sharing the car 196

Plan ahead **198**
75. Embrace embodied energy 200
76. Buy good wood 202
77. Generate your own power 204
Enter the electricity advocates 206
78. Alternative fuels 208

6 OUTSIDE **210**
79. Take only photos, leave only footprints 214
80. Be a sticky beak 215
81. Let's water carefully 216
82. The dog walks with you 218

We need to talk about … **220**
83. Going on a picnic 222
84. Barbecue fuel 224
85. Your inner pyromaniac 226
86. Getting fed without giving a fig 228
87. Food that grows on trees 230
88. Nature on the strip 232
89. Planting a local 234
90. Handmade watering systems 236
91. Where babies come from 238
92. The dinosaur family 240
93. Feeding the chooks 242
94. Helping out nature 244
95. Our community garden 246

Plan ahead **248**
96. Fertilise naturally 250
97. Don't fence me in 252
Enter the apiarists 254
98. Host a hive of bees 256
99. Put some water in your tank 258
100. Double glaze 260
101. Intelligent design 262

ANTIKYTHERA **264**
Glossary 266
Ready reckoner 270
Personal carbon target 276
Personal water target 279
Work-environment-life balance 280

Acknowledgements

A vibrant team of eco-warriors and communicators birthed this book.

Huge thanks go to Alette Nalder, queen of the reviewers, who collected comments and co-wrote large slabs from her tiny house while also running her sustainable cleaning business. To the team of reviewers, text wranglers and fact checkers: Marcela Ramirez, Wolfgang Kessler, Henrietta Ebbs, Tallulah Ebbs, Claire Tracey, Rhiaan Leckie, Lisa and Malcolm Mackenzie. Thanks for slaving away in a damp cave over winter for a few mouldy breadcrumbs as we sought the first glimpse of spring and a complete manuscript.

I cannot thank enough the experts who provided valuable input, new ideas and salient facts. Some of them feature prominently in this book and on the website, YLYP.news; some of them are mentioned in passing. Their knowledge and experience is broad and deep, and I have simplified and summarised it in ways they may not appreciate. All omissions and errors are mine so, if you know better, sympathise with them and save your ire for me.

Finally, the publishing teams at Ebono Institute, Woodslane Press and Australian Geographic who launched the project and provided the wherewithal to make it possible. Editor Maryanne Philips has worked alongside me for 35 years. Publisher Andrew Swaffer's patience and diplomacy nursed us all through many dangerous shoals, designer Christine Schiedel made this book a thing of beauty, and impresario David Scott published my first book in 1993 and has believed in me ever since.

Without all of you, these would just be the scratchings of a life-long tech-nerd and environmentalist who dreamed of a gentler world but was never sure how to realise it.

Hopefully our combined effort will help you, dear Reader, take a step in that direction.

Gaia knows we need it.

INTRODUCTION

The accumulated impact of billions of resource-hungry humans on the natural systems that support us seriously disrupts our daily life.

Extreme weather now regularly wreaks havoc in every corner of planet earth. Unprecedented heat caused catastrophic bushfires that ravaged eastern Australia and killed 34 people as the new year of 2020 rolled around.

More dramatic events unfolded as the year progressed. The Covid19 pandemic is a stark reminder of how vulnerable our social systems are to the harsh realities of nature.

Our global economy is extremely fragile, depending on the cooperation and coordination of many different systems in many different nations, all working in harmony to keep things running smoothly.

The future is very uncertain.

The **carbon dioxide** that we produce when we run machinery, use electricity, grow food or travel is heating the oceans and the atmosphere. Global heating causes chaos in climate systems, sea levels to rise and sea water to become acidic.

The planet has a fever of one-and-a-half degrees above the last few millennia and the rapidity of the change is causing extreme stress to many ecosystems and some human environments.

Introduction

The cheap energy that we rely on to manufacture low-cost goods, generate a comfortable and convenient lifestyle, and make travel simple and affordable, is proving to have hidden costs and long-term impacts.

New forms of energy are more difficult to extract than the petroleum oil that fuelled the last century of growth.

The economic growth that we have grown up (see related image, this page) with relies on cheap energy, population growth, increased consumption, and the exploitation of people and resources. It cannot be sustained.

Advanced economies, like Japan's, have learned to live with limited growth to maintain their preferred lifestyle.

We, too, are finding different ways to live. We are learning to live more lightly on our planet. It's the only home we have.

The good news is that we have practical solutions to deal with most of these changes. Technical innovations provide more sustainable ways to live, every day. The real challenges are in our attitudes and behaviour.

We will have to give up some convenience and forgo a few luxuries. We will probably travel shorter distances and throw things out less often. It is likely that we will spend more time at home and less at work.

That's not bad news, though. It also means that we have more time to spend with our loved ones, that we better nurture our creativity and our relationships, and that we can build stronger and more resilient communities to help us thrive in uncertain times.

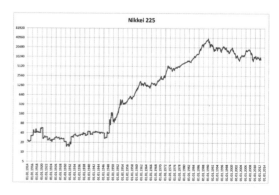

How to use the book

This book contains 101 tips to help you build a better future. They are grouped into quick tips that let you fix something straight away without having to think too hard or spend any money, things that you need to talk about before you launch into them and bigger challenges that require you to plan ahead.

LET'S FIX IT

These tips are simple steps that you can take with next to no effort, straight away. They are at the beginning of each chapter headed, *Let's fix it*.

These things generally do not make a huge impact on their own. Their main value is in changing your habits and raising your awareness of your impact on the environment.

WE NEED TO TALK ABOUT ...

... the impact of our lifestyle. Many tips are easy to do but require you to buy something different or plan and coordinate with the other members of your household. The section *We need to talk about* ... in each chapter also deals with changes to our behaviour that might be quite challenging.

PLAN AHEAD

Then there's the big stuff. Insulating the house, installing solar hot water, deciding what to do when your current transport hits its use-by date. These *Plan ahead* sections need some serious thought. You will probably want to budget them, prioritise them and work towards them.

Finding stuff in this book

Website addresses like yourlifeyourplanet.news are underlined. The *Look it up* section in each tip gives #hashtags, <search terms> and web addresses without any text decoration. Each tip also points to other tips that extend or complement the one you are reading under the heading *Now try this!*

The tips are organised into different areas of your house.

Whether you live in a studio apartment or a 19-room mansion you'll be able to navigate the tips by the activities you do every day. It will not exactly match your house because

I have taken some liberties. I put all the wet areas together in the chapter called *Bathroom, Toilet & Laundry,* for example.

You can easily scan all the tips using the table of contents, on pages iv-v, or you can browse at random and follow the pointers that take your interest.

Of course, you can let a search engine do its work and head over to ylyp.news to find out more about anything contained in these pages. We'd love to see you there and know more about how you are thriving in these challenging times by nurturing your life and your planet.

Your Personal carbon target

It's one thing to have a bunch of bright ideas, the real challenge is putting them into practice. That's why we measure the tips against infographics such as your **Personal carbon target**. (Words in **bold** are defined and discussed in the Glossary.)

The body of the target represents the carbon footprint of individual humans in different countries. The numbers given are in kilograms per day for particular countries. The average Australian, for example, emits 46 kilograms of CO_2 per day, about the same as someone in the USA, nearly four times as much as the average Thai, and 15 times as much as the average Tongan.

Let that sink in for just a moment.

Your personal target is the area in the line just outside Tonga. That is 5.5 kilograms of CO_2 or its equivalent (CO_2e) every day. That is two tonnes per year — we are aiming for a **two-tonne lifestyle**. If we all reduced our emissions to one eighth of what they are now, we would be able to keep temperatures at around the present level, which is already pretty hot.

Now let that sink in.

Where this gets really interesting is when we show the impact of a specific tip as a hole in the target. If you stopped throwing away clothes, for example, the polyester you take out of production would remove about 0.8 kilograms of CO_2e each day, shown here as a star burst hole in Australia's emissions.

There are two sobering facts that this makes obvious.

1. You can see at a glance that we need to make a lot of these holes to get our emissions down to an appropriate level. About 50 equivalent actions, in fact.

2. Just the polyester in the clothes thrown away by the average Australian pumps about as much carbon dioxide into the atmosphere as the average Kenyan or Nigerian does with all their activities. Your shirts are more polluting than their entire life.

Other infographics are introduced in the relevant chapters. The **Personal water target** makes its first appearance in Chapter 2, *Bathroom, Toilet & Laundry*, and the **Work-environment-life balance (WELB)** appears in Chapter 3, *Bedroom*.

CARBON DIOXIDE AND ITS EQUIVALENT

Living things contain carbon. When we burn wood, or alcohol or coal (fossilised plants) the carbon combines with oxygen to create carbon dioxide (CO_2). That carbon dioxide forms a blanket around the earth that works like the glass in a greenhouse. It lets sunlight in, but traps the heat generated when that sunlight is reflected.

Carbon dioxide is not the only greenhouse gas. When you burp, the digestive gases in your stomach contain methane, which is carbon and hydrogen. Methane is produced by digestion. The bacteria in a cow's stomach, a swamp, a sewage treatment plant, or rubbish dump full of waste material produce methane as they digest the carbon-based organic matter that was once living things.

So, burning or breathing produces carbon dioxide, digestion produces methane.

Luckily methane is a very useful gas. We burn it every time we turn on the gas stove. What we call natural gas is methane trapped in the earth when ancient plants were fossilised. Biogas is the name we use for methane captured from rotting material and used for transport, heating and cooking.

When we burn methane, the energy of the fire is generated by separating its carbon and hydrogen atoms and combining them with oxygen to produce water and carbon dioxide. That is the great cycle of life. Plants capture sunlight to convert water and carbon dioxide into carbohydrates, while fire and living things use that captured energy by

digesting the plants and releasing water and carbon dioxide.

Both methane and carbon dioxide have a greenhouse effect, but the effect of methane on global warming is 25 times more powerful than carbon dioxide. In terms of global heating, one tonne of methane is the equivalent of 25 tonnes of carbon dioxide.

In conversation, and throughout this book, we often talk about greenhouse gas and carbon dioxide as if they are the same thing. What we are really talking about is the amount of warming that would be caused by the equivalent amount of carbon dioxide. So if we produced five tonnes of carbon dioxide and one tonne of methane we would say we have generated the equivalent of 30 tonnes of carbon dioxide in greenhouse gases, abbreviated to 30t CO_2e.

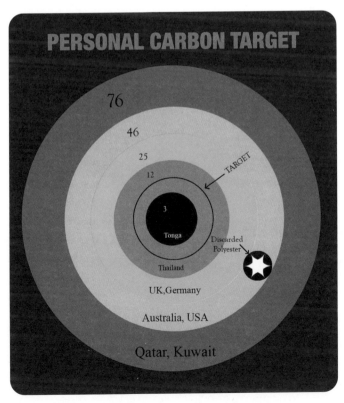

PERSONAL CARBON TARGET

76

46

25

12

3

Tonga

TARGET

Discarded Polyester

Thailand

UK, Germany

Australia, USA

Qatar, Kuwait

Let's fix it

Save energy at the
touch of a button

1. An empty room does
not need a light
2. Turn down the air-con

We need to
talk about …

… the effect our choices have on the environment

3. Those packaged drinks

4. The snacks I love

5. Paying it forward

6. Indoor plants

7. Our high-speed lives

8. Buy green power

9. Control the airflow

10. Ordering in food

11. A no-spend day

12. The nature of time

13. Our alcohol consumption

Plan ahead

Invest in the future of your life
and your planet

14. Meet your heater

15. Get a better light

16. Insulate your home

17. Get active with your community

18. Hire a human

19. That doggy in the window

20. Invest ethically

LIVING ROOM

Baby, it's wild outside.
Nice to kick back in
the cave, snuggle into
the comforts of home
and restore our souls.
Unfortunately, some
of the things that keep
us comfortable do not
contribute to the greater
good. Here's why.

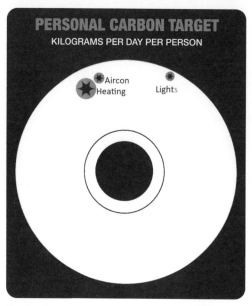

PERSONAL CARBON TARGET
KILOGRAMS PER DAY PER PERSON

Aircon
Heating

Lights

Heating has greater emissions than air-conditioning

The problem

Back in the day, we burned wood to keep the cave warm in the neat fireplace we made using river rocks. That meant chopping down trees and ripping up the local creek bed. (Not to mention pumping carbon dioxide into the atmosphere.)

The modern equivalent is reverse-cycle air-conditioning, a comfortable lounge suite, a large plasma screen and one smart digital assistant to rule them all. Our comfort is costing the earth.

GADGETS

The gadgets we use today are marvels of modern engineering. Problem is, they take a lot of rare resources and energy to make; they can't be easily repaired; and e-waste is pretty toxic, precisely because of all the rare elements that went into making them so wonderful.

ENERGY

Aside from the electricity that you pay for every quarter, there is an enormous infrastructure supporting your online connection. The servers that deliver your movies, social media, work meetings, directions, emails, phone calls and so on consume about three terawatts of electricity every year.
That is one hundred times Australia's total electricity consumption during summer afternoons.

FURNITURE

Lots of energy was spent making and delivering all the stuff that keeps our current caves comfy. Australia's more than eight million households spend more than $10 billion on furniture each year. Only about one quarter of that is manufactured in Australia, so has to be shipped here. Cheap furniture lasts less than five years.

COMFORT AND CONVENIENCE

That's the challenge, my friends. We make life easy and comfortable for ourselves at someone else's expense.

Let's fix it

Let's start with the no-brainers. You don't need to spend any money or make any effort to do the first two tips in this chapter but the benefits are immediate. They are not going to stop the world catching on fire, but you've just walked in the door. It makes sense to take a few baby steps to start with.

YOUR PERSONAL CARBON TARGET

The impact of these tips can be seen here by the holes they make in the Personal carbon target.

The target was introduced and described in detail on page 5. The simplified version of it, shown opposite, is used throughout the book to visually show the impact of particular tips. The outer circle of the target represents 46kg per day or 17 tonnes per year, the per capita emissions of each and every Australian. You can read up on the details of that calculation in the Antikythera.

The line drawn around the bulls-eye is our personal carbon target of 5.4kg each day. We are trying to blow away pieces of the target by making holes in it with each tip. The inner black circle, the bull's eye of just under 3kg per day is typical of Tonga and other Pacific islands. That is provided for reference, just to remind us that one billion of the world's population produces less carbon now than we are aiming to produce in the future.

The holes that have been blasted in this target represent the two tips in this section.

The lights in a typical Australian home are responsible for about 5% of electricity use. If we can save, say, one fifth of that use by turning off the lights we do not need, we reduce our carbon footprint by 60g each day. It's not a great big hole in the target, but it's an easy win.

Turning down the heater is a much bigger deal. It saves over 600g every day, about the same as produced in total by the average citizen of sub-Saharan Africa.

1. An empty room does not need a light

This is not rocket science; it's just one of those obvious things that most kids and many adults are too slack to pay attention to. Get real, guys. This one is obvious.

If you are not in the room, turn off the light.

Those of us with older lighting systems are just burning energy for nothing. Only turn the lights on when you need them. If you are aware of the energy used by lighting, you are more likely to switch off standby devices and other energy wasters. It is important to take responsibility for your energy use.

Glentworth in Brisbane by dion seminara architecture. Copyright 2020 dsarchitecture.com.au

Here's a plan

- Pop reading lamps and other low-energy lights around the place to avoid bumping into the furniture and only use the bright lighting when you are in the room for a period of time. This means you can shift between lighting environments and reconfigure a space quickly and easily.

- If you're really feeling inspired, look into some motion sensor lighting. Not only with this reduce your need to physically turn off the lights, it can give you that 'Welcome' feeling when arriving to an empty house.

- You can also dot candles around the place, especially beeswax candles that are the longest burning, cleanest burning, and highest quality candle material available and have been around since the Egyptians built the pyramids. LED based e-candles are also atmospheric, low-energy light sources.

Look it up
Light globe emissions
Domestic energy consumption
cleanenergyregulator.gov.au/NGER
Paraffin soy beeswax
earthhour.org

Reality check

Wander around the neighbourhood after dinner one night and have a look at who has their lights searing into the darkness — even after going to bed or leaving!

Some advisers recommend using timers to save you the trouble of remembering to turn off your lights. The makers of digital personal assistants like Siri, Alexis or Google Home offer to manage your household electrics on your behalf or allow you to do it remotely.

Purchasing a device to do the job for you seems to mimic the approach that led to the problem in the first place. We are not going to solve the problem by repeating bad behaviour. Just turn off the light!

Now try this!
8 Buy green power
15 Get a better light
55 Energy-efficient appliances
77 Generate your own power

HARD FACTS

CANDLES AND KIDS ARE NOT ALWAYS A GOOD MIX
(cue *Burning Down the House*).

Paraffin,
made from fossil fuel,
IS MIXED WITH MOST SOY CANDLES TO HELP THEM BURN.

Palm oil,
ANOTHER COMMON INGREDIENT IN CANDLES, IS OFTEN GROWN ON PLANTATIONS THAT replace tropical rainforests, which is to be avoided at all costs.

LEDs
are manufactured from metals and plastics.

Candles
can be manufactured from natural ingredients
LOCAL BEESWAX CANDLES HAVE A LOWER FOOTPRINT THAN AN
LED lighting solution

2. Turn down the air-con

Australia spans a range of climates, from the tropics to the Antarctic Ocean, but most capital cities have reasonably comfortable climates. Nevertheless, the energy we use to heat and cool our homes remains one of the largest sources of household emissions.

Little wonder that heating and cooling our homes accounts for 35% of domestic greenhouse emissions. Air-conditioning on its own is responsible for about 14% of the electricity used in buildings. The crazy thing, though, is that we don't just reduce the temperature to a bearable level. Instead, we refrigerate our houses in summer and toast them up in winter.

It makes much more sense to use the temperature control to just take the edge off the heat in summer and the chill in winter. Most of us simply don't think about the environmental cost of air-conditioning.

HARD FACTS

DEMAND FOR ELECTRICITY IN AUSTRALIA has increased by less than 1% each year over the last decade.

DEMAND PEAKS AT 4:00pm on hot afternoons.

Wholesale electricity prices are measured in megawatts per hour (MWh) based on demand. At 4:00pm about 20 times each summer, **WHOLESALE ELECTRICITY PRICES RISE FROM $90/MWh to a whopping $5,000/MWh.**

Photo by andrea-davis- on Unsplash

A personal story

From Far North Queensland, "Hotels in Townsville use air-conditioners more than their counterparts in Cairns, despite the climate being dryer and less tropical. There seems to be a cultural effect."

Here's a plan

Go for a 10-minute walk to get used to the ambient temperature and get your blood moving.

When you come back, put on your inside clothes and walk around the house to check out where it really is too hot or too cold for comfort and where you really need to be for the next couple of hours. Then you can adjust the temperature of the rooms you will use to the current need.

Adjust the temperature minimally, set it to the recommended two or three degrees above or below the outside climate.

Close all windows and ensure that energy is not being wasted through badly sealed doors.

Reality check

Australian homes are not well insulated and modern houses are often not designed to take advantage of local conditions.

Tasmania, Victoria and parts of South Australia have pretty cold winters and need heating. Even residents of sub-tropical cities could put a bit more effort into winter insulation. Even though the cold snaps are relatively short and mild, they matter when they happen.

The extreme summer temperatures are becoming unbearable right across Australia and so air-conditioning is increasingly considered essential.

As well as being conservative with the thermostat we need to pay attention to how heat moves through our homes. The *Now try this!* tips that follow go into more detail about these approaches.

Look it up

Heat islanding

Peak demand electricity

Passive cooling

Ceiling fans vs air-conditioning

Evaporative technology

Now try this!

9 Control that air flow

14 Meet your heater

16 Insulate your home

We need to talk about ...

... the effect of our choices

Photo by Stephanie Harvey on Unsplash

The big contributor to your carbon footprint in the living area is cooling and heating. Our efforts to control the climate in our homes potentially drives the global climate out of control.

Cooling and heating are responsible for 37% of our energy use, and contribute 35% of our household emissions and 14% of our total carbon footprint. Because it is such a big part of our footprint, many of the tips in

this chapter deal with how we cool or heat our homes or how we can make ourselves comfortable without sucking so much energy from the grid.

Of course, the actions that we take have impacts on other areas of our lives, summarised in the Tip summary table shown on the next page. We build on these in later chapters. But first, here is a graphical key to reading the *Tip summary* tables.

Tip summary key

The impact of each tip is measured against six criteria

FIRE	WATER	BODY	SOUL	TIME	MONEY
MEASURING:	MEASURING:	MEASURING:	MEASURING:	MEASURING:	MEASURING:
Carbon target saving	Water target saving	Physical health	Wellbeing	Impact on your time	Financial cost
UNITS: CO_2e kg/day	UNITS: L/day	UNITS: Rating	UNITS: Rating	UNITS: m/day	UNITS: $/day
EXAMPLES: ✓✗	EXAMPLES: ✓✗	EXAMPLES: ✓✗	EXAMPLES: ✓✗	EXAMPLES: ✓✗	EXAMPLES: ✓✗

Tip summary

#	Tip	Page	🔥	💧	🧍	👁	⏱	$
3	Those packaged drinks	16	✓	✓	✓✓	✓		✓✓
4	The snacks I love	18	✓	✓	✓✓	✓	✗	✓✓
5	Paying it forward	20				✓✓		✗✗
6	Indoor plants	22	✓	✗	✓	✓✓	✗	✗✗
7	Our high-speed lives	24				✓	✓✓	✗✗✗
8	Buy green power	26	✓✓✓	✓				✗✗
9	Control the airflow	28	✓✓✓✓	✓	✓✓		✗✗	✗✗
10	Ordering in food	30	✓	✓	✓✓	✓	✗✗	✓✓
11	A no-spend day	32				✓		✓✓
12	The nature of time	34				✓✓	✓✗	
13	Your alcohol consumption	36	✓	✓	✓	✓	✓	✓✓

3. Those packaged drinks

Packaged drinks are a perfect example of how cheap energy has encouraged us to consume resources for no good reason. We pay over 1,000 times the price of tap water to drink essentially the same water from a plastic bottle.

How can this hurt? Let me count the ways.

1. The packaging is waste.

2. Bottling wastes water.

3. Preservatives added to packaged drinks are bad for you.

4. Transporting packaged drinks adds to global warming.

The amount of sugar in the soft drinks we consume every day has medical practitioners calling for a sugar tax.

Reality check

Drink bottles are a huge waste problem. Only about one third of the bottles sold in Australia are recycled — high by world standards — and the rest end up in landfill or the oceans. Because they are hollow, they take up a lot of space in landfill (around 30%) and provide a reservoir for microbes to lurk in wait for future generations.

Here's a plan

Some of us need a sugar hit every now and then and like to have a sweet drink to offer guests: here's a method for making simple syrup.

- Nearly fill a saucepan with white sugar and cover with water. Simmer that until clear and let it cool, then bottle the syrup in glass bottles. Make cordials by mixing the syrup with fresh fruit juice. Make iced tea by mixing cold tea with lemon juice, the syrup and ice. Home-made cordials have all the negatives associated with sugar, but not the packaging.

- If it's the chill you love, freeze your home-made drink and pop it in the lunch box to keep your lunch cool and have a cold drink. Keep bottles of frozen water in the freezer for summer walks and picnics.

- If you don't like your tap water, get a filtration system. There are ceramic and charcoal filters for different budgets and different levels of concerns.

- The major chemical used to keep tap water free of bugs is chlorine. Boiling tap water is the fastest way to get rid of the chlorine. Empty the boiled water from the kettle into your drink container before you go to boil it next time.

From mountain spring to your lips

EVERY 600ML BOTTLE OF WATER CONSUMES AROUND 1.5MJ (MEGAJOULES) OF ENERGY.

MANUFACTURING 1KG OF PET PLASTIC CONSUMES 17.5L OF WATER AND AROUND 3L OF OIL

DRINK FACTORIES USE UP TO 3.5L OF WATER FOR EVERY LITRE OF DRINK THEY SELL.

HARD FACTS

We currently drink

75L OF PACKAGED DRINKS

PER PERSON, PER YEAR.

Each year, Australia disposes of
373 million PET bottles.

Only 36%

OF PET BOTTLES ARE RECYCLED.

GLOBALLY, BOTTLED DRINKS ARE RESPONSIBLE FOR AROUND

100 million tonnes of carbon dioxide annually.

Now try this!

7 Our high-speed lives

10 Ordering in food

56 The packaging we purchase

65 The problem with recycling

Look it up

Rotten troubled water

Edible water blob

Bottled water waste

PET recycling

Oil bottled water calculate

4. The snacks I love

From sweet biscuits to cheese platters, potato chips to trail mix ... those nibbles between meals keep us going while we get through the day. The healthier that snack is for us, the more likely it is to nurture our planet.

The sort of food that makes us fat is convenience food that contains corn syrup, white sugar, trans fats and highly processed foods. The trick is to find local, easy to get snacks that are yummy and don't break the bank.

Here's a plan

The cheapest snacks are popcorn, flat bread, plain biscuits or traditional snacks from other cultures. These are easy to make with a minimum of ingredients. Your local bulk food store or food cooperative will have lots of options.

POPCORN: To make popcorn you need corn kernels, a spoonful of oil or butter, salt, a saucepan and a stove. Heat the oil, put in the corn kernels and pop on a lid. Shake it every now and then until the kernels starts popping. Add butter, salt, sugar or flavouring to taste.

FLAT BREAD OR PLAIN CRACKERS: Take some flour (any flour) and add water a teaspoon at a time until you get a stiff dough. Roll, or press it, as thinly as possible. Heat the dough on a hot plate or frying pan. Turn it over before it burns. Crackers are not much more complicated. Make the mixture wet enough to spread, put drops onto a baking pan and bake in a hot oven. Crisp and crackle!

TZATZIKI: Yoghurt, cucumber and finely chopped onion. Grate and drain the cucumber, mix all the ingredients together, then salt and spice to taste. I put a splash of olive oil on top and sprinkle with red paprika.

PESTO: Basil (or other tasty leaves), olive oil, nuts (pine nuts are traditional), garlic and parmesan cheese (or yeast flakes).

Photo by Eduardo Casajús Gorostiaga onn Unsplash

A personal story

Alette writes, "My mum used to make a big deal about making popcorn at home. We even ended up getting one of those old-school popcorn machines. As a kid, we learnt how to do it ourselves, easy peasy, giving us a relatively healthy snack with almost no waste!

Mash it up in a food processor or chop it up finely with a knife.

BABAGANOUSH AND HOUMOUS:
Either roasted eggplant pulp (for babaganoush) or soft-boiled chick peas (for houmous), with tahini, lemon juice and garlic. Mash ingredients in a food processor and eat.

Costs

Here's a general guide to what you'll pay for produce that make great pantry staples.

Chickpeas, $3/kg

Sunflower oil, $2.50/L, Olive oil $10/L

Peanut butter $8/kg, Almonds $15/kg, Cashews $25/kg, Pine nuts $45/kg

Milk $1.50/L, Yoghurt $4/L

Processed tasty cheese $10/kg, Parmesan cheese $3/120g, yeast flakes $15/100g

Now try this!

10 Ordering in food

54 Baking bread

46 Where the kitchen herbs grow

60 Things that grow in the dark

Look it up

taste.com.au

delish.com

Food cooperatives

Dried pulse providers

Homemade dips

Homemade crackers

5. Paying it forward

You're rich, they're poor. They've got little, you've got more. Send something their way and make a connection. Remind yourself how the other 90% live.

Poverty goes hand in hand with higher birth mortality rates, the spread of disease and political instability. Investment in education, healthy nutrition and access to financial opportunities helps people overcome the negative impact of poverty and empowers them.

You can help the poorest people on the planet by sponsoring a child, helping build a school, or giving a goat. Or you can start at home, working with local indigenous groups to try and close the gap that exists here in Australia.

Here's a plan

Use Christmas or your birthday to encourage people to gift a cause instead of you. "Hey instead of buying me another decoration to put on top of my window pelmet box, make a donation to PayTheRent."

In Australia, First Nation people die eight years younger, are 12 times more likely to go to prison and earn two thirds of the average Australian. This systemic racism against them is not only inhumane, it denies a thousand centuries of accumulated knowledge about living sustainably on this continent. ANTaR, PayTheRent, Reconciliation Australia and IAHA are all organisations that welcome your financial support.

Check out the causes you want to support. Some charities do not get the money to those in need and some forms of aid result in unexpected outcomes. Voluntourism, for example, can increase costs for locals.

HARD FACTS

THE LIFE-EXPECTANCY GAP
First Nations people
die younger
than immigrant populations
AUSTRALIA: 13–17 YEARS
New Zealand: 6–10 years
Canada and USA: 0–5 years

From little things, big things grow: PM Gough Whitlam pours sand into the hands of Vincent Lingiari at Dagaragu in 1975

Look it up

Global poverty

Close the gap

numbeo.com

Purchasing power parity

Voluntourism

paytherent.net.au

antar.org.au

iaha.com.au

reconciliation.org.au

Now try this!

16 Get active with your community

20 Invest ethically

33 Put down the phone

Reality check

The richest 1% of the world's population own 50% of the world's resources. In 2005 it was the top 5% who owned half the wealth. They are all millionaires. On the other hand, half the world's population own only 1%.

Global trade is making the situation worse. In 1750, India manufactured 24.5% of the world's goods and Britain less than 2%. By 1880 the situation was reversed. Colonialism in India did not take a 'primitive' country and advance it, it took the resources and markets from a rich country and impoverished it. This has been the Game of Empires since King Nebuchadnezzar.

Australia is the beneficiary of centuries of colonisation. Instead of feeling guilt at the greed of your ancestors, use your privilege to pay something forward. We cannot undo the past, but we can build a better future by learning not to repeat it.

Back in the day

Traditionally Australian charities have raised money for poor countries overseas. As awareness grows about the extent of the gap between the descendants of immigrants and First Nations people, we have become more concerned about cleaning up our own act first.

6. Indoor plants

Pot plants are the new pets: cheap to feed, undemanding but still responsive to tender loving care. They improve the atmosphere of our homes as well.

Air-conditioning is really not good for us. It dries out the air, circulates germs and can breed some pretty nasty bugs in the cooling water. A few plants dotted around the place can freshen the air, injecting soothing negative ions into the area, and add a splash of colour for a fraction of the fuss and finance.

They might also have a positive psychological impact for the majority of us who spend 80% of our time indoors. Popular movements such as Forest-bathing have emerged to overcome the concern that we might be suffering en-masse from a nature-deficit disorder.

Unlike manufactured, low-cost home decor that breaks quickly and need to be replaced, indoor plants look good, grow and multiply all on their own.

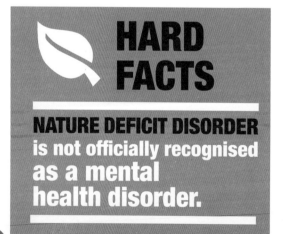

HARD FACTS

NATURE DEFICIT DISORDER is not officially recognised as a mental health disorder.

Oxygen per hour

HUMANS CONSUME 5L O$_2$/H.

AN INDOOR PLANT PRODUCES ABOUT 5ml O$_2$/H

Reality check

Mixing it up with nature will always encourage a few stray bugs. If you really cannot bear to share the air with tiny creatures, quarantine the pot plants on the back patio. Look into natural repellents as well, like neem oil and apple cider vinegar.

Charged particles (ions) attract other particles and are an active ingredient effecting air quality. Because plants emit relatively simple molecules, including water vapour, they tend to improve air quality. The science shows that the effect varies widely for different plant species.

Here's a plan

Check out your neighbours and your friends to find indoor plants you like. Then look a bit more closely and see if their plants have multiplied. You might be able to get a baby plant for nothing. Many plants are surrounded by a forest of babies from seeds they have dropped or where their leaves touch the ground.

You can also try cutting off a branch of their plant and keeping it in a glass of water for a week or two. Most plants will start to grow roots as long as they have adequate light and water. Remember to keep filling the glass with water as the plants drink it!

A pot plant needs a saucer. It helps retain the moisture and stops it leaking out all over the furniture. If you are a home décor nut, you can put some rewarding time and effort into selecting the right pots. If you are flat broke or frugal, the plants themselves are the décor.

Don't forget the culinary benefit of a few herbs when you are scrambling eggs or making a sandwich. Potted herbs are a great way to spice up your life without spending a cent.

Costs

A potted plant from a nursery: $20+.

A cutting from a neighbour: $0.

Look it up
Building ecology
Forest bathing
Nature deficit disorder
Plants sick buildings

Now try this!
46 Where the kitchen herbs grow
89 Planting a local
47 Mung beans and love

Photo by Stephanie Harvey on Unsplash

7. Our high-speed lives

A silver lining to the pandemic may be that we learned to slow down. Working from home has been fun for some and the four-day week looms as a serious possibility. Slowing down gives us more time to nurture ourselves and to live more lightly on our planet.

The Slow Food movement started Piedmont, Italy, in 1986 as an organisation dedicated to preserving traditional food and food culture. There are now 1,600 Slow Food convivia (communities) around the world, including 19 in Australia. Slow Food is just one organisation in a broad movement to incorporate traditional values and rituals into modern life, and improve our physical and emotional wellbeing. When was the last time you made a fresh loaf of bread?

Slow fashion is a movement designed to divert us away from cheap clothes designed to be worn a few times and then discarded for the newest shiny thing. It is discussed in detail in Tip 37 *Fast Fashion*.

"People are unaware of the sheer volume of waste caused by fast fashion. Handling a tonne of discarded clothes is one way to create a physical understanding," Tenfingerz told YLYP.

Selling time savers to busy parents is not a new idea

Here's a plan

Check out local events around slow food, slow fashion, community connection and sharing. How can you slow down in your local area?

Explore food trees in your neighbourhood, or join a community garden or local crafting club. These new hobbies cannot only slow you down happily, but encourage you to nurture your planet.

Through our actions, we shape our lives, through slowing down we create connections with each other and build a richer, more balanced lifestyle.

Reality check

Working from home might slow things down a bit but it also shifts the responsibility of workplace safety, and raises complex questions about insurance and liability. How safe and ergonomic is your equipment? Where does the workplace end and the household begin?

The volume of on-screen meetings and training sessions has caused many employers and employees to think seriously about the structure of work. What can you do to restructure your working environment into healthy practices and structures?

Costs

Cost of home office: $5,000+. Paid by employer? Cost of commuting: $3,500 a year. Paid by worker.

Look it up
Telecommuting statistics Australia
Food/harvest festival
Telecommuting
Four day week
Wine trails
slowfood.com
slowmovement.com
communitydevelopment.org.

Now try this!
11 A no-spend day
54 Baking bread
73 Cycle to work

HARD FACTS

ALMOST A THIRD (3.5 MILLION) of working Australians regularly worked from home in 2016.

About 1 million OF THEM WERE CLASSIFIED AS **telecommuters.**

Australians spend **34%** (ONE THIRD) OF THEIR **food budget on fast food.**

6,000kg OF FASHION WASTE goes to landfill in Australia **every 10 minutes.**

Four fifths of the textiles produced **ARE THROWN OUT WITHIN A YEAR.**

8. Buy green power

Renewable electricity is now the cheapest form of new energy in Australia. Large-scale solar is coming online to compete with wind. You can speed up this process by refusing to pay for power generated by burning fossil fuels.

Fossil fuels still provided 80% of Australia's electricity supply in 2018. Coal provided 60%, gas 19% and oil 2%. Renewables contributed 21%. It's getting better but not fast enough. Most new electricity-generation projects are renewable because investors see their costs fall and customer demand increase. New technologies, like MGA Thermal, will eliminate fossil fuels.

You can speed that process up by insisting on renewable energy from your electricity supplier.

PERSONAL CARBON TARGET
KILOGRAMS PER DAY PER PERSON

Green power

On average 14% of our electricity is already renewable. Greening the rest significantly reduces our footprint.

Here's a plan

Find out from your current electricity supplier's website how much it costs to buy 'green power' and find out what range of options they offer.

Before you sign up, compare their offering to other suppliers. A table comparing the various energy companies and how green they are is available online at the Green Electricity Guide.

Comparing exact prices is a bit trickier. Pick a provider from the Green Electricity Guide, or find the price of green energy from a company advertising in your area, or search for <green electricity> and compare the prices.

If you switch, your new provider will look after the switchover from the old company.

HARD FACTS

DOMESTIC ELECTRICITY consumption accounts for a little **over 25%** of all electricity used

Wind power COSTS AROUND **$36/MWh to produce, large-scale solar around $50/MWh**

Reality check

Buying green power really does work. Consumer demand has forced suppliers to invest in renewable energy. With around one quarter of the electricity supply across the country now renewable, the supply in the south eastern states was more than 50% renewable on occasions during 2020.

Electricity providers are still charging an additional 5c per kilowatt hour for Green Power on top of the 25–50c that they charge for traditionally sourced electricity. As prices continue to fall and more green power comes online, this charge will be dropped as it becomes completely illogical. You are only paying it because you want to speed up the process of driving energy generators away from fossil fuel. That amount added to your bill is then invested in building new renewable energy.

Wind power has been the cheapest form of electricity generation until now, but large-scale solar is catching up fast. It has fallen from $135/MWh in 2015 to around $50 in mid-2020.

Some sites offering to compare prices want you to register all your details before they will reveal the comparison.

Carbon offsets, where you buy dirty power and then your supplier pays someone-else to plant trees to clean up your carbon footprint is less effective than generating clean power. You are still pressuring your supplier, though.

Look it up
Green power
Renewable energy certificate
Renewable funding
greenpower.gov.au
greenelectricityguide.org.au

Now try this!
35 The standby lightshow
29 Switch off the lights
36 Better light globes

9. Control the airflow

Heating and cooling without throwing a switch? Think the shady courtyard of a Mediterranean villa, the snug stone cottage of northern Europe or a curtain of glass capturing the winter sun. These approaches are known as passive heating and cooling.

In the southern parts of Australia, we shut the house after Easter, light the fire, then open the house again in September for a good spring-clean. In the north, we shut it down for summer, turn on the air-con, then open up again after Anzac Day. There are more subtle ways to control our domestic micro-climate by managing the airflow.

Here's a plan

Keep your house open as much as possible in mild weather, and keep track of how the air flows through your home and what areas are naturally cooler or warmer.

Use doors and curtains to separate the warm and the cool areas so that you can manage the temperature better as the weather becomes less comfortable.

Frills around doors and windows, door sausages (draught stoppers) and heavy curtains (Pass 3 blackout backing is what you need) might seem old-fashioned, but they serve a purpose.

Those boxes above the windows that cover the curtain rails? They are called pelmet boxes (helmets for windows). They do not exist to put unwanted Christmas presents on top of; they help control the airflow.

The little shade rooves over the outside of the northern windows of your neighbour's house let in the winter sun, which is lower in the sky then, but keep out the summer sun beating down from overhead.

Take advantage of regular breezes. There is usually a breeze before sunset, especially in coastal areas. Open and close your windows during the day to capture the breezes as you need to.

In winter, arrange your room so that you are not sitting in the airflow, say between a door and a heater. Not a cosy seat selection.

Prevent all the warmth collecting upstairs or at the ceiling where you can't feel it. Put your

Reality check

Electricity use peaks at around 4:00pm on summer days when its blazing hot outside, school's out, workplaces are still pumping and we are all trying to keep cool.

Heating and cooling consumes about 10% of the electricity we produce, so contributes significantly to global warming. It is worth learning to learn to control our climate naturally.

Look it up

Pelmet box circulation

Greenhouse curtain

Draught stopper

yourhome.gov.au

energy.gov.au

greenhouse.gov.au

apps.epa.vic.gov.
au/AGC/home.html

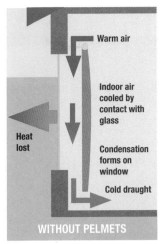

Warm air

Indoor air
cooled by
contact with
glass

Heat
lost

Condensation
forms on
window

Cold draught

WITHOUT PELMETS

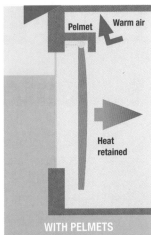

Pelmet   Warm air

Heat
retained

WITH PELMETS

fans on the winter setting by flicking the little switch (usually on the fan itself) from S (Summer) to W, and turn the fans on low so that it gently moves the air down into the room.

A personal story

Alette writes from sub-tropical Brisbane: "I open my windows up in the morning and shut up the house when I go out. I pull the blinds in summer to keep the house cool through the hottest part of the day. Then, when I get home, I can often open the house back up again to enjoy the cooler evening air."

Costs

Solid curtains cost upwards of $100 per window. Old blankets are a cheap alternative.

If you're thrifty, head to your local opp. shop and dive into their piles of fabric.

Now try this!

11 Turn down the
air-conditioning

14 Meet your heater

100 Double glaze

HARD FACTS

More than one third of the energy used in the average house **(40%)** IS USED FOR HEATING AND COOLING.

Up to 14%
OF AUSTRALIAN DOMESTIC GREENHOUSE GASES
are due to heating and cooling.

IN AUSTRALIAN HOMES,
wall areas made of glass range from 15% to 40%.

UP TO 40% OF A HOME'S HEATING **can be lost in winter and up to 87% of its** heat gained in summer through windows.

10. Ordering in food

You have locked yourself in; it's tempting to have food brought to you and enjoy delicious cooking rather than performing miracles with an empty cupboard. Always remember, though, convenience costs.

The costs of delivery and the packaging involved are the biggest reasons not to go there. Don't forget, delivery is cheap because the delivery driver is probably earning less than the minimum wage.

Cooking can reconnect us to the seasons, to our bodies and to our families. Cooking is an old and potent way of showing love; treat it as a pleasure, not a chore.

Add up the amount you spend over a month ordering-in food. Cooking at home makes sense for the budget.

It's good for our health. MyDr.com.au says preparing meals at home reduces the risk of type 2 diabetes. Take away food is high in salt, sugar and fat, and comes in large serves. We are less active when not preparing our own meals.

Here's a plan

Preparation is the friend of convenience.

Cook more, less often. Keep the leftovers and eat them when you can't be bothered cooking. You can use leftovers as a filling in a sandwich, a sauce on pasta or rice, or as a side dish with a simple meal.

Keep yummy, nutritious and easy-to-prepare food in the fridge, like corn on the cob or eggs (that only need to be boiled for a couple of minutes).

Pre-boil or roast potatoes, or pumpkin, sweet potato, brussel sprouts and broccoli, so you can simply warm them up when you want a quick meal. You can do the same thing with meat, too.

Keep your favourite topping on hand – white sauce, mayonnaise, a rich red tomato puree – and make your warmed up pre-cooked vegies into a gourmet dinner.

If you are really hankering after comfort food, you can throw your favourite oil or fat into the frying pan and stir fry a few of these goodies tucked away in the fridge.

A personal story

The industrialisation of food has got us disconnected from the food we eat and the world we live in (tomatoes for $5/kg in the middle of winter?).

Sneak in some extra nutrition for fussy ones. Cauliflower in mashed potatoes? Use some real tomatoes and boiled carrots in the bolognaise. Blend some fresh fruit into their OJ. They'll hardly know.

Look it up
Footprint takeaway containers
#trashlesstakeaway
Real wages gig economy
returnr.org
mydr.com.au
delicious.com.au
healthyfoodguide.com.au

On those occasions when there seems to be nothing in the fridge and no-one can be bothered rattling the pots and pans, fresh herbs or garden greens on pasta, rice (or any other carbs in the back of the pantry) goes a long way to filling the spot.

Costs
At $15 each, a couple ordering in once a week spends $1,500 a year.

Now try this!
7 Our high-speed lives
48 The things we eat for lunch
54 Baking bread
56 The packaging we purchase
61 Things that grow in bottles

HARD FACTS

Minimum wage
IN AUSTRALIA (JULY 2020):
$20 an hour

Gig-economy
WORKERS (JULY 2020):
$15 an hour

ADD UP THE PACKAGING INVOLVED IN A TAKEAWAY MEAL FOR A COUPLE: 3 containers, 2 drink bottles, cutlery, sauce packets, 2 plastic bags and serviettes. NOW CALCULATE YOUR throwaway packaging for a week, a month.

Two thirds
OF PLASTIC PACKAGING IN AUSTRALIA
is not recycled.

11. A no-spend day

One way to reduce our environmental footprint is to pause our consuming. Saves money too. Spend a day without spending a dollar and check the effects. It might benefit our lifestyle as well as our wallet.

The amount of energy and resources that go into what we consume is roughly in proportion to the money we spend. Just have a look at the Hard facts, at right.

Constantly consuming is seriously costing the planet as well as our mental wellbeing. It is an addiction deliberately exploited and perpetuated for profit. Actively going cold turkey can be hard, but oh so rewarding.

Okay, it's not that simple, but there's no doubt that snapping shut the wallet for one 24-hour trip around the sun could save a tidy bundle.

Here's a plan

Literally leave the plastic and the cash at home. Temporarily turn off the contactless payments on your phone. Do a trial run for a day and see what inevitable expenses you might have forgotten. Things like your weekly contribution to the lunch-room biscuit fund might be a tad embarrassing if you are not prepared. Make sure you have the supplies you need.

Any food, drinks or other treats you normally buy yourself during the day will need to come out of your kitchen. That might include taking snacks, lunch and a water bottle with you, sipping peppermint tea in the lunch room instead of buying a coffee, and putting together a meal from leftovers and pantry items instead of buying something on the way home for dinner.

The point of going cold turkey is to see how often you habitually reach for the phone, debit/credit card or bag of gold dust (gold coins), and to take mental notes. And pay attention to the tolls, fares, parking fees and other payments that come out of apps or cards preloaded with your money.

HARD FACTS

The Australians who buy **LUNCH SPEND** approximately $15 per day.

On average, each year:
PEOPLE LIVING IN AFRICA PRODUCE
1.1 tonnes of CO_2 and
EARN LESS THAN
$AUD1,000.

THE AVERAGE AUSTRALIAN PRODUCES
22 tonnes of CO_2 and
earns $AUD90,800.

Look it up
Thrift
Stop spending
Buy nothing
Global footprint income
thethriftyissue.com.au
moneysmart.gov.au
sustainableliving.com.au

Reality check

Many of the services we use are now billed as we go: everything we stream, electricity, phones, and the Internet. Others are paid on account: think public transport, parking, and tolls.

Turning off contactless payments for a day is a little clunky; leaving the phone at home, unrealistic.

One criticism of no-spend days is that we tend to binge after fasting; like abstaining from drinking until Wednesday so we can go wild for the rest of the week. Look at it more as an opportunity to learn a little about yourself than a way of balancing the books.

A personal story

A sailor writes, "I love this about sailing. I go to sea for a couple of days and don't spend a cent. When I come back my bank account is reconciled because all the tap-and-go payments have been processed."

Now try this!

3 Those packaged drinks
7 Our high-speed lives
10 Ordering in food
48 The things we eat for lunch
54 Baking bread
61 Things that grow in bottles

12. The nature of time

Unless you are Hermione and have a Time Turner, making time is impossible.

Unfortunately, none of us seem to have gotten our letter from Hogwarts, and so we are trapped in a high-speed but shallow world: quick bedtime stories for kids by busy parents, three-minute noodles, fast fashion. Convenience implies speed and ease. Faced with the choice of doing something quick and easy or something long and difficult, convenience wins hands down, every time.

So, how are we supposed to create the additional time to focus on quality? Extra preparation creates convenience but requires some time management.

Jumping in the car to buy the morning loaf of bread seems harmless enough. That 1km round trip consumes 50–100ml of petrol, producing 150–300g of CO_2. Doesn't seem like much until you add up the 20 million Australians who average three trips each day of less than 3km … and that's just the car.

We order goods online and if they don't fit, we send them back and order something else. How convenient. How resource-intensive.

Here's a plan

One way to create time is to avoid soul-destroying activities, like sitting in peak-hour traffic or unproductive meetings.

To stop wasting time on negative actions without slowing to a crawl, we can creatively combine activities, and I'm not talking about multitasking. Despite the hype, we don't multitask well. Have you watched someone shaving and driving?

Catch public transport and read and work on the train. Work from home; we know how now. Come and go from work outside peak hour! Get ready for tomorrow and do those pesky chores between screen time and bedtime.

Another way is good, old-fashioned planning.

You know that a morning walk is good for you, but you never have time. Plan ahead.

- Find a place to shower near work
- Pick a day without an early meeting
- Pack breakfast, instead of eating at home
- Walk part of the way to work that day.
- Shower, change and eat breakfast after your walk

Huzzah! A morning walk, a great start to the day, and no impact on your schedule.

Photo by James Coleman on Unsplash

Back in the day

The Roman philosopher Seneca said: "It is not that we have a short space of time, but that we waste much of it."

Reality check

The car is at the centre of modern suburbia. It is a serious change of pace to ditch it. Public transport takes roughly twice the time and in most Australian cities costs the same or more as driving and parking.

Only a handful of workplaces have 'end of journey' facilities for you to change out of your sweaty gear after jogging to work.

Look it up

Time ecological footprint

Environmental convenience

Seneca time

Now try this!

47 Mung beans and love

49 What's wrong with the supermarket

54 Baking bread

62 Shank's pony

13. Our alcohol consumption

Nature has blessed us with the grape and the grain. We have harnessed the humble yeast to transform old fruit into delicious and intoxicating drinks. What could possibly go wrong?

The good news is that local breweries, distilleries and vineyards have become a feature of the Australian drinking culture. Most bottle-shops carry a range of organic wines and beers that reduce the amount of chemicals going into your system as well as our waterways and atmosphere.

The greatest impact of our alcohol consumption on the environment comes from transport, refrigeration and packaging, rather than brewing, fermenting and distilling the drink itself. Find your local boutique brewery, vineyard or distillery and drink a toast to your planet.

The killer is price. The industrial-scale manufacturing plants, distribution and retail outlets give the handful of major alcohol companies a significant price advantage. If you can make that investment in nurturing your planet, please do, because the more of us that support our local food processors, the more competitive they become and the more resilient our communities.

A personal story
"As a local to Western Australia, I really enjoy spending a day out visiting multiple vineyards and coming home with a selection."

HARD FACTS

A 2008 study by the New Belgium Brewing company **IN THE USA SHOWED THAT ALMOST ONE THIRD** of its greenhouse gas emissions came from refrigeration and 22% from glass manufacture.

Major brewers promote their boutique brands at
HALF THE PRICE OF LOCAL BREWERS.

Here's a plan

Check the label. Opt for brewskies from your local area and avoid international imports with their huge transport footprint. This doesn't mean you'll never drink saké again! There are many distilleries in Australia.

Think again. Do you need that third glass? Cutting back will do more good than harm. And hey, that might mean you can splurge on the good stuff.

Make your own brew. It's a great thing to share with friends. Head to Tip 61 about starting your own backyard brewery.

Reality check

The ecological footprint of a big brewer is easier to control than that of a local brewery. The Yatala plant of Carlton and United Breweries is world renowned for its water and energy management. The real difference comes about through the reduction in food miles and the social benefits of supporting the local economy.

The big brewers are creating craft beers that use the more rustic brewing methods that give boutique brewing its distinct flavours. The downside is they still use national transport networks and distribution services.

Be mindful of misleading statements like 'Packed in Australia'; often times this means it's been shipped here from yonder.

Costs

Boutique beer: $7+/375ml can
Organic wine: $15+/750ml bottle
Spirits: pick a number!

Look it up

craftcartel.com.au
fabulousladieswinesociety.com
bucketboys.com.au
#craftbeer
#winetournearme
#brewerynearme
#organicwine

Now try this!
3 Those packaged drinks
61 Things that grow in bottles

Plan ahead

To really make a difference to the impact we have on the climate, the environment and to take control of our future, we are going to have to change more than our day to day habits.

We can implement some structural changes that require serious planning, a budget and a timetable.

In the living room, with our focus on heating and cooling, those structural investments include the heater, the air-conditioner and insulation. If you do not have LED lighting in your home already, there is another opportunity to significantly reduce your footprint.

These all require a bit of planning but put a serious dint in your Personal carbon target.

A broader summary

Tip 16 looks at ways we might engage in coordinated activities to amplify our effort.

Tip 18 looks at the more complex issue of economic exploitation, how it impacts on us personally and how we might respond.

These things are hard to quantify. So we have summarised the impact of the tips under different headings.

Every tip has some impact on your Personal carbon target (PCT), or a similar impact on your water usage. Those tips that are significant in either area will have the PCT or the Personal water target (PWT) infographic on the page with the rest of the information.

Most tips require some effort on your part. We have identified the Time and Money that you might spend on that tip using a simple infographic. Because one of the major costs of modern life is energy and energy leads to greenhouse gas emissions, many tips will save you money by reducing the resources used. The money indicator in those tips is green. When the tip costs you money it is red.

The cost is given as an estimate of whether it will cost you hundreds of thousands of dollars, rather than entering a specific number. *X X X X* means the tip will cost you thousands, *✓✓✓* means you will save hundreds. Some tips, like solar panels, will cost thousands to set up and will save thousands over their lifetime. They get red and green marks.

We have applied a similar approach to Body and Soul, grouping together physical impacts like pollution, health benefits and comfort into the Body column and social benefits like community, wellness and calmness under the Soul column.

#	Tip	Page	🔥	💧	👫	👁	⏰	$
14	Meet your heater	40	✓✓✓	✓	✓✓			XXX ✓✓
15	Get a better light	42	✓					XX ✓
16	Get active with your community	44				✓✓✓	XX	
17	Insulate your home	46	✓✓	✓	✓		X	XXX
18	Hire a human	50				✓✓	✓✓	XXX
19	That cute little dog in the window	52	✓			X	✓	✓✓✓
20	Invest ethically	54	✓✓✓	✓				✓✓✓

14. Meet your heater

The hearth is the heart of the home because heat heals and nurtures us. Sharing a fire is a natural bonding experience for humans even when we can't look into the flames.

Except for tropical Australia, the nip of winter warrants some external warmth. Victoria and Tasmania face chills that may make you ill unless you turn on the heater.

Here's a plan

Other tips deal with keeping the house warm by insulating it, plugging leaks and double glazing, or suggest you accept a slightly cooler house and wear warmer clothes inside. When you need a heater, the type you choose will have a big impact on your footprint.

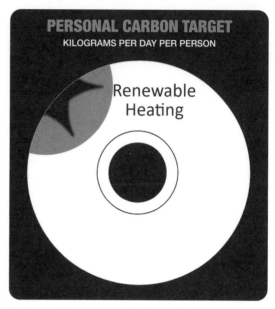

PERSONAL CARBON TARGET
KILOGRAMS PER DAY PER PERSON

Renewable Heating

Southern states have larger footprints due to heating. This represents the impact on the average national footprint.

Choose your fuel

Burning the ancient sunlight stored in fossil fuels is a great way to get warm quickly, but we need to get smarter about keeping warmer.

Burning natural gas is less polluting than burning coal, but it's still a finite resource and it's increasingly produced by fracking coal seams which damages the water table and the surface environment.

Wood contains recently captured carbon, so can be renewed, but we need to preserve our forests and keep smoke out of cities and towns. Wood heaters recycling waste timber in pellet form and m/ethanol burners mimicking fireplaces are more environmentally sound.

Renewable electricity is by far and away the best source of energy to create heat at home. Biofuels or renewably generated hydrogen are not yet practical in most regions.

Reality check
The efficiency of your heater is much less significant than the heat efficiency of your house.

Select the source

To get the maximum efficiency you need to match the heater to your circumstances.

Floor heating or hot oil heaters use lots of energy to warm up but can be efficient if you use them to warm a well-insulated area for long periods of time. Don't use them to crank up the heating when you come home to a cold house.

Radiators and fireplaces warm up objects close to them. That works well in small spaces where you can get close to the source of the heat. Once you are warm, turn them down to maintain a comfortable temperature.

Most heaters warm up air which then travels around the house by convection. To use them efficiently, control the amount of air you are trying to warm up. Read up on controlling the airflow.

Small portable heaters are not efficient, but they are handy and cheap to buy.

A personal story

One of our Sydney-based eco-warriors writes, "The most efficient, cost-effective and sustainable way to keep warm is to warm yourself instead of an entire room. Put on an extra thick pair of socks, a thick jumper and use a hot water bottle. I make a hot water bottle to keep in my lap while I study. This keeps me nice and toasty while it's a chilly 6°C."

Costs

Oil-filled column heater: $40

Portable alcohol burner: $60

Gas heaters: $950

Wood pellet heater: $1,990

Look it up
Wood pellet heaters
Oil filled column
Tile heated floor
Ceramic heater
environment.gov.
au/climate-change
ecosmartfire.com
homeheat.com.au

Now try this!
9 Control the airflow
16 Insulate your home
77 Generate your own power

15. Get a better light

Lighting creates atmosphere and good workspaces. LED lights use relatively little electricity, but most homes still use lights that suck power and pump out carbon dioxide and heat. Check out your lighting to set the mood you want.

Power-hungry halogen globes, harsh fluorescent tubes, and cold compact fluorescent globes still dominate many homes, so we have the opportunity to improve our lighting choices, especially when retrofitting an old home, or renting a property with single light fittings in the middle of each room.

Here's a plan

Start slowly. Use desk lamps, bedside lamps or floor lamps to vary the lighting around the house. You might want bright lights when cooking and cleaning, and warmer, more intimate lights when eating, for example. Find fittings that can easily be plugged into the existing light sockets and power points. This is both cost effective and ensures you can get the effect you want in your dimly lit rental.

Once you have an idea of the lighting you would like you can develop a clear lighting plan to discuss with an electrician (if you own your home).

LED lights are replacing fluorescent and filament lights in cars, streets and signage as well as our houses. There are huge savings in energy consumption as a result. LEDs have relatively long lifespans so need to be replaced far less often.

Modular lighting systems allow you to simply install panels, strips or points of light that can be controlled by touch, remotely or the more traditional switch in various colours and brightness to create mood, ambience and dramatic effect. HeliosTouch, nanoleaf, LiFX and Smartbunch are just some examples.

A personal story

Alette really loves fairy lights. "My whole house has one tucked away somewhere. Solar-powered lights are a cheap and flexible option. You can charge them during the day, and they have more than enough life to last until bedtime. Leave the charging panel on a sunny windowsill when you wake up and voila, free ambience lighting! And yes, even on overcast days, your light will be able to charge!"

Smartbunch is one of many modular lighting systems announced in the last five years

Back in the day

The incandescent tungsten light globe was banned in Australia in 2009, with compact flourescents taking up the slack. Since then, LED lighting has advanced in leaps and bounds.

Reality check

LEDs use rare earths which, as the name suggests, are non-renewable resources. They are also mined in a small number of countries that do not always employ good hiring practices.

LEDs are difficult to take apart and recycle. Keep an eye out for future LEDs designed to be taken apart for recycling.

Don't let the units on the packaging confuse you. The amount of electrical power it uses is measured in Watts; the amount of light it produces is measured in Lumens. The so-called Temperature of the light refers to the colour.

Look it up

LEDs rare earths
Modular lighting systems
Touch panel light
Liter of light
Fairy-light footprint
Solar-powered lighting

Now try this!

1 An empty room does not need a light

35 The standby lightshow

77 Generate your own power

16. Insulate your home

So, you've turned down the air-con, controlled the airflow and selected the right heater, but the energy bills are still ridiculous. You can make an enormous difference by insulating your home. That is like the difference between sleeping under the doona or under a sheet.

Drive across any Australian metropolis. The landscape outside the inner-city and the established, leafy suburbs is dominated by homes on concrete slabs, with small eaves and little shade. Reverse cycle air-conditioning is the way that we manage the temperature in our typical Aussie homes.

On average, 40% of an Australian's energy bill is spent on climate control. The extreme summers of the last five years have made air-conditioning an essential consideration for many people, especially those medically vulnerable to the heat.

Instead of burning precious energy to control your environment, insulation helps create a pleasant environment and keep it that way. View it as an investment and enjoy the returns in comfort as you watch your energy bill go down.

Here's a plan

Every house is different, so here's some general principles and a personal story.

Your house will need its own plan, but the elements will be the same. Insulate the ceilings as soon as possible, the walls when you can and shade the western and northern walls from the summer sun. If you can't do that structurally – say with eaves or a patio – do it with plants. Deciduous plants shade the house in summer and let the winter sun in. How handy is that?

Reality check

Insulating a ceiling is relatively easy, the walls are hard. You have to take off one side of the wall.

Any property manager, plumber or maintenance person will groan at the mention of using plants for shade. Plants play havoc with plumbing. Choose your shade plants carefully.

A personal story

A young family got the keys to their 50-year-old timber house in mid-August when the cold winds blow but the temperature in the north-west corner of the house was 31°C! The room had been unusable in summer after the trees on the western wall had been chopped down.

Before moving in they replaced the asbestos cladding with weatherboard and, while the walls were open, stuffed them with a wool–polyester blend insulation. They installed ceiling fans and planted grapes (deciduous) on the west wall.

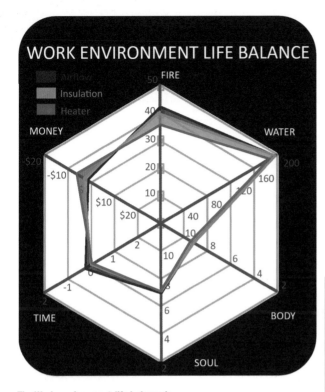

WORK ENVIRONMENT LIFE BALANCE

- Airflow
- Insulation
- Heater

FIRE, WATER, BODY, SOUL, TIME, MONEY

The Work-environment-life balance is explained on page 67

The standard AS/NZS 4859 rates insulation. R4 insulation is the maximum necessary for a home. Lower ratings are less effective.

Costs

Insulation: $**XXX**

Installation: $**XXX**

Payback time: 5 years

Now try this!
2 Turn down the air-con

8 Buy green power

9 Control the airflow

You get what you pay for. Air flow, insulation and new heaters compared. See also page 67

Look it up

Insulation emissions

Space cooling

Wool insulation

environment.gov.
au/climate-change

HARD FACTS

Stop heat leaks
AT HOME
Reduce energy bills by one third

POWER RATING OF ROOM COOLERS

Overhead fan: 40W

Air-conditioner: 2kW

That's 50 times
more power

17. Get active with your community

There's only so much you can do on your own, but waiting for government has not proven terribly effective. Getting together and doing it as a community hits the sweet spot.

Our power as individual consumers or investors can influence corporate decision-making, but only when lots of us do it in a coordinated way. As well as changing our own habits, we can get together and do things as a community, without waiting for the big end of town.

Reality check

Avoid activities that drain your soul. If a group does not feel right for you, don't hang around. You don't owe them anything.

Don't let the perfect get in the way of the good. Alette quotes the Zero Waste Chef: "We don't need a handful of people doing zero-waste perfectly. We need millions of people doing it imperfectly."

Here's a plan

Sing in a choir, join a community garden, home brewing club or repair café. Get involved in an activist group like the Youth Climate Coalition. Get active with your community. Join a group discussing future approaches and lobbying political parties. Pick a group that matches your passion.

The hive-mind of our virtual community is a great tool for building the future. Start asking for advice on which sustainable deodorant works, which shampoo bar sucks, or ditching the razor to save up for a safety razor (and lots of hair!) to get the ball rolling.

Search a platform like meetup.com and find local groups that interest you. Look online for groups like Permablitz, CropSwap. SpareHarvest, FreeCycle and LETS that use technology platforms to enable communal networks.

Find traditional groups, like community gardens, home brew societies or repair cafés who do physical activities together. Other groups discuss ideas and approaches and still others to engage in activism to raise awareness.

The Climate Angels greet Kayak4Earth at Evans Head

Look it up
Environmental/Climate/
Social activism
Non government organisations
Lobby influence
Corporate political donations
meetup.com
change.org
getup.org.au

Now try this!
80 Be a sticky beak

HARD FACTS

IN 2018/2019 THE
fossil fuel industry
DONATED OVER
$85 MILLION
TO AUSTRALIAN POLITICAL PARTIES

Enter the ... app watchers

Share what's spare —
Helen Andrew

Spare Harvest is a peer to peer app that started as a solution to a mandarin problem that I had and has grown organically by word of mouth. Now people share food hydrators, mowers, cuttings, food scraps, coffee grounds, eggshells and cartons.

The platform is just a facilitator, connecting people who have or want something. I see it as a global community acting at a local level; the way the members connect is quite unpredictable. I have had people meet in a city courtyard in their lunch time. I thought it had to be hyper local to survive, but we have had people from

Mildura in Victoria and the Sunshine Coast in Queensland share jams and chutneys by meeting up on holiday.

Mainstream apps that deliver cardboard boxes and use web cams to monitor them skew us away from what it means to be human beings. We have used technology to change what we as humans typically do. What we have to do is go back to what is innately inside every one of us: the desire to connect and trust another person. Food grown at home will generally be pesticide free, nutritionally rich because it is picked at the time of consumption and lovingly looked after with organic fertilizers and mulches.

One challenge to establishing these networks is that we get busy in our lives and forget that we have spare stuff in our kitchens and gardens and that sharing that stuff may help us connect.

One way we plan to overcome that is to support businesses and organisations that see a benefit in bringing their people together through sharing. They will contribute to the development of the platform so that it remains free.

Starting at a micro level, we are working with community gardens to share what they have spare, to generate some income for their garden and to find people to join their community garden. A level up from that is the lovely partnership we have with a sustainability school organisation to connect students across grades and classes, and share what they have at home or have grown in the school garden with the community while they learn about circular economy, sharing economy and social enterprise.

www.spareharvest.com

Helen Andrew with the mandarins that launched Spare Harvest

Pay what's fair —
Debra Weddall

Debra Weddall has produced over 400 videos and television segments promoting solidarity and equality for the labour movement. She is a founder member and National CoSecretary of the Rideshare Driver Network, an organisation of app based drivers in Australia.

"The network coordinates with the trade union movement and internationally with organisations like the International Association of App-based Transport Workers (IAATW) to get drivers industrial coverage under the law.

"The relationship between drivers and app-based transport companies is covered under the Trade Practices Act. Drivers' work is heavily directed by the companies. Drivers are allocated trips by algorithmic selection, therefore drivers cannot make any real decisions that might increase their hourly take.

"What is required is a third category of worker under the law that has industrial rights despite being employed using casual contracts.

"International and Australian research has revealed that the tech companies developing the apps make more money from data mining than they do from the services they provide. In the long term, robots are likely to replace drivers and so the companies have little incentive to invest in their workforce."

18. Hire a human

Every time you use a ride share app or have food delivered, you are hiring a human. But a slice of the money goes off-shore to the owner of the app. Why not keep that money in the community and pay each other to do this stuff?

Hard work is unpleasant and so we have harnessed the power of machines to do it for us. That means we live in great luxury, but a lot of us don't have much meaningful work to do. Because the wealth is not shared very evenly, some of us can get other people to do the jobs that we don't want to do ourselves. That's nice for the people with money, but pretty revolting for the rest of us.

Local networks build community and provide satisfaction through meaningful work.

Here's a plan

Find the local tailor or seamstress and get them to take in that extra-large dress from the local opp. shop.

The gig economy disrupts industry by having workers bid for jobs as independent businesses

Advertise the tasks you cannot do on your own; promote your skills, produce and creations.

So, you have a lawn mower and a washing machine? Find someone who doesn't. Offer them the use of your gear to do their chores in exchange for helping you do yours.

Throw a street party and get all the neighbours to bring food. Offer to buy the food you like next week, instead of ordering in from a restaurant.

Find your local beekeeper and buy their honey. See if they sell their beeswax to a

A personal story

"I thought delivering Uber Eats could be a simple way to make some extra cash when in between jobs. After about a month and a half of racking obscene kilometres on my car, refuelling three to four times as much as I used to, and only making around $14 an hour (before all the expenses), I stepped out. Those on bicycles make even less and can't get to anywhere near as many orders as I could in a car."

Look it up
Energy slaves
Rideshare wages
Real wages gig economy
Energy work units

local soap maker or make wax wraps to use instead of cling wrap.

Don't worry about the price; just barter. Play fair by making sure you would be happy to reverse the exchange.

Reality check

The two-speed economy is not an equitable or sustainable solution. We actually need to share the work around to benefit each other, not rip someone off so we feel better.

While you may be tempted to pay cash, 'under the table' this can come back to bite you. The tax department uses big data to detect money leaking unexpectedly around the economy.

This is not an invitation to rip off your neighbours. Sharing is caring. Be fair.

Global Green Tag helps companies monitor product supply chains to eliminate slavery.

Now try this!
10 Ordering in food

36 A stitch in time

53 Feeding friends

69 Borrow power tools

70 Repair café

95 Our community garden

HARD FACTS

AUSTRALIAN WAGES — $/H:

Minimum: ≈$20
Median: ≈$25
Average: ≈$45
Aussies earning > $100/h: ≈1mil

THE HUMAN MACHINE
A petrol engine produces
200 times as much work as a human, and uses
100 times the fuel.
OVER ONE DAY, A HUMAN labourer consumes
3.2kWh
(2750cal in food) to deliver
0.6kwh of useful work.
A SMALL PETROL-POWERED DIGGER
consumes 340kWh
(37L of petrol) to deliver
113kWh
of useful work.

19. That doggy in the window

Our companion animals improve our mental health, palliative care and immune systems. Dogs and cats, though, are not great for the environment. Here's how to get your cuddles sustainably.

You can have great fun getting to know your local wildlife. Birds enjoy sharing your garden and you can attract them with a birdbath. If you prefer furry things you can plant trees for the possums and other local wildlife.

Here's a plan

Resist the temptation to buy your own pet. Share one with a friend or neighbour or get to know the wild creatures around your home.

Wildlife rescue organisations like WIRES need volunteers to help look after rescued animals.

Organise a pet-friendly environment where you can offer to look after your friend's animals. Do it as a favour, a business or just for fun. Look into fostering. Give rescued animals an opportunity to get used to living a 'comfy home life' before being adopted into their own family.

Buy your pet dry food and cook your own pet meals by boiling pet meat with vegetables and rice. Do some research on DIY pet food and ensure it's got everything they need. Meat and canned pet food is about 80% water and importing water has an enormous carbon footprint.

If you are getting a new pet, adopt a rescue animal. There are millions of surrendered animals who won't see the other side of the pound. Purchasing from breeders, even registered ones, condemns the deserted pets to death. Most importantly, never buy a pet from a store. They are often bred in horrendous conditions at puppy mills or kitten farms.

Cost

A pet costs more than $500 a year.

HARD FACTS

Pet food facts, 2019
Australia spends: $3 billion
Per Australian: 37kg
Increase: 4.5% each year

ABANDONED PETS:
200,000
abandoned dogs are euthanised in Australia each year

A personal story

Sharing pets only works on a part-time basis. Pets are loyal and devoted to one family. When you share animals, make it clear that there is one owner.

Feeding wild birds and animals disrupts their wild life. Vary the routine to make sure they fend for themselves some of the time.

600 unwanted dogs are euthanized in Australia every day

Look it up

Imported pet food

Raw pet diet

Supplements for dogs/cats

Adopt don't shop

Puppy mills

Foster a pet Australia

Feed wildlife

wires.org.au

adoptapet.com.au

petrescue.com

Now try this!

24 What the cat does each night

92 The dinosaur family

94 Getting out into nature

97 Don't fence me in

20. Invest ethically

Superannuation has made us all investors. As shareholders we can have more influence over corporate behaviour than we do as consumers. Make sure your superannuation is invested in companies that look after your life and your planet.

Corporations exist to generate value for their shareholders. That value is measured in dollars, not in the impact on the environment or the people who work to create that profit. Some companies have actively opposed investment in renewable energy and environmental regulation.

One way to influence companies is through your superannuation fund and by moving your bank account to an ethical bank.

Here's a plan

Investigate the policies of your bank and superannuation fund and then compare that to those that claim to be ethical. Some super funds allow you some control over where your money gets invested. If you have to rollover (move) your superannuation to one of these funds, make sure you do your research first. You need to balance what is going to work for your retirement as well as making sure there is a liveable world to retire in. There are also life insurance and taxation implications around your super.

Managed funds offer a different mix of investments to ensure your money is safe. A fund may invest 20% in property, 20% in loans and 60% in 'bluechip' shares, for example. You might have the opportunity to adjust that spread of investments, or you might be able to specify ethical or environmental issues that you wish to support.

You can take maximum control if you set up your own super fund and put it all in an ethical, green sector that appeals to you. You need a big chunk of superannuation to make that worthwhile. Most advise that you should have $250,000 in your super before considering a self-managed super fund.

Investing money independently of your superannuation gives you more control but less protection from taxation on your earnings.

HARD FACTS

THE RESPONSIBLE INVESTMENT ASSOCIATION OF AUSTRALIA reported that responsible (ethical and green) funds **returned 12.9% over 10 years,** COMPARED TO 8.9% FOR THE ASX TOP 300.

The impact is less dramatic on a global scale.

Reality check

Many free trade agreements allow companies to sue the Australian government if it passes regulations that restrict their profits. Philip Morris, for example, tried to sue the Australian government for its plain packaging rules on tobacco products, using a clause in the Free Trade Agreement between Australia and Hong Kong.

Your super fund may not reveal what companies it invests in.

Check the impact on your life insurance before you roll over your super.

Smaller banks do not offer all the services provided by the four big banks and some international banks operating in Australia.

The source of all wisdom, as far as superannuation rules go, is the Australian Tax Office (ATO).

Costs

Fees for rolling over your superannuation may be as high as 4%.

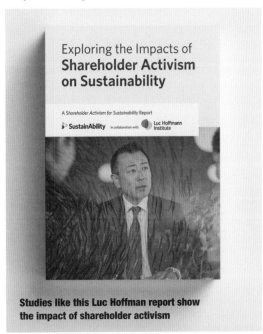

Exploring the Impacts of
Shareholder Activism on Sustainability

A Shareholder Activism for Sustainability Report

SustainAbility   In collaboration with   Luc Hoffmann Institute

Studies like this Luc Hoffman report show the impact of shareholder activism

Look it up
Ethical investment
Responsible investment return
Sue plain packaging
1millionwomen.com.au
australianethical.com.au
futuresuper.com.au
industrysuper.com.au

Now try this!
5 Paying it forward
16 Get active
with your community
18 Hire a human
45 What's on the label
74 Sharing the car

Let's fix it

As well as saving water,
let's save the energy used to heat
the water and pump
it to your house.

21. Take a shorter shower

22. Lighten the laundry load

23. Recycled toilet paper

24. If it's yellow let it mellow

We need to talk about ...

... THE CHEMICALS WE USE

We tip chemicals and water down the drains
of the wet areas of our house. Many of them
are not good for us, or the environment.

25. Those dripping taps

26. Essential oils

27. Home spun hair care

28. Lotions and potions

29. That toxic detergent

30. Oil and vinegar

Plan ahead

Pumping and heating water are
big users of energy.
We can make a big difference to
our personal carbon and water
targets with a little forward planning.

31. Process greywater

32. Solar hot water

## CHAPTER 02

BATHROOM, TOILET & LAUNDRY

Australia is the driest continent on earth and we regularly suffer drought. Those droughts have become longer and drier as the impacts of global warming kick in. We need to keep a lid on our water consumption.
We also use a lot of chemicals in the wet areas of the house. Many of these are quite dangerous and need to be carefully managed.

How we'll fix it

We'll reduce demand by each using less water, being more efficient in industry and agriculture, and recycling water better.

During the most recent drought, water-saving measures reduced our consumption to under 200 litres per person a day. As well as having shorter showers, many people showered with a bucket and used the captured water to keep essential plants alive. Most people gave up on the thirstier parts of their gardens.

Australians became acutely aware of the amount of water that goes into growing and processing foods and textiles. These skills should not be forgotten.

PERSONAL WATER TARGET
LITRES PER DAY PER PERSON

2014 Average
2020 Average
Target
Stanthorpe
Sailor

Your Personal water target

In this chapter we will make use of the **Personal water target** to measure the impact of each tip on your overall water usage.

Water is a national, rather than a global, issue. As a result, your Personal water target is compared to average Australian use.

- The outer area of the target, 360 litres a day, is at the upper end of per person consumption; it represents someone in an affluent suburb with a swimming pool in times of no water restrictions.

- The white drop represents the national average of 199 litres per day.

- The target of 144 litres per day is about the middle of the personal targets in cities in 2018.

The town of Stanthorpe in Queensland, for example, had a target of 100 litres per day after its water supply ran dry and water was trucked into town for people to collect in large containers.

As with the carbon target, P5 smaller is better. Again, the savings described in each tip are calculated based on the average household, as defined in the Anitkythera.

The impact of a specific tip will depend on your current habits and your current

water usage. For example, you might be frugal in the bathroom but use a lot of water in the garden. The next tip *Take a shorter shower* will have a small impact on your large water usage, whereas Tip 60 *Handmade watering systems* might reduce your water use considerably..

Let's fix it

These first tips are easy to do and require very little time and money. As well as saving water, they save the energy used to heat the water in your shower and to pump the water to your house.

Laundry detergent consumes energy and contains pollutants and if your toilet paper is not recycled it involves cutting down forests. As well as the impact on your carbon footprint these affect the health of the ecosystem, so that impact registers in the tip summary provided here.

Left: Water restrictions have become a permanent feature in many regional areas

#	Tip	Page	🔥	💧	🧒🧒	👁	⏱	Ⓢ
21	Take a shorter shower	60	✓✓	✓✓✓			✓✓	✓✓
22	Lighten the laundry load	62	✓✓✓	✓✓			✗✗	✓✓
23	Recycled toilet paper	64	✓					
24	If it's yellow let it mellow	65		✓✓				

21. Take a shorter shower

A long shower is a luxury that costs the earth. Spend more time in bed, instead; take a bath every now and then.

Here's a plan

- Make sure you have aerated taps and shower heads. They insert air bubbles into the stream of water, reducing the water while still getting you thoroughly wet.
- Set a timer to ring after three or four minutes or put on your tunes and have a one-tune shower. Make it a household rule.
- Don't shave, clean your teeth or cut your toenails in the shower. At least turn the water off while you are doing those things or putting product through your hair.
- Share a shower or bath. Big families do this for practical reasons. Line 'em up and run 'em through. It saves time as well as water.

PERSONAL WATER TARGET

LITRES PER DAY PER PERSON

shorter shower

A 10-minute shower with a traditional water head uses half your average water consumption

showers and then hops in the bath for 10 minutes of R&R.

One eco-warrior turns off the tap as she soaps up, "I kind of do this out of necessity as I only have a tiny water heater, so hot water runs out pretty quickly. Especially if my household has showers around the same time. I was annoyed at first but now I'm used to it."

A personal story

The traditional way in Japan is to run a hot bath for the whole family. Everyone

Back in the day

The Romans, Turks, Koreans and Japanese have all been famous at various points in human history for their bath houses. A long hot scrub in a steam-filled room is good for

Look it up
Potable water

Water saving tips

savewater.com.au

Aerating shower heads

Ginseng bath house

the soul as well as the epiderm. If you're in the mood for a good soak of the sort that takes an afternoon, head to a bath house.

Australians are apprehensive about a saunter to the sauna, but there are options for those craving bath-time. Sydneysiders can head to the Ginseng Bathhouse in Kings Cross. Melbourne has the recently refurbished City Baths. The rest of us might have to find a Day Spa with hot pools. Your body will love it.

Reality check
A four-minute shower is an efficient use of water. A 10-minute shower, even 15 minutes with a water efficient shower head, uses similar amounts of water as running a bath.

Now try this!
25 Those dripping taps

31 Process greywater

32 Solar hot water

89 Planting a local

HARD FACTS

AN AERATING SHOWER HEAD USES
6-9 litres
per minute

A TRADITIONAL SHOWER HEAD USES
15-20 litres
per minute

A BATH TAKES
150-200 litres of water

THE AVERAGE FAMILY USES
70,000 litres
of water to shower
each year

THE SHOWER ACCOUNTS FOR AROUND
20% of the water
used in the average family home

22. Lighten the laundry load

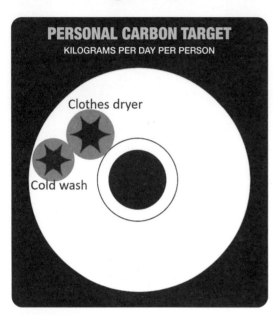

PERSONAL CARBON TARGET
KILOGRAMS PER DAY PER PERSON

Clothes dryer

Cold wash

In a typical home, the clothes dryer has more impact than washing clothes in hot water

Photo by jeremy-sallee on Unsplash

To keep you stepping out in style, the laundry tumbles, spins, dries and presses its way through the week, at some cost in energy. Working with nature can lighten the load.

The washing machine and the dryer are big-ticket electrical appliances. They consume enormous amounts of energy to keep your whites crisp and clean.

The amount of energy required to heat the water is up to 25 times that required to agitate and spin the clothes. Heating 30 litres of hot water to 40°C uses around 1.3 kilowatt hours of energy. Unless you have a solar hot water service, use cold water for your regular loads. The dryer uses energy to turn the clothes, heat the air and blow the air through the clothes. If you have the space and the sun is shining, hang your clothes outside. If you're not blessed with the warm winter sunshine, consider stringing up some laundry lines in your house, or use portable laundry racks.

Here's a plan

- If you have a solar hot water service installed, you may have plenty of hot water with no **embodied energy** at all. You can wash your clothes at a temperature you choose.

- Washing in cold water most of the time and only using hot water for really dirty loads goes a long way to reducing your energy consumption.

- Forget the clothes dryer altogether if the weather allows. The sun disinfects, whitens and makes your clothes smell good. Use those indoor laundry racks if the day isn't as sunny as you had hoped.

- Another way to lighten the impact of your laundry on the planet is to share the appliances with the neighbours.

HARD FACTS

A CLOTHES DRYER PRODUCES ABOUT

3 kg of CO$_2$ an hour.

WASHING IN

COLD WATER

generates 300 grams OF GREENHOUSE GAS PER WASH.

HEATING THE WATER

for a hot wash

GENERATES UP TO

4 kg of greenhouse gas.

Applying sensitive laundry practices saves energy and water

Reality check

Some washing liquids and powders work better in cold water than others. Other tips explore detergent and soap.

Some apartment blocks and strata title developments have policies against hanging clothes outdoors. This tip might help get that policy overturned.

Washing and caring for fabric is hard work. In most cultures it is a task that is delegated to the down-trodden. Washing machines, powerful chemicals and hot water considerably reduce the required effort. If you are not actually doing the washing yourself, I suggest you pass this tip on rather than boasting you have a better way to handle the laundry.

Now try this!
18 Hire a human
29 That toxic detergent
55 Energy-efficient appliances

Look it up
Spin cycle washing bike
Cold water wash
Solar hot water

23. Recycled toilet paper

The great toilet paper crisis of 2020 showed just how obsessed Australians are about wiping our bums. Quite a few enterprising environmentalists will deliver high-quality recycled toilet paper to your door.

 Don't get me wrong, high quality here does not mean soft, strong, fluffy, fragrantly smelling and appealing to the eye. Most of eco-friendly toilet papers are plain and simple without being scratchy or flimsy.

A personal story

Alette writes, "Toilet paper was one of the first sustainable changes I made — when I was six years old. My Year 2 teacher taught us all about the oceans and what was being filtered into it. My family used to get the scented stuff with printed purple flowers on the paper. That night, I banned my mum from buying toilet paper with dye on it. She has never bought it since (and lets me know about it)."

Here's a plan

- **Check out the brands at your local shops and compare the price per hundred sheets of the most eco-friendly brands with the more glamorous items.**
- **Buy in bulk to reduce the impact of delivery emissions.**
- **Consider the options of a bidet, or washing your nether regions in some other way, or using sponges, cloth napkins or something else that can be washed and sterilised.**
- **Many toilet papers are only 50% recycled. Look for 100% on the label.**
- **The labelling laws also let you see just how many squares you get for your dollar.**

HARD FACTS

EACH AUSTRALIAN USES
20kg of toilet paper per year.
THE GLOBAL AVERAGE IS 4kg/Y.

Look it up
Toilet paper recycled
Gompf stick
World toilet culture
whogivesacrap.org
toiletpaperhistory.net

24. If it's yellow let it mellow

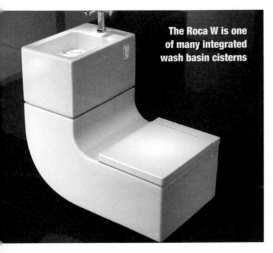

The Roca W is one of many integrated wash basin cisterns

A personal story

Allete says, "I lived in a tiny apartment in Japan, and its toilet had a little sink on top of the cistern. Every time you flushed, the tap filled the cistern's sink. This meant you washed your hands with clean drinking water, then used that water to flush. More exciting than the bidet."

Look it up
Cistern fills tap sink
Yellow mellow brown down
Scour velocity sewer
thomas-crapper.com
japanese tap cistern

Flushing the toilet more than necessary wastes water and the energy required to pump it. Pop the lid down to avoid offending the eyes and nostrils.

We can no longer afford to use drinking water to wash away our wee.

Consider the old fashioned 'brick-in-the-cistern' trick. The brick takes up more space so that less water is used to fill the cistern. However, this is pointless if you have to flush twice to get the solids to flow away.

Reality check

There will be the occasional odour and the porcelain may need an extra polish.

It's all very well to save water at home, but it might not be welcome at work or other shared spaces.

HARD FACTS

TOILETS USE BETWEEN
3 & 13 litres
of water per flush.

DUAL FLUSH CISTERNS are law in all states except NSW.

... the chemicals we use

We wash nearly all the lotions, potions, product and poisons we use down the drain. These chemical, microplastics and nanoparticles build up in the oceans. The load of active pharmaceuticals ranging from recreational drugs to antibiotics in our city's sewers is large enough to reveal what recreational drugs are most popular on what days of the week! Wastewater (sewage) treatment plants were recently used to identify the presence of non-symptomatic cases of Covid19 in regional communities.

It was the explosion in chemical use that led to the 1962 book, *Silent Spring*. Since then, we have paid much closer attention to what each particular product does, how it does it and the options available to achieve that same affect more sustainably.

Waste water treatment plants reveal much about the lotions and potions we use
©Simmonds & Bristow

Tip summary

The tips in this chapter have an impact across most aspects of our daily lives.

#	Tip	Page	🔥	💧	🧍	👁	⏱	$
25	Those dripping taps	68		✓✓	✓	✗		✗✗ ✓
26	Essential oils	70			✓	✓		✗
27	Home spun hair care	72			✓✓	✓✓	✗	✓✓
28	Lotions and potions	74			✓✓	✓✓		✓
29	That toxic detergent	78	✓		✓✓	✓✓		✓
30	Oil and vinegar	80	✓		✓✓	✓✓	✗	✓✓

Introducing the WELB

We can visualise that summary on a diagram by adding each separate index along the spokes of a wheel, or web. The shape of the wheel reflects the areas that are being most impacted.

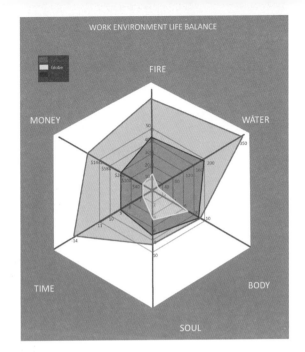

WORK ENVIRONMENT LIFE BALANCE

FIRE

WATER

MONEY

BODY

SOUL

TIME

Work-environment-life balance (the WELB)

As with the previous infographics, the WELB visualises the work-environment-life balance of the average Australian. Here we compare Australians in the top 10% of income, with the average Australian and the global average. This provides a graphic representation of what we mean by a two-speed economy.

The environment is represented by the fire and water symbols and is positioned along the axis using the carbon and water figures discussed in detail in earlier chapters.

The time and money figures are based on UN and OECD surveys and represent daily income and spare time per day. A bibliography of the sources is available through YLYP.news.

The personal physical and social wellness scores are taken from the UN Human Wellness Index and the Household Income and Lifestyle Dynamics in Australia (HILDA) survey conducted by the University of Melbourne every year. They are discussed in more detail in the Anitkythera at the end of the book.

We are wealthier and healthier than most other nations, so it is unsurprising that we find little to complain about in that regard. That being said, the health of the Australian environment is largely due to the fact that a relatively small number of people live on a rather large landmass that has been sustainably managed by First Nations people for not far short of a thousand centuries and we have only spent two centuries ignoring their good work.

More information about how the WELB is used within the book is provided at the beginning of Chapter 3, *Bedroom*.

25. Those dripping taps

A slowly dripping tap loses 9 litres a day; that's around 60 litres a week, 250 litres a month, or 3 kilolitres a year. Most taps can be fixed with a washer that costs $1.60. Just do it!

Old houses, or houses connected to old water supplies, tend to suffer from dripping taps.

One reason is that particles of rust or dirt get caught inside the tap and allow water to sneak through. This carves a channel in the tap washer, which needs to be replaced. Every tap needs the washer replaced from time to time.

Other leaks need to be checked as well.

Pipes in the garden and on roofs are particularly hard to check. Make sure all the taps are turned off and check the water meter — if it is ticking over you have a significant problem.

Keep your eye out for unusually lush or wet spots in the garden.

Check the downpipes coming from your roof. If any of them has a permanent dribble

PERSONAL WATER TARGET
LITRES PER DAY PER PERSON

Stop leaks

A dribbling tap has a significnat impact on your water use

of water coming from it, you have a leak somewhere upstairs.

A personal story

I keep a tap reseating tool handy. They are easy to use, once you know how, but it is better to get someone to show you than try and describe it in a book like this.

Reality check

The rate of a dripping tap speeds up quickly as it wears a channel through the tap. Put a bucket under the tap if you want to see how fast your tap is actually dripping.

A house with a few dripping taps will soon double its water consumption. A street full of houses like that and you have a major leak in the water supply.

HARD FACTS

| SOME AUSTRALIAN CITIES HAVE REDUCED THEIR **water pressure to reduce leaks.** | SOME CITIES IN AUSTRALIA **lose over 40%** of their water **SUPPLY THROUGH LEAKS.** |

Reality check

Not all taps are easily fixed. Single-handled taps, the ones that blend the hot and cold water, are notoriously difficult (read expensive) to repair. Most home handy-people replace the whole unit.

Spring-loaded and 'cushioned' washers work well for a short time but may need regular attention.

Older plumbing presents a variety of challenges. Fittings can be buried deep in the wall; sometimes they have been reseated so often that special tools are required to fix them any further.

Plumbers are expensive. Plumbing is tricky if you don't know how. Bribe a handy friend.

Some European cities turn off the water supply at night to prevent losses through leaks in the mains supply.

Look it up
Dripping tap litres
Reseating tool
savewater.com.au
sydneywater.com.au

Costs

A dribbling tap loses 27 litres a day; that's around 180 litres a week, 750 litres a month or 9 kilolitres a year.

Most taps can be fixed with a new washer, costing $1.60.

A simple reseating tool is available in most hardware stores

Now try this!

21 Take a shorter shower

31 Process greywater

99 Put some water in your tank

26. Essential oils

Oils from many plants have medical properties, are soothing or simply pleasant. Essential oils can deliver their benefits through your skin, stomach or your nostrils via a room with scent.

The greatest damage done by cosmetics and medicines happens when we wash them down the sink. Toxins in the lotions and potions we use accumulate in our waterways and in aquatic life.

Some products are made from palm oil grown at the expense of rainforest and others are tested on animals.

Here's a plan

Where appropriate you can use essential plant oils instead of manufactured products. Some powerful and commonly available oils are included here.

EUCALYPTUS: A cleaner and a cure for chest complaints, eucalyptus oil is the active ingredient in many cough lollies, syrups and chest rubs due to its expectorant properties. Eucalyptus oil also acts as a disinfectant and penetrative agent to carry other substances into the skin. Citronella is a eucalyptus oil that repels insects, protecting health in the tropics and sub-tropics.

TEA TREE: Made from the *Melaleuca alternifolia* tree and widely available as an oil, tea tree is used as an ingredient in antiseptic, toothpaste, deodorant, hand sanitiser and insect repellent. It is a fungicide as well as anti-bacterial and so useful against tinea, dandruff and for ridding fruit and vegetables of mould.

LEMON MYRTLE: An even more powerful disinfectant, expectorant and anti-fungal agent than either tea tree or eucalyptus oil. It is widely recommended for mouth and throat infections. Its scientific name is *Backhousia citriodora* reflecting its powerful lemon scent.

CLOVE: The dried bud of the tropical tree *Syzigium aromatica* has anaesthetic, anti-bacterial and anti-fungal properties. Relieve toothaches by popping a whole clove into the mouth and allowing it to rest against the sore tooth.

PEPPERMINT: Used to flavour toothpastes and foods, peppermint also relieves headaches, muscle-pain and itching. Peppermint tea is a refreshing, uplifting and relaxing drink that energises without stimulating and is useful for irritable bowel syndrome and nausea.

LAVENDER: Often placed under pillows as a relaxant and soporific in the form of a pot-pourri, lavender is also recommended by naturopaths as a relaxant and possible anti-depressant. The Drug and Food Administration does not recommend it clinically due to insufficient evidence.

CANNABIS: Widely used for pain relief, pleasure and medical conditions such as the control of seizures. Although historically commonplace, cannabis oil currently has a complicated legal status.

Back in the day

Mrs Winlow's Soothing Syrup was an opiate promoted in 19th century America as suitable for babies. It was advertised using a drawing of a young mother teasing a naked baby who reaches for an eye dropper of the drug.

Reality check

While you can extract essential oils using a simple still, the first step is to explore essential oils off the shelf. Buy them from small, local manufacturers to keep your dollars in the community. Some essential oils are more expensive than others; start with the basics that help around the home.

Look it up
aromatherapy

Now try this!

28 Lotions and potions

30 Oil and vinegar

46 Where the herbs grow

27. Homespun hair care

Hair care ads promote bounce, shine and curl at considerable cost. You can replace these highly packaged products with simple, natural ingredients and a little extra effort.

Like all lotions, potions and cleaning products, shampoos and conditioners have one impact on the environment during manufacture and another when you wash them down the drain. They are detergent- rather than soap-based, glossily packaged, sometimes tested on animals and contain substances that accumulate in the food chain.

Here's a plan

The easiest thing to do is to shampoo less. Your natural oils will give your hair some gloss and bounce and you can wash the grime out without completely stripping out the good oil.

Some people simply rinse their hair under the shower, giving it a good scratch and combing in clean, hot water. Others, with fine or fragile hair, skip the shampoo and just wash the hair in conditioner.

If you can't ditch the detergent, have a look into natural saponin makers. Soap berries are fantastic alternatives. Make up a batch of 'mother' soap and use it for your hair, body, dishes and more. They last a couple of months if kept in the fridge.

Other alternatives include lemon juice, vinegar, olive oil and aloe vera. Most of them can be applied by simply brushing through the hair and rinsing them out the next day. The pulp from inside the aloe vera leaf foams and can be rubbed into the wet hair like shampoo. You can get aloe vera extract from organic stores but, of course, that comes with a bottle.

Many cultures use a paste made of plants, similar to henna. Rub the paste through your hair and let it do its work, then rinse it out. Most of these treatments will work in cold water if you can brave the chill.

Conditioner can also be created from many household products: day-old rice water, apple cider vinegar, eggs.

If the natural route isn't your dig, look into shampoo and conditioner bars. They contain some blend of the approaches already described and are simple to use with less packaging but for a slightly higher cost. The market for them is growing rapidly, with products for blonde hair, curly, frizzy, dry ...

Photo by jiangxulei1990-elzzwtkBjU on Unsplash

A personal story

A curly headed gal mentions, "Curly girls can often get away without shampoo. Since I started reducing the amount of silicones on my hair it feels lighter and I can go longer between washes. It did take about three months for my hair to get used to my new shampoo and conditioner bars, though."

Look it up

Surfactant hair

Hemp oil shampoo

Non-plastic shampoo pods

Soap berries

Shampoo bars

Conditioner bars

Cider vinegar rinse

Rice water rinse

Now try this!

29 That toxic detergent

22 Lighten the laundry load

40 Use clean detergents

41 Cleaning products

65 Skip the supermarket

94 Helping out nature

28. Lotions and potions

We put weird and wonderful concoctions on our skins and inside us to keep us well, sane and apparently youthful. Some are tested on animals or have a negative impact on the environment. Some of them are not that great for us, either.

The over-prescription of antibiotics and 'feel good' drugs such as painkillers is a social and a health problem. Holistic medicines nurture the whole human being and the environment; investigate natural wellness supplements. Seek expert advice on medicines and cures when you need it.

Here's a plan

Look into ethically made and sourced cosmetic products. There is a plethora of locally made products to reduce the transport emissions of your beauty regime. Seek out plastic-free alternatives – often these are organic or ethically sourced products into the bargain.

Bulk stores have their own lines of refillable toiletries and body care products. Consider investing in a sturdy caddy and refill as you need to.

Or, get gung-ho and make your own from natural ingredients: coconut oil, jojoba oil, shea butter and your favourite essential oils. They can usually be found in bulk stores, so BYO jars!

Many cosmetic companies add natural ingredients to industrial products, but you are looking for products that are organically grown, do not contain palm oil or petroleum-based products. Look for labelling such as Fair Trade that defines the source.

HARD FACTS

THE PHARMACEUTICAL SECTOR IS ESTIMATED TO PRODUCE OF 52 megatonnes of CO_2 equivalent.

THEIR MAJOR IMPACT, THOUGH, IS ON THE water rather than the air.

Photo by Tijana Drndarski on Unsplash

Reality check

One of the biggest problems with cosmetics is the ingredient palm oil, which to grow usually involves mass destruction of rainforests. It is often described as vegetable oil on cosmetic labels.

Sunscreens contain Oxybenzone (also known as Benzopehnone-3) which sucks up the sun's UV rays, protecting your skin, but also harming the reef.

Waste antibiotics released into the environment are a major contributor to the emergence of drug-resistant super bugs. More of them come from farming than our bathroom cabinets.

Making your own cosmetics can be time consuming.

In February 2018 many natural products were removed from Therapeutic Goods Register and, more recently, from private health insurance.

Buying basic ingredients in bulk resolved issues of transport and packaging

Back in the day

For our great grandparents, simple infections were often a death sentence. A bad wound obtained while playing sport or working outdoors often led to illness and death. In 1914 the Australian Medical Journal reported that infection was only responsible for one quarter of deaths and tuberculosis for one in 10. Hygiene, disinfection and better sanitation were largely responsible for the decrease.

Look it up

Naturopathy

Osteopathy

DIY skin care

Bulk food

Toothpaste pills

Holistic health care

Floraandfauna.com.au

Biome.com.au

Now try this!

6 Indoor plants

26 Essential oils

29 That toxic detergent

46 Where the herbs grow

60 Things that grow in the dark

Analysing the ingredients —
Ken Goonengerry

We asked Dr Ken Goonengerry* to analyse a typical list of ingredients from the back of an 'organic' shampoo bottle. Here is an example, followed by an abridged explanation as to what those names mean.

Water (Aqua), Ammonium Lauryl Sulfate, Disodium Cocoamphodiacetate, Polyquaternium-39, Cocamine MEA, Stearic Acid, Dimethicone, Laureth-8, Succinoglycan, Glycol Distearate, Persea Gratissima (Avocado) Leaf Extract, Hydroxypropyl Guar, EDTA, Dimethlypabamidopropyl Lauryldimonium Tosylate, Propylene Glycol Stearate, Citric Acid, Fragrance (Parfum), DMDM Hydantoin. Not tested on animals.

Shampoo is basically detergent that strips out grease and dirt, combined with a series of compounds that deposit a film onto the hair to add shine and body.

Detergents allow other chemicals to penetrate the skin more easily. Concerns have been expressed that because surfactants break down skin cells they can accelerate the ageing process. Some classes of surfactants – the nonylphenols – have been reported to interfere with the sexual development of wildlife.

The surfactants in this shampoo include Ammonium Lauryl sulfate, Laureth-8, Disodium Cocoamphodiacetate and Cocamine MEA.

Cocoamphodiacetate is a surfactant derived from coconut oil with a very good toxilogical profile.

MEA (monoethylamine) is considered responsible for creating carcinogenic compounds that are absorbed through the skin. It is considered less dangerous than DEA (diethylamine) which has been banned in the US but is prevalent in Australia.

Other active chemicals that are not involved directly in the cleaning process include EDTA (ethylenediaminetetraacetic acid). It is used to soften the water by depositing mineral salts and locking them up in the shampoo foam. It also preserves the shampoo.

DMDM Hydantoin is a preservative that works by releasing formaldehyde into the shampoo to prevent mould, fungus and bacteria growing in it. Formaldehyde is a known carcinogen.

The second group of compounds are those left behind on the hair to replace the natural oils. These compounds are relatively inert, though their manufacture may cause industrial pollution.

Stearic Acid is made from blasting animal fat or saturated vegetable oils with water at high temperature and pressure and is used

Photo by jiangxulei1990–eIzzzwtkBjU on Unsplash

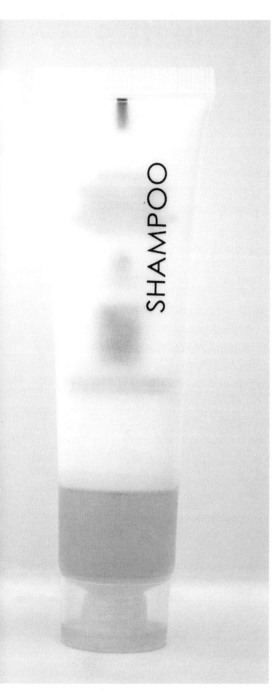

to give body to the shampoo. *Propylene glycol Stearate* and *Glycol Distearate* are related compounds.

The addition of avocado oil, *Persea Gratissima* (Avocado) Leaf Extract, into the mix does little to interfere with the underlying chemistry of the shampoo.

This shampoo contains *Polyquaternium-39*, which is cellulose derived from cotton, the silicone-based *Dimethicone*, as well as *Succinoglycan* and *Hydroxypropyl Guar*. *Dimethlypabamidopropyl Lauryldimonium Tosylate* is included to protect it from ultraviolet radiation.

The third main group of compounds are used to add fragrance. This shampoo label simply labels that group as Fragrance. Over 4,000 chemicals are used to manufacture fragrances, 95% of them derived from petroleum and 84% which have never been tested for safety. Fragrances are considered trade secrets so do not have to be declared on product labels.

This is just one shampoo product. Conditioners contain a similarly strange mix of chemicals, and hair-colouring products that use synthetic dyes are probably even worse. For example, they may contain coal tar colours, listed on labels as FD&C and D&C, and made from bituminous coal. Or, they may contain *phenylenediamine*, another cancer-causing agent. Some even contain lead. This is not only bad for you, but also the environment.

*Dr Ken Goonengerry is a pseudonym used for this book.

Commercial shampoos have a range of chemical ingredients

29. That toxic detergent

Detergent is a modern miracle and a curse. It appears in almost every cleaning product from shampoo to oven cleaner, as well as industrial products and food. It has the power to change the nature of water and anything that contains water, such as skin.

Detergents have largely replaced soap in every cleaning product we use, because it is soluble in water and chemically stable. Detergents are made from petrochemicals and so are dependent on a finite resource. Some detergents are toxic, but they are not used in household products.

Here's a plan

Use detergent sparingly. Don't aim for a thick layer of bubbles on every sink full of dishes or bath you take.

Dilute it! Most dishwashing liquids are so concentrated you only need a few drops to fill your sink with suds.

Buy washing powders that are phosphorus and fluorescent free. Liquid detergents and washing powders are 'complemented' or 'boosted' by chlorine-based bleaches, phosphorous-based cleaners and fluorescent brighteners. All these chemicals have an immediate and measurable impact on the environment.

Bio-surfactants are less harsh environmentally but relatively new; look out for them.

Don't forget about the wonders of soap. One way to keep a handle on it, literally, is to put it in a soap cage. This is a wire box on a handle that you plunge into a sink full of hot water and swish around before you do the dishes. Easy.

Use soap instead of body wash. Ignore the scare mongering by chemical manufacturers about bacteria living on soap. Their sole aim is to sell more detergent.

Photo by MD Duran on Unsplash

HARD FACTS | **BLUE GREEN ALGAE ARE REALLY** cyanobacteria | **Phosphate content** of detergents ranges **FROM 0% TO 8.7%**

Reality check

Strong detergents do clean more thoroughly. You may need to use them sometimes to shift stubborn stains.

Soaps are harsh on metal objects like washing machines. You may want to read up on your manufacturer's recommendation before you ditch the detergent altogether.

Using hot water makes your soap or detergent more effective. If your water is heated by renewables it is environmentally friendly to wash in it.

Detergents cause problems if they build up in waterways

Look it up

Phosphorus blue algae

Detergent waterway

waterwatch.org.au

planetark.com

simplesavings.com.au

Now try this!

30 Oil and vinegar

32 Solar hot water

40 Hemp and bamboo

Bathroom

30. Oil and vinegar

The cupboard under the sink contains a toxic cocktail of chemicals. Replace it with a bottle of vinegar, a box of bicarbonate of soda (bicarb or carb soda) and a little elbow grease. Natural polishes, waxes and oils are all back in a big way because they do the job without damaging our planet.

Reality check

Can lemon juice, vinegar, salt, talculm powder and bicarb soda really cut the mustard when it comes to cutting grease? You betcha. They worked for centuries before TV commercials sold us industrial cleaners made from fossil fuels.

They do not poison you, release aerosols, or endanger the lives of those rummaging through the middle drawer.

A personal story

Alette runs a cleaning company and says: "I've completed bond standard cleans with bicarb, vinegar and a razor. The mix has

Here's a plan

- Dampen metal surfaces such as pots and ovens then sprinkle bicarb soda over them. Wait an hour and then scrub.
- Sprinkle bicarb on a damp cloth to wipe down benches, chopping boards, the fridge or metal fittings.
- Keep the fridge sweet smelling with an open container of bicarb soda in the main body.
- Sprinkle bicarb then splash vinegar on drains, toilets and stained surfaces. Wipe while the mixture is still frothing. Then pour boiling hot water over the surface to give your drains a better rinse.

- Vinegar on a damp cloth is a great way to wipe mould and mildew off walls and smooth surfaces.
- Vinegar, or lemon juice, with olive oil makes a great furniture cleaner and polisher.
- Lemon juice is a natural bleach and can be used to lighten most stains. Adding some crushed eggshells puts a bit of calcium in the chemistry and grit in the mix.
- Talcum powder sprinkled on oil stains in clothes will soak up the oil and prepare the cloth for cleaning.
- Borax, or boracic acid — the two are not identical — can be used as a cleaner in place of bicarb soda and mixed with white sugar or honey to kill ants and cockroaches.

Photo by joanna-kosinska on Unsplash

Great for salad, furniture, hair and skin. Where would you NOT put oil and vinegar? ©myolive.ca

citrus peel, steeped in the vinegar, for two or more weeks. Strain and add it to an empty spray bottle, 50:50 with water, and you've got your very own spray 'n' wipe. And don't stop at citrus. Rosemary, eucalyptus … if it smells good put it in some vinegar."

Reality check

If you move into someone else's house, inherit a barbecue or come in contact with years of greasy grime, these simple remedies may leave you disappointed. Try scraping the surface with a sharp tool and leaving the detergent to soak in before you reach for the nuclear-grade oven cleaner in a spray can.

Look it up
Safe cleaning products
Sodium bicarbonate
Boracic insects
Propoxur
Natural furniture polish
Vinegar spray
ecoshop.com.au
biome.com.au

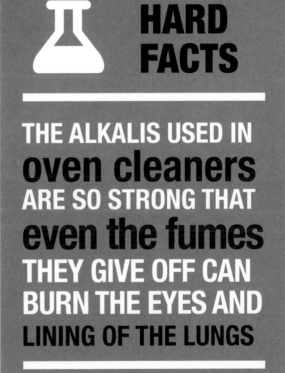

HARD FACTS

THE ALKALIS USED IN oven cleaners ARE SO STRONG THAT even the fumes THEY GIVE OFF CAN BURN THE EYES AND LINING OF THE LUNGS

Now try this!

29 That toxic detergent
70 Repair café
96 Fertilise naturally

Plan ahead

The big infrastructure items for the bathroom, toilet and laundry are unsurprisingly about water. *Process greywater* is about saving water, Tip 32 *Solar hot water* about saving energy by heating it renewably. The details are dealt with in the tip itself.

Before you make major investments, you are entitled to think seriously about the return that you will get. What difference will a renewable hot water system or a greywater processing plant actually make? This goes to the

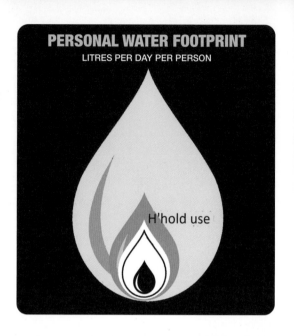

PERSONAL WATER FOOTPRINT
LITRES PER DAY PER PERSON

H'hold use

#	Tip	Page	🔥	💧	👦👧	👁	⏱	Ⓢ
31	Process greywater	84	✓	✓✓✓*		XX		XX ✓
32	Solar hot water	86	✓✓✓					XXXX ✓✓

fundamental issue of the difference we can each personally make.

Let's put that in context. We each use, on average, 199 litres per day, but our total water footprint is 3,562 litres a day. That is the water used in Australia each day divided by the population. Of this, 2,494 litres is used in the production of food (30% of which is wasted before it is sold) and 667 litres is used by industry (partly to make things that we use, and partly in inter-industry activity that cannot be attributed to us personally). Of the

remaining 401 litres, 127 is used in urban water management, largely processing sewage but also washing streets. There is leakage in all these activities, usually somewhere between 5% and 20% that is then returned to the environment or lost down the drain.

When we map that onto the Personal water target, we see that our personal impact is reasonably limited. There is a similar calculation, somewhat less dramatic, for the personal carbon target; that is detailed elsewhere.

Photo by Erwan Hesry on Unsplash

The point of raising this is to be perfectly clear-headed about the context in which we operate. We cannot simply give up, do nothing and blame someone else. That leads nowhere. But neither can we take it upon ourselves to turn the whole ship around using our tiny little life-raft.

Once we understand the scale of what we are trying to achieve, we can then focus on the actions that do make a difference, coordinate our responses to multiply their effect, and make as much noise as possible to get government and industry to follow our lead. Look at the impact of roof-top solar on the generation of electricity as an example.

Tip 31, *Process greywater*, is based on the average Australian using around 33% of their daily 274 litres of water in the shower, 26% in the toilet, 23% in the laundry, 6% in the kitchen and 12% in the garden. We can capture as much as 56% of our daily water from the shower and the laundry as greywater and so provide an extra 154 litres per day of water to the garden. That's great; it will increase the amount of food or flowers that the garden can support.

We capture our greywater, then, not to salvage the urban water supply, but to help make us independent of that central system. Your independence protects you from the possibility of systemic failure and allows you, with your neighbours, to build the resilient community that you might need if more Covid-scale shocks come our way.

An example of the potential significance occurred during the recent fires. When the power went off, water supplies failed. Without electricity to pump water up to the towers dotted around our suburbs, nothing comes out of the taps. The more independent your water supply, the more robust your future.

31. Process greywater

nstead of a bucket in the bath, put a purple pipe under the path. Put your greywater in the ground and enjoy lettuce all year round.

Each minute in the shower uses around 10 litres. Washing the dishes, clothes, the muddy dog, watering the garden: the list goes on. To achieve the Personal water target of 144 litres a day, we have to capture some of that water and use it twice.

Greywater is the water from the shower, the sink and the laundry. It's 'grey', because of soap, body oils, bits of food and flakes of skin. Most of us produce about 150 litres of greywater a day

PERSONAL WATER TARGET
LITRES PER DAY PER PERSON

Greywater

Water the garden completely with reused greywater

Here's a plan

The simplest way to make use of greywater is to take the pipe from the bathroom, laundry or kitchen sink and divert that water into the garden. As long as the water does not sit on the ground or leave a scum behind, you will not create a health risk. It's not that easy, though, in a small urban garden.

If your house is higher than the garden, you can let it run downhill, otherwise you will have to store that water and pump it up to the garden beds. You then need to treat the water to remove the soap and bacteria that might breed in the storage tank.

Using less soap or detergent can help with that, of course. Filtering the water on its way into the greywater tank is important, and all regulations insist that you regularly empty the tank completely to ensure bugs are not sitting there for long periods of time. Commercial systems are built this way.

Natural treatment systems involve running the water through reeds or other plants to filter out most of the biological matter. Some variations use fish and insects to speed up that step. The nutrients are then released slowly, after breaking down.

A personal story

The hilarious Korean TV show, Human Condition, involves a group of comedians facing a 'sustainability' challenge in a share house. The water-saving episode is a hilarious and creative way to explore this topic. It's free on YouTube with English subtitles!

Reality check

One billion people in the world live on less than 50 litres of water a day. Almost one quarter of the world's population do not have clean, safe drinking water.

As well as the water you use directly, water is used on your behalf to process sewage and garbage, wash the streets and, most importantly, to grow your food.

Costs

DIY? In the $100s
Bought? $1,000s

HARD FACTS

In 2019 **55%** of the water used in AUSTRALIA WENT TO AGRICULTURE

In 2007 it was **70%**

The food you eat consumes more water THAN YOU USE IN THE HOUSEHOLD

Now try this!

21 Take a shorter shower

81 Water carefully

87 Food that grows on trees

32. Solar hot water

PERSONAL CARBON TARGET
KILOGRAMS PER DAY PER PERSON

Solar hot water

Sunshine is free and most Australian cities get around seven hours a day, even in winter. Perth gets 11 hours in summer! Don't burn coal to heat water for your shower; let the sun do it for you.

Solar hot water saves you money while reducing your footprint. You can let the sun do it directly, use solar panels and do it electrically, or use a heat pump to maximise your efficiency. However you do it, turn off the clunky old off-peak electric system.

Heating water consumes a lot of energy. Let the sun do it.

Here's a plan

One quarter of all household emissions are generated by heating water.

Solar electricity (photovoltaic or PV) is now so cheap it is actually more cost effective to use those panels to power an electric hot water service. Combining solar electricity with a heat pump is the most efficient, but the most expensive option In Victoria, most people use gas..

A solar hot water service is easy to maintain and it is yours for years. It pays for itself. Quickly.

It converts sunshine into hot water directly through collector panels on the roof. The water tank can be on the roof (simple to operate but requires a strong roof) or the water can be si-phoned from a tank near ground level. These systems need boosters if you are in REC Zone 4, as illustrated.

If you live further north than Zone 4, marked on the REC Zone plan, you can use a heat pump. This works like a refrigerator in reverse. This uses between one sixth and one third of the energy required to heat the water directly using a heating element.

Reality check

Solar hot water gets very, very hot. To prevent you being scalded, a solar hot water service has a temperature relief valve. Make sure that the overflow valve from your hot water is not hidden on the roof, but is on a wall where it can be maintained. All hot water services are insulated. Make sure the pipes are as well.

Melbourne only gets four hours of sunshine a day in winter. You need a booster.

Choice magazine describes a typical four-person household as needing a 270 to 315-litre tank.

Back in the day

When coal-fired power was new, electricity companies encouraged people to use electricity at night to use up the baseload power generated while the power station was idling. The encouragement was cheap electricity at night, 'off peak pricing'. Now, those same electricity companies use the idea of baseload power to justify the need for 24-hour power stations.

Costs

A heat pump costs from $2,700 to $5,000, fully installed. Passive solar costs about $3,000 to $7,000 but uses almost no electricity to run. Standard hot water systems are around $2,000 to $4,500.

HARD FACTS

HOURS OF SUNSHINE: 7 HOURS
POWER OF SUNSHINE: 1KW/M$_2$
SIZE OF PANEL: 2M$_2$
TANK VOLUME: 320L
INCREASE OF TEMPERATURE: 40°C
NUMBER OF SHOWERS: 8

Government rebates go up and down with election cycles, but you might get $500 to $1,000 back.

Expect to save 10 to 20% of your electricity bill.

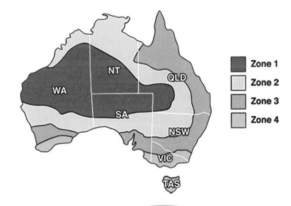

Zone 1
Zone 2
Zone 3
Zone 4

Now try this!

14 Meet your heater

21 Take shorter showers

55 Energy-efficient appliances

77 Generate your own power

Look it up

Choice solar hot water

Temperature relief valve

Heat pump water

www.environment.gov. au/climate-change

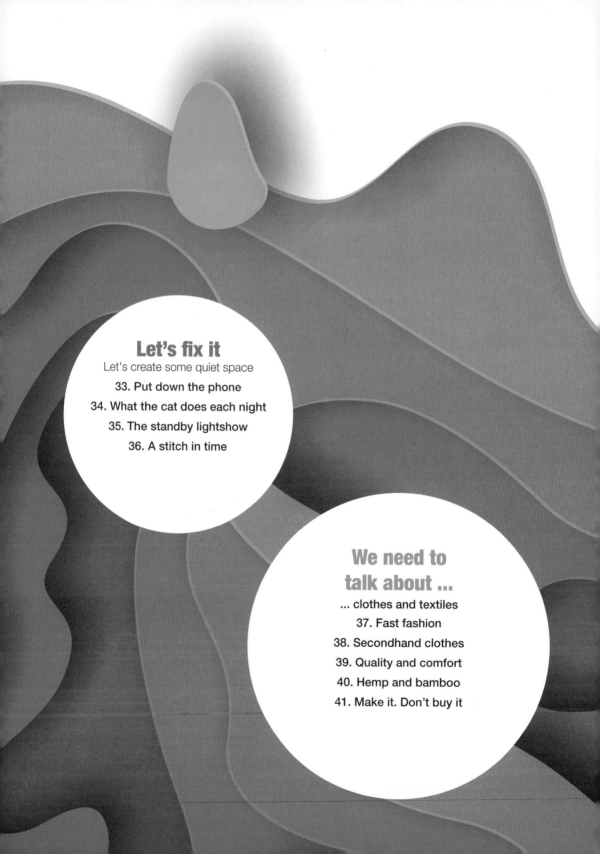

Let's fix it

Let's create some quiet space

33. Put down the phone
34. What the cat does each night
35. The standby lightshow
36. A stitch in time

We need to talk about ...

... clothes and textiles

37. Fast fashion
38. Secondhand clothes
39. Quality and comfort
40. Hemp and bamboo
41. Make it. Don't buy it

03

BEDROOM

And so, to bed, to healing sleep.
Bathed in the dark and silence deep.

Bedrooms are our private spaces, the refuge where we recharge our batteries. The bedroom is also a room adorned with textiles: bed linen, floor coverings, clothes. In this chapter, we get ready for bed and reflect on the way our wardrobe can best nurture our life and planet.

Let's fix it

The quick tips in this chapter are about the things we do before bed, to close down the day and get us in the best zone for sleep. Ideally, we could make the bedroom an electronics-free zone, but that is difficult for those of us who study or have screen-time in the bedroom.

This chapter also considers the impact of allowing our pets to wander at night and the chores that we can do before bed, with all that extra time we have after turning off our screens. The impacts of these actions are summarised using the Work-environment-life balance (WELB).

Tip summary

#	Tip	Page	 🔥	💧	🧍🧍	👁	⏱	Ⓢ
33	Put down the phone	92	✓✓		✓	✓		✓
34	What the cat does each night	94				✓		✗ ✗
35	The standby lightshow	96	✓			✓	✗	
36	A stitch in time	97	✓				✗	✓

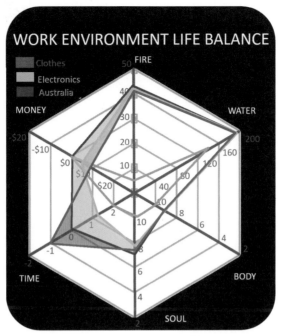

Using the WELB

The WELB was introduced on page 67 in Chapter 2 Bathroom; we will make good use of that tool in this chapter.

Reducing our footprint nurtures the planet, but we also want to nurture our lives. The 'b' in WELB is the balance between the various aspects of our life.

Just as the **triple bottom line** used by corporations balances profit, planet and people, so the WELB balances work (Time and Money), the environment (Fire and Water) and life (Body and Soul). The scales for Time and Money are hours and dollars per day. The Body and Soul axes show a rating out of 10.

By comparing the impact of a particular activity on our WELB we can make decisions about the relative importance of a specific activity to us individually.

In this book we compare the impact of an activity against the average Australian home as described in the *Antikythera*.

The WELB shown here assumes you will put away the phone for a couple of hours, keep the cat in overnight, turn off all devices in your bedroom (and as many as possible in the rest of the house) and spend half an hour repairing any items that are beginning to come apart or show some signs of wear. It maps the benefits in your physical and spiritual wellness as well as the health of the biodiversity in your area. It acknowledges that you would have to invest some time into doing these activities, but that would save you some money. Those actions are going to have a small impact on your carbon and water imprint, through the reduction in the clothes you buy caused by repairing what you already own.

This is shown visually by the red and green shading on the WELB. The green zones are areas where the reduction in your footprint provides a positive benefit. The red zone is where you sacrifice some time.

Photo by James Hollingworth on Unsplash

33. Put down the phone

Our telephones engage and inform — addictively. Turning your phone off will give you extra time to improve your planet. Become engaged by your immediate surroundings. Remember things you have not photographed.

If you can't do it now, do it half an hour before you settle down for sleep.16

We spend an average of 11 hours a day looking at the world through a screen. This warps our perception, is not good for our physical or mental wellbeing and consumes resources. Your phone might not use much power, but the network it connects to consumes up to 10% of the electricity globally. Now, that's a serious consideration.

Screen-time before bedtime hypes you up, just when you need to be calming down.

Here's a plan

Get in the habit of giving yourself some phone-free time every day. You could talk to people face to face who live close to you and who you normally ignore. You might play games and eat dinner with your friends and family, instead of sitting

Reality check

Our phone is an important part of our identity and identification. It's not a cigarette. You are not actually harming yourself or anybody else by using it (not directly, anyway). No government authority is going to come around and check why you have gone offline. Not this year, anyway.

Research into gambling indicates that games are designed to engender a dopamine response. That is the hormone that provides comfort and pleasure and keeps us hooked.

There does not appear to be a serious connection between over-indulgence in screen-time and mental health. A report published in Nature Human Behaviour in 2019 indicated that it was about as dangerous as eating potatoes.

on your own with a screen. You might read books or start doing some of the things in this book! Now there's a novel idea.

We have migrated so many services online that it is sometimes hard to do anything without a connection. One source of information still available during the 2020 bushfires was the radio. Mobile phone towers and Internet services went down but people with radio sets could still tune into the local radio station. Cars still have analogue radio sets. Radio alarm clocks are useful as alarms as well as information services. Get in the habit of checking into the radio as a back-up.

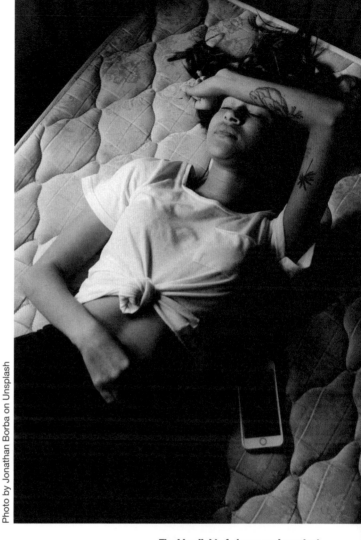

Photo by Jonathan Borba on Unsplash

The blue light of phones and constant notifications interrupt our natural cycles

Look it up
#digitaldetox
Dopamine phone addiction
Screen time IQ
screentimenetwork.org
digitaldetox.com
itstimetologoff.com

Now try this!
7 Our high-speed lives
26 Essential oils
54 Bread baking
61 Shank's pony

34. What the cat does each night

Natural as it is, if you're a cat, to prowl about the place in the moonlight killing small animals, it is a trifle traumatic for the local wildlife. It is estimated that each domestic cat kills one animal a week.

Cats are patient, powerful and persistent, watching carefully and planning their attack over long periods of time. She might be lying on the end of the bed looking like butter wouldn't melt in her mouth in the morning, but the fragments of feather between her teeth explain that contented Cheshire grin.

Here's a plan

Give puss a pedicure that will prune her predatory prowess and protect the parrots on your patch. I'm suggesting that you clip her claws, trim her talons, neutralise her nails.

Vets can provide you with a neat nail clipper for pets with a guard that prevents you trimming her toes instead.

Is it really necessary?

Well, yes, it is. Those razor-sharp talons will shred living things as effectively as they do your furniture. Once every two or three weeks will do the trick. An alternative is cat 'socks' that keep her weapons sheathed.

SHUT THE DOOR: The cat door that allows her to come and go in her own good time is a lovely notion but it spells disaster for those small birds and animals outside. Keep her in at night but train her to do whatever business you don't want inside, outside, in the evening while you are still awake.

BELLS AND BOWS: It may be beneath her dignity, it may not be how you'd present 'best of breed'; regardless, a collar with a bell gives a sporting chance to those birds, lizards, frogs and small marsupials that may be appetisers to the can 'o' cat food.

NO SEX, PLEASE: It is no coincidence that philandering is colloquially known as 'tomcatting'. Make sure all your animals are desexed. If you adopt from a rescue,

HARD FACTS | **One in 10** CATS OWNED BY AUSTRALIANS **is not desexed.**

or from a registered breeder, they will have done the deed. The RSPCA folk who euthanise 300 cats each week will thank you. Councils and other organisations have to destroy even more.

Photo by raphael-schaller on Unsplash

A personal tale

Cat woman comments, "I have indoor cats and deal with their burst of energy when the sun goes down using toys and walks. I have an eight-foot cat tree and toys littering my floors. I also take them to the tiny public courtyard in harnesses and leads. They get their limited freedom when I'm home —and it's been a lot this year! They know, when I'm crawling into bed at 7:00pm, it's time to sleep."

Costs

A collar and bell: $3

Claw clippers: $20

Harness: $15

Cat leads: Pretty pricey! Get creative with the leads!

Desexing: A small fortune. Consider pet insurance or funding programs.

Look it up

Cat claws trim

Bell cats birds

Cat leads harness

Last litter programs

rspca.org.au

petnet.com.au

animalsaustralia.org

pets4life.com.au

Now try this!

19 That doggy in the window

44 Pause before breakfast

75 Wildlife care

82 The dog walks with you

CATS CAN HAVE A LITTER AT four months old.

Over 50,000 cats are euthanised IN AUSTRALIA EACH YEAR.

35. The standby lightshow

The modern house is never dark. Twinkling lights indicate devices on standby, cameras and microphones alert to our every move, ready to jump to attention. That not only consumes power, it subtly influences our state of mind.

Most of our devices assume they will be always on. They have enough battery power to chug along overnight, but night-time is when a lot of devices update their software and recharge their batteries.

Reality check

Many of us are seriously unable to wake up without some form of alarm. You might need to buy yourself a clock. A busy business owner observes, "owning a business means you never switch off. We organised to charge our phones in the kitchen and bought a digital clock radio. So simple!"

Here's a plan

Keep the charging station out of the bedroom. Organise your power boards and power points so that groups of devices can be turned off using one switch. Get power boards with switches, or put 'in-line' switches on the power leads so you can turn off all those devices with one switch.

To test how much power standby is using at night, read your own electricity meter at night and in the morning.

Declare the bedroom a standby-free zone. Keep the twinkling lights, buzzing chargers and eavesdropping robots out of the bedroom.

Look it up

Electronic smog
One watt initiative
Greenhouse standby
Vampire appliances
greenhouse.gov.au
environment.gov.au
energyrating.com.au

HARD FACTS

EVERY WATT OF STANDBY POWER
adds 2kWh
TO YOUR QUARTERLY ELECTRICITY BILL
(that's about $11)

36. A stitch in time

Photo by Darling Arias on Unsplash

A loose thread means something is coming undone. Fix it now and it will go no further. Do it now, before you go to bed. You might not have time in the morning.

We throw out clothes because they fall apart. Our clothes literally fall apart at the seams. Notice problems as they emerge and stop them getting worse.

Own the patch

Tear off the sleeves and sew some bling around the arm holes. Cut 10 centimetres off the bottom of the pants and match them with good boots or interesting socks.

Reality check

If you travel a lot, keep a basic sewing kit in your luggage so that you can make repairs on the road.

Here's a plan

Being able to repair clothes is a life skill that will save you money, protect your favourite garments and ultimately save you the time spent replacing them.

Small holes can be darned and larger ones patched. A skilled tailor or seamstress can make a patch practically invisible. Many tailored clothes incorporate a spare piece of fabric sewn into a seam, often with a spare button attached.

A fraying hem or cuff, worn knees, elbows and the seats of pants might mean moving that garment into the housework drawer.

Look it up
Darning
Yarning place
Sewing lessons
French seam

Now try this!

12 The nature of time

18 Hire a human

41 Make it. Don't buy it

70 Repair café

We need to talk about ...

... clothes and textiles

Photo by Keenan Constance on Unsplash

The monsters in the bedroom usually hide in the wardrobe. Our clothes bloat our environmental footprint. They silently hang there, waiting for their moment of fame when we ask them to show us in our best light. Clothing, like food and shelter, is a basic human need. We have let fashion, though, drive our clothes shopping out of control. We need to rein in our clothing's oversized footprint.

More than half a million tonnes of clothes are thrown away in Australia every year. Cotton farming still sucks our rivers dry (see what's happened to the Aral Sea?) and cheap labour in poor countries is exploited to put the latest fashion on your rack. Because there are so many ways to approach this problem, this chapter examines a handful of ways to review your wardrobe.

Using the Personal carbon target to visually show the impact of each action gives us some idea of one part of that equation. We can then decide for ourselves if the sacrifice we are being asked to make is warranted.

Tip summary

#	Tip	Page	🔥	💧	🧍‍♂️🧍‍♀️	👁	⏱	Ⓢ
37	Fast fashion	100	✓✓✓	✓✓✓				✗✗ ✓
38	Secondhand clothes	104	✓✓✓	✓✓✓			✗	✓✓
39	Quality and comfort	106	✓✓✓	✓✓✓	✓✓	✓		✗✗✗ ✓✓
40	Hemp and bamboo	108	✓✓	✓✓	✓	✓		✗✗
41	Make it don't buy it	110	✓✓✓	✓✓✓		✓✓	✗✗✗	✓✓✓

The WELB, discussed at the beginning of this chapter, allows us to think more broadly about the impact on our lives and on the planet. Context is important. For example, we initially resisted wearing face masks because it was a significant cultural shift. In the face of ongoing lockdown, though, it seemed a small sacrifice to make.

The context of our environmental footprint is extraordinarily complex. How do you rate the extinction of the Bathurst grassland earless dragon against the reduced cost of grass-fed beef? If you know that farmers who regenerate bushland to offset emissions from their cattle are also protecting endangered species then it becomes an easy decision, but it is impossible to maintain that level of detail when looking at the broad picture.

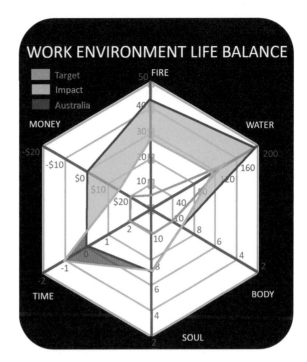

Once the fourth largest lake in the world, the Aral Sea covered 68,000 km$_2$. It dried out in 2014 due to cotton farming in Uzbekistan and environmental programs have since restored it to one tenth its original size.
©2007 Philip Micklin, Western Michigan University

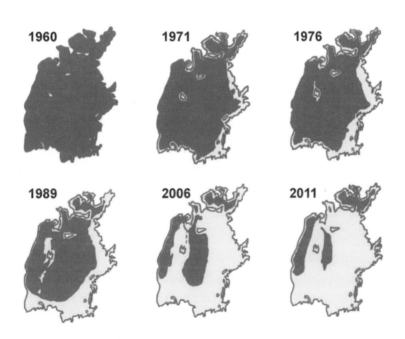

Bedroom

37. Fast fashion

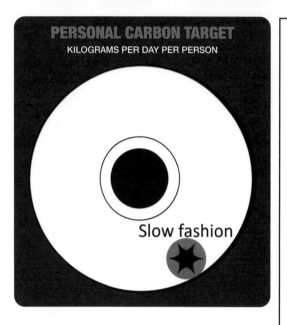

PERSONAL CARBON TARGET
KILOGRAMS PER DAY PER PERSON

Slow fashion

The fashion industry generates our desire for a new look every time we go out. Artificially cheap textiles and manufacturing have fed this fashion fetish. To stop exploiting the people who make our clothes and the land that produces the textiles, we need to slow down and think.

How do clothes harm us?

Globally we manufacture over 100 million tonnes of textile each year and throw away four fifths of it. One third is lost in production or never sold. This wastes resources including water and fossil fuels and creates huge amounts of pollution, including 10% of global greenhouse gases. We need to buy less clothing.

Here's a plan

The simple rule is stop shopping. Problem is, the cheap clothes we bought last week probably won't last more than three wears, so we have to make a bit of a plan:

- 1. Buy better clothes, less often and wear them for longer.
- 2. Repair and enhance existing clothes.
- 3. Make your own.
- 4. Use tattered clothes as sewing scraps or cleaning rags.
- 5. Consider the employment and environmental policies of the manufacturer.
- 6. Dispose of clothes appropriately when they wear out.

Upcycling is a movement of creating new clothes from secondhand clothes or other materials. Many recycling outlets, like Reverse Garbage, support upcycling efforts, and some local councils run competitions and exhibitions supporting upcycling artists.

The distinctive layered style modelled by Tenfingerz and Sebastian is wildly popular on many social media platforms, and is a specific outcome of this playful interaction between fast fashion and upcycling.

It's getting worse. Textile production has doubled in the last 15 years and is currently growing at around 7% per year. Overall, our fashion obsession consumes one quarter of the world's pesticides and produces around one billion tonnes of CO_2. It is also responsible for the bulk of the plastic microfibres in the oceans.

On average we keep our clothes for less than a year.

Reality check

Lobbying manufacturers to pay their workers better wages may lead to a better outcome than refusing to buy any clothes manufactured in poor countries. This is similar to the 'better meat' discussion in Tip 50.

Costs

A 2nd hand shirt: $5

A cheap new shirt: $30

A quality new shirt: $120

Look it up
slow fashion
upcycle
reverse garbage
etsy clothing

Now try this!
7 Our high-speed lives
12 The nature of time
18 Hire a human
70 Repair café

HARD FACTS

UP TO 20% of fabric is wasted **as leftovers in the cutting process.**

Another 15% IS THROWN OUT without being sold.

In OECD countries, WE EACH THROW OUT an average of **40kg** of clothing each year.

Of that, **25%** IS INCINERATED **and 57%** ends up in landfill.

Enter the ... designers

Tenfingerz and Famous Artist Sebastian Berto

Exploring the 'pile' —
Tenfingerz and Famous Artist Sebastian Berto

This duo recently launched an online magazine, FastFashun.com, showcasing their Fast Fashun events, artists active in the space and a directory of responsible fashion brands.

"We ran a project during the 2020 Melbourne Fashion Festival that introduced people to the perils of the fashion industry both environmentally and in terms of the effect on people's lives.

"It grew out of runway shows that showcased local, responsible fashion brands. I felt at the time that it wasn't hands-on enough and we needed to engage people more.

"We get a tonne of opp. shop waste, that is 10 bales of 1,000 items each, all destined for landfill. We cut open the bales in the exhibition space, create some installation art, and then invite the public in to rummage through the 'pile' and create their own fashion or artwork out of the waste.

"It is very confronting for many people to come face to face with a tonne of waste; to see what is being thrown out, why things are unsaleable, how broken zippers or a small cut can condemn a garment to landfill.

"We provide craft materials, sewing machines and designers to help people make new outfits. We make it all happen very fast, hence the name Fast Fashun, by holding runway shows every hour on the hour for people to showcase their creations.

"We encourage people to use shortcuts, like safety pins, so they can make things as quickly as possible. People get silly and try to create haute courture by placing a chair on their head."

**Professor Alice Payne
researches the industry**

1. Design out waste

2. Design with waste

3. Dematerialise.

"Design out waste means using less fabric; designing and cutting more carefully, thinking about re-use and we must not forget the most powerful choice: not to make, or buy, the garment at all.

"Design with waste means upcycling, using clothing in different ways, and thinking seriously about recycling. We need to think about the natural stream as distinct from the technical stream. The natural stream is about biodegradability and returning the nutrients to the earth. The industrial stream is about effectively capturing the resources, like polyester, that can be re-used infinitely and so maximising their benefit.

"Dematerialise is to think about ownership and material differently and to focus on the service rather than the product. Clothing is not simply functional, it is about our appearance, our ego, the cultural statements we wish to make, a form of expression. It is possible that owning an outfit is not essential to these outcomes.

Prof. Payne also pointed out that the consumer cannot address issues that may be systemic. "'Monstrous hybrids' like cotton and polyester are extraordinary difficult to separate and recycle, but they solved real world problems. Before cotton–polyester blends were invented, women spent hours each week washing, ironing and preparing garments. These blends released them from that intense and time-consuming labour."

Researching the future —
Professor Payne

Associate Professor in Fashion at the School of Design at QUT, Prof. Payne writes and researches about innovation that reduces waste in fashion.

"The main problem is that fashion has encouraged us to consume so much. In earlier times, fabric was considered valuable and every scrap, literally, was treasured. Clothes were cut very carefully to minimise waste and then the fabric re-used in many different ways through its life. As far back as the Renaissance, clothes were modular, so components could be re-used.

"There are different approaches that address this:

38. Secondhand clothes

The opp. shop, pawn broker, secondhand shop, thrift store, boot market or trash and treasure market is a powerhouse of fashion, a source of unusual fabrics, unique designs and unexpected serendipity. You go in looking for a waistcoat and you come out with a pair of lined leather boots.

Here's a plan

Buying secondhand clothes is cheap, fun and good for the environment. Of course, you don't get the latest fashions, but you get the best of the blasts from the past.

There are lots of reasons to love opp. shopping, markets and vintage stores.

IT HANGS TOGETHER: The clothes designed to fall apart after the first couple of outings are not in the secondhand store. They have already disintegrated. You're looking at a store full of items built to last.

QUALITY SHINES: You'll come to quickly recognise quality and seek that purr of satisfaction from a well-tailored piece with spare buttons, double seams and rolled hems.

YOU'VE SEEN IT BEFORE: You are not guessing if this electric blue sheath is a fickle whim that will look ridiculous next season or a stunning piece that has your name on it.

5 REASONS WHY YOU SHOULD START BUYING SECOND HAND

It's cheap

UNIQUE

CHARITY

REWARDING

SAVING THE PLANET

YOU'RE HELPING SOMEONE ELSE: The sector is dominated by charities. By shopping at the opp. shops run by Lifeline, Vinnies, the RSPCA, the Asthma Foundation, your local church or neighbourhood centre you are helping a good cause. You may also have a retro-store or secondhand shop run by local entrepreneurs. All these stores keep the money in the community.

Reality check

There is not much difference between secondhand prices and the cost of cheaply

A personal story

The grumpy old man with his name on the cover refuses to give his kids money to go clothes shopping in the mall. "They have to want something new for two weeks before I hand over the cash."

made goods imported from the other side of the world. You do get quality that lasts.

With high fashion items at the local opportunity shop occasionally breaking the $20 price point and the pre-loved fashion store being double that, you can dress in style for much less than the average Australian.

Beware mega charities disrupting the sector with media contracts, free warehouses and data mining apps. Look up the traditional opp. shops listed below.

Look it up

Secondhand shopping

Opportunity shop

Secondhand markets

Lifeline

vinnies.org.au

RSPCA

Asthma Foundation

Now try this!

40 Hemp and bamboo

45 What's on the label

56 The packaging we purchase

HARD FACTS

AUSTRALIANS SPEND

$27.50

a week on clothes.

That's more than health care!

The fashion industry produced

1.3 billion tonnes of CO_2 and used 79 billion cubic metres of water globally in 2015.

Globally, each kilogram of cotton (a t-shirt and jeans) consumes

20,000L of water.

ABOUT HALF OF THAT IS IN PRODUCTION.

Cotton farming deploys

24% of the world's insecticides

and 11% of pesticides, even though it only occupies 3% of the world's farmland.

Polyester manufacture creates 14kg of CO_2e

PER KILOGRAM OF POLYESTER.

About half

THE POLYESTER FIBRE PRODUCED

ends up in polyester cotton blends which are difficult to recycle.

39. Quality and comfort

You can own clothes for longer and love wearing them more if you buy better, less often. Quality clothing looks good, is designed to last and easy to repair. Classic fashions earn their reputation because they have stood the test of time. They don't go out of style.

Fast fashion wastes resources and exploits labour. One way that you can get off the treadmill is to look out for clothes that last. Well-made clothes in classic styles are easy to accessorise and will become staples of your wardrobe.

Here's a plan

A wardrobe with a range of classic basics provides the foundation for any good wardrobe. Coco Chanel famously quipped in 1926, "One is never over-dressed or underdressed with a little black dress."

Mixing and matching what you already own is how you can get away with wearing that shirt twice! Have fun with it! Basics don't have to be black, white and nude. Love orange? Have an orange t-shirt, skirt and dress! Any colour t-shirt goes well with a good pair of jeans.

A tiny home enthusiast says: "When I downsized to fit into my tiny home, my wardrobe had to shrink as well. No more cheap and cheerful summer dresses only relevant to that year. I bought myself a bunch of basics, and maintain them through sewing and repairs. Opp. shops are my best friend for less worn pieces like dinner dresses or ball gowns!"

Be original

"Don't be into trends. Decide what you are, what you want to express by the way you dress and the way you live." — Gianni Versace

Following fashion is a consumer trap. We follow the fashion because we want to fit in.

Get out of the basement

Elle Australia pointed out in its 2020 Affordable Brands piece that "good quality clothes cost more".

The bargain basement discount store can be a dollar trap, taking your money for very little return. These are places where fast fashion goes to die. Tempting as it is to buy new items at rock-bottom prices, keeping your eyes out for other ways to get a good deal can be a much better option.

Embrace your inner individual. Own it. You are so uniquely you. The way you dress or style yourself might turn some heads, but ultimately, if you feel good, you're doing better than the rest of 'em!

Quality can afford to be fair

Send a message to the manufacturer, designer and retailer that your consumer dollar will do good in the world. The familiar Fairtrade mark makes sure your clothes are not enslaving people in poor countries. No Sweatshops, Sweatshop Free and Ethical Clothing Australia are some of the movements that have emerged to implement this approach.

Look it up
Truecost movie
Apparel impact
ethicalclothingaustralia.org.au

Now try this!
18 Hire a human
36 A stitch in time
45 What's on the label
66 Holding a garage sale

40. Hemp and bamboo

Cotton is lightweight, breathable and lovely to wear, though environmentally questionable. Hemp and bamboo have become popular fibres because the plants do well without vast amounts of water and fertiliser. Feel good wearing them and nurture your planet.

About half the textile produced in the world is a mix of cotton and polyester, which is very difficult to recycle. Cotton is grown in hot, dry climates, and consumes vast amounts of water and lots of pesticides. Polyester is responsible for the bulk of the microfibres in the ocean, which are released from our washing machines.

Here's a plan

Replace the cotton and polyester clothing in your shopping bag with other natural fibres, recycled plastics or the latest microbial synthetics.

Hemp is a fast growing and versatile plant that is naturally pest-resistant and produces strong fibres. It lasts a long time, appears in fine weaves as well as more traditional coarse fabrics and holds dye well.

Bamboo is a relatively recent source of fibre for textile. Traditionally used for construction and culinary purposes, modern manufacturing techniques have released the strong-as-steel fibres of bamboo for the textile market.

Outdoor clothing company Patagonia pioneered a movement to produce high-quality synthetic cold-weather gear from recycled plastic. There are now a wide range of such fabrics in various brands. They harness the inherent advantage of plastic; it lasts forever. While that is a problem in the ocean, it is a great advantage in the circular economy.

A more recent source of synthetic fibres is microbes (microbial plastics). While indisputably industrial, biosynthetic fibres do not harm the land and require minimal resources to produce and process.

Traditional fabrics like silk, wool and linen maintain their natural advantages, breathing well and breaking down rather than polluting the environment, but are generally more expensive to produce.

HARD FACTS

About half THE TEXTILE IN THE WORLD CONTAINS COTTON. It makes up one third of the weight of all textile produced.

Look it up
ocadvantage.com.au

braintreehemp.com.au

sheethouse.com.au

Now try this!
20 Invest ethically

22 Lighten the laundry load

38 Secondhand clothes

45 What's on the label

A wide range of eco-cotton producers sell organic and environmentally sensitive cotton as quality fabrics.

Reality check

Laws still restrict the farming of hemp because it is a variety of cannabis.

Be wary of catching the fast fashion wave of bamboo love. Bamboo plantations can be grown in very unethical ways and sometimes parallel cotton in their emissions.

Australia's cotton industry is one of the most efficient in the world. It uses about seven megalitres per hectare to grow 1.5 tonnes of cotton, half what it did in 1992. Nevertheless, the cotton farms still make the Darling River flow backwards when they turn on their irrigation pumps. Production of cotton fabric also consumes huge amounts of water.

Back in the day

Those very fine bible pages are made from hemp.

The oldest industrial artefact in the world is an 8,000 year old piece of hemp fabric.

Money was made from hemp until the plastic bank note was invented, in Australia, in 1988.

Rope is traditionally made from hemp or flax.

Costs

Recycled wool sweater: $200

Recycled polyester: $120

Hemp or bamboo t-shirt: $25

POLYESTER PRODUCTION PASSED
50 million tonnes in 2015,
releasing the equivalent of 706 million tonnes of CO_2

41. Make it. Don't buy it

Break the fast fashion cycle by creating your own unique style. If you feel more like Cinderella right now than the Fairy Godmother, you can indulge in the simple art of upcycling.

Department store fashion was originally designed to be tailored. You'd buy something that was relatively your size, and adjust, take in or nip to suit your actual body shape. As we became busier, we gave into mass-produced fashion. Today's cheap fashion is made with pretty average material, designed to last a mere season, with little to no room for larger breasts or longer torsos.

No. 182 March 1968 2'-

PINS AND NEEDLES

A Christine Veasey Magazine for Smart Needlewomen

Care Free Family Knitting
Supplement to pull out and keep

Machine Knitted Cover Suit

Smocking Made Easy

2 Bargain Offers
all-cotton sheets and pillowcases: Summer bulbs

The art of making clothes is not as common as it once was

Here's a plan

Some of us learned to sew, knit and crochet when young by the side of a kindly relative and can whip up anything from a pillowcase to a ball gown while watching Project Runway. If you did not get that early head start, find a local seamstress or tailor, a sewing circle or needlecraft class and stretch your ability.

Alternatively, you could take a shortcut and refurbish old favourites. Modern technology means you don't even need to pick up a needle: iron-on patches, fabric glue, hot glue guns and staples are rough and ready ways to whip up a little glamour.

Rip the arms off a business shirt, sew some bling on the collar or around the shoulder. Cut off the thigh of your old pants, arrange it on your head and decorate it with whatever takes your fancy. Unique hat, new style.

Costs

It costs nothing to cut up your old wardrobe.

Beginner's sewing kit: $20

New printed fabric (3 metres): $20

Photo by Vera Davidova on Unsplash

A personal story

A 20-something millennial says: "I learnt to sew out of curiosity. Home ec. classes at school never inspired me to make my own clothes, but it taught me how to use a sewing machine. In my teens, I suddenly found myself spending hours in the fabric aisle. I just started sewing. No YouTube tutorials back then. Some pieces worked; I received (a lot) of help from my mother and grandmother. I learnt to make patterns from tracing clothes I already owned and making something with the fabric I'd collected.

"For my 22nd birthday, I received my very own sewing machine and the family collection of sewing patterns. I moved interstate and Mum's overlocker came with me. I've used old pillowcases for bread bags, tattered t-shirts for masks. I always get a bit of a kick from telling people I made it myself."

Look it up
Upcycle
Refurbished fashion
Yarning circle

Now try this!
11 A no-spend day
36 A stitch in time
66 Holding a garage sale
70 Repair café

Let's fix it

Just press pause for one second.
Have you thought about
your life and your planet?

42 Half fill the kettle

43 Turn off the dishwasher

43 Pause before breakfast

We need to talk about ...

... the cost of food.
Environmental and social cost, that is.

45 What's on the label

46 Where the herbs grow

47 Mung beans and love

48 The things we eat for lunch

49 What's wrong with the supermarket

50 Eating better meat

51 The power of the bean

52 A vegan lifestyle

53 Feeding friends

54 Baking bread

55 Energy-efficient appliances

56 The packaging we purchase

57 Silicon and beyond

Plan ahead

Don't waste that food. With a
little planning it could
become a treat.

58 Salt and sugar

59 Smoke your own

60 Things that grow in the dark

61 Things that
grow in bottles

KITCHEN

Food keeps us alive. We need air
and water more, but food makes us
feel good and sharing food
connects us. The kitchen is the
heart of the house, usually the first
stop when we come home, the
source of *yum* — a refreshing drink,
a satisfying snack,
a nourishing nibble.

Kitchen

The problem

It takes a huge amount of energy to feed us.

We use considerably less water in the kitchen than the bathroom: about 3% of household usage occurs in the kitchen. Letting the water run while we rinse the dishes and fresh vegetables is about the biggest crime committed at the kitchen sink.

The energy we personally use to cook is a fraction of that spent on heating and cooling. The only real challenge in the energy department is our love affair with the raw flame. Gas burners get oil and water hot enough to process food fast. From an environmental point of view, it is easier to green your electricity; burning gas releases greenhouse gas emissions and, in a nutshell, that's a really bad idea.

However, it still takes a huge amount of energy to feed us.

So, where's the problem? Fundamentally it is food.

Agriculture accounts for around 17% of global emissions, food production, packaging and distribution accounts for another 16%. In Australia, agriculture is responsible for 13% of our emissions and uses 65% of the water that we capture in Australia. Some of that goes on textiles, but the vast majority on food.

But wait, it gets worse. We throw out one third of the food that is produced. If global food waste were a country, it would be the third largest emitter of greenhouse gases behind the USA and China. Food waste

in Australia exceeds 8 million tonnes a year and produces methane equivalent to 15 million tonnes of carbon dioxide. On its own, that is another 3% of our carbon emissions.

We really need to get the environmental impact of our food production under control.

Photo by Dane Deaner- on Unsplash

Let's fix it

The good news is that engaging more closely with our food not only helps us manage our environmental footprint, it is also good for our health. It's also a great way to connect with people and more broadly with the planetary ecosystems that nurture us. The kitchen is where you can engage in a fun and functional way with creating a circular economy, a sharing economy and build that robust community that is going to save your behind, when the going gets tough.

There is some cost in time with eating well, but that could be considered time well spent. And while an individual item of organic, local food is more expensive than the industrially produced equivalent, we can balance our budget by preparing more food from basics. Food only gets expensive when we expect other people to do the preparation for us.

Get in touch with your inner peasant, take delight in the power of hand-made food and release yourself from the chains of endless consumption.

As always, these initial tips are simple, quick and prepare the way for more substantial actions later on. We are going to do more with less and we are going to let nature do as much of our work for us as we can arrange. Let's start by going easy on the appliances and giving ourselves a little time to breathe.

#	Tip	Page	🔥	💧	👨👩	👁	⏱	Ⓢ
42	Half fill the kettle	116	✓				✓	
43	Turn off the dishwasher	117	✓✓	✓	✓	✓	✗✗	✓
44	Pause before breakfast	118			✓	✓✓	✗✗	

42. Half fill the kettle

Only put the amount of water into the kettle that you need to boil. A classic no-brainer, but you'd be amazed how many people still fill the kettle every time.

This is one of those obvious things that everyone knows instantly—as soon as you say it. It seems trivial to mention in the same book as hydrogen cell cars and global poverty.

Here's a plan

You are saving electricity by only heating the water you use.

Pay attention to all your energy uses, not just the kettle. Get used to thinking in watts.

Your kettle probably has a power rating of two kilowatts. It chews up juice as fast as the toaster or a portable heater. After all, the aim is to heat water as quickly as possible.

Reality check

What difference will controlling your kettle-filling fetish actually make?

The honest answer is, 'not much'.

If your kettle boils in three minutes (one twentieth of an hour) you have used (2000/20)=100 watt hours of **energy**. (The physics says that it takes just under 85 watt hours to boil a litre of water. That is the same as leaving the plasma screen running for 20 minutes.

If you do that twice a day for 320 days a year, that is 55 kilowatt hours. For the average Australian that's about 63 kilos of CO_2e, more or less equivalent to 24 litres of petrol.

It illustrates an important principle, though. Efficiency is an important part of reducing our impact on the earth.

The same applies to complex systems. Make every stage as efficient as possible and the overall savings can be dramatic. We have simply not been used to conserving energy.

Now try this!
8 Buy green power

35 The standby lightshow

25 Those dripping taps

Look it up
Energy conversion

Joule degree water

43. Turn off the dishwasher

Dishwashers consume energy when in use and substantial resources to manufacture. They waste energy, water and use strong detergents that pollute our waterways. Chat as you wash the dishes by hand, instead of retreating to your screen.

HARD FACTS

EACH YEAR, AUSTRALIANS throw away 2.5 million WHITEGOODS. That's 100,000 tonnes of steel.

Here's a plan

Those of us who have grown up with a dishwasher view a sink full of hot soapy water as a mountainous chore. In fact, many chores can provide a period of gentle concentration followed by the satisfaction of a job well done.

Rinse first so the food scraps get to the compost, not on your clean dishes. Wash in hot water and then rinse the suds off after you're finished so that you are not eating detergent.

Make it a social occasion.

Divide the roster into rinsing, washing and drying. Someone can tidy up the kitchen and dining room while others do the dishes.

Some studies argue that dishwashers save energy because they efficiently heat their own water, allowing you to turn down the hot water service. Generally, these studies seem to be comparing a dishwasher with the European habit of washing up under a flowing hot tap for up to 15 minutes (rather than in a filled sink). It also entirely ignores the energy used to make the dishwasher and dispose of it after it breaks down.

Look it up
Hand washing dishes

Major appliances material project

energyrating.gov.au

Reality check

There are places where dishwashers make sense. The office is one, hospitality is another; hygiene rules and the volume justifies automation.

Now try this!
7 Our high-speed lives

18 Hire a human

55 Energy-efficient appliances

44. Pause before breakfast

"**W**hy is it always eggs? Who decides?" Spymaster Carolyn Martens, before ordering her 7:00am gin and tonic. *Killing Eve.*

Many spiritual traditions ritualise the breaking of the fast by insisting that cleansing rituals and worship are the first order of the day and have been properly observed, prior to the first feeding of the face. Modern wellness guides also point out that exercise taken early has more impact than the same effort taken late in the day and that the nutrition absorbed at breakfast is more efficiently utilised (creating less fat) than the same nutrition eaten later.

Breakfast, then, is important.

Here's a plan

Even workaholics can linger over breakfast. Allow yourself time to explore a variety of foods and digest them. Just organise a breakfast meeting, every morning, and work while you live well. Talk to your accountant before you try claiming it as a tax break.

Juggling a busy family with different departure times, dietary preferences and morning moods offers its own challenges. The combination of creative approaches to food and forward planning might be a significant part of the solution. Look to lunch tip 48 for hints on combining food preparation for busy families.

Plan ahead. Many breakfasts you can make in bulk nowadays, so you can grab and take with you. Many are 'prepare the night before' and then you have an awesome breakfast in the morning (overnight oats, anyone?).

One of the simplest ways to make time for breakky? Wake up earlier. Shock! Horror! Over three days set your alarm half an hour earlier, then another half hour earlier, then another. Mornings are amazing for embracing the stillness of the world and the slowly warming sun. That little time of peace can bring you solace in the rat race of the working week. You might also find your earlier rises lead to the earlier bedtimes you've been swearing to start doing.

Once you get good at it you will have time to attend to the animals, have that morning workout and start that loaf of home-made bread.

Photo by Brooke Lark on Unsplash

HARD FACTS A 2013 study compared two groups EATING THE SAME WEIGHT-LOSS DIET WITH THE BIG MEAL AT BREAKFAST OR DINNER. The big breakfast eaters lost **50%** more weight.

Better breakfast choices

If you are going to load up on carbs, breakfast is the time to do it. You have the whole day to burn them off and you are not going to drop straight into a stupor, like the post-lunch slump.

The key is to mix it up a little, follow the food pyramid, get in some wholefoods and fibre, and go easy on the sugar and fats. Toast with butter and jam, muffins, croissants and pastries give you the hit of fat and sugar that you crave right now, but have a think about these options:

- Put your morning eggs on a bed of spinach instead of a slice of toast.

- Eat a fruit salad with a sprinkle of your favourite cereal as a topping instead of the main meal.

- Have a fruit smoothie loaded with your home-grown herbs and spices.

- Halve your serve. Shed a few kilos because, hey, it's good for the planet too.

Reality check

Yep, white bread is cheap and spinach is not. Check out the section *Eating weeds* in the Garden chapter.

Throw cheap fruit in the blender for a morning smoothie.

Look it up

Benefits morning prayer

Early exercise

Big breakfast better

ENERGY DRINKS CONTAIN UP TO 300mg OF CAFFEINE

COFFEE & MANY energy drinks contain 80mg OF CAFFEINE

We need to talk about ...

... the price of bread

Simple Sourdough $6.00   Ancient Multigrain Pan Bread $6.00

Photo by Mae Mu on Unsplash

Julius Caesar defined the central role of government as keeping the price of wheat low enough that the people would not riot and high enough that the farmers would grow it.

Feeding our ever-growing cities continues to be a challenge.

Little wonder that 70% of our water usage and 35% of our greenhouse emissions come from food production. As a society, we can change our agricultural practices to sequester carbon in the soil, minimise emissions and waste, and grow food closer to our cities, but this book is about what you and I can do at home.

The aim is to do as much as we can ourselves. The food energy hierarchy is:

- Make it, don't buy it
- Share it around
- Use fresh or dried foods
- Grow your own.

But we need to use common sense. We cannot all do everything ourselves. For a start, we do not want to. Secondly, it is not terribly efficient for us each to make everything from scratch every day.

What we can do is organise ourselves to distribute the tasks among ourselves, so that we are not all lining up together at the supermarket or the soup kitchen, but are looking after each other. In terms of energy efficiency, we need to reduce the length of the supply chain, the so-called food miles. We need to buy less packaged, frozen and canned food, and we need to start picking up the food that is literally growing on the trees we walk past every day.

Tip summary

The baker's dozen of tips in this chapter looks at the food we choose, how we prepare it and share it.

Most dietary advice can be summarised in three words, 'Eat more vegetables'. That's a good way to nurture our planet and our lives.

In each case we want to understand what is involved in getting that food onto our plate and how to maximise the benefit for us. This is useful now, while the shelves are stocked and we have lots of choice, but these skills could well be invaluable on those occasions when things are not working quite as expected.

As is made clear by the work-environment-life balance (WELB) of these tips, there is a big benefit in all areas, except your time. These tips will have you spending longer in the kitchen.

Underpinning this approach is the notion that the more independent we can be, the more empowered we are as well. Instead of being a node of consumption you will transform your home into a hub of production. That will make you happier, healthier and reduce the load you place on the environment.

Now that's a great notion.

#	Tip	Page	🔥	💧	👫	👁	⏱	$
45	What's on the label	122						XX ✓
46	Where the herbs grow	124		X	✓	✓	X	X
47	Mung beans and love	126			✓		X	✓
48	Things we eat for lunch	128			✓		X	✓
49	What's wrong with the supermarket	130	✓✓		✓		XX	XX
50	Eating better meat	132	✓✓	✓✓✓	✓✓ X			✓✓
51	The power of the bean	134	✓✓✓✓	✓✓✓✓	✓✓		X	✓✓
52	A vegan life	138	✓✓✓✓	✓✓✓✓	✓✓		XX	✓✓
53	Feeding friends	140	✓			✓✓	XX	X
54	Baking bread	142	✓			✓	XX	✓
55	Energy-efficient appliances	144	✓✓					XXX ✓✓
56	The packaging we purchase	146	✓✓	✓✓			X	✓
57	Silicon and beyond	148	✓	✓				X

Kitchen

45. What's on the label

Australian Certified Organic

UTZ Certified

Photo by Gyan Shahane on Unsplash

Labelling laws are designed to protect your health, the environment and people in poor countries working to produce the products we buy. Get used to scanning the label for symbols and logos that mean it's good for your life, for others and for your planet. The same principles apply to textiles, timber and other manufactured products.

Many of our low-cost products are produced by people working for unbelievably low wages. We not only exploit the environment for our convenience and comfort, we exploit other people, just like us, who are born in poor countries.

If we shop on price alone, the retailers put pressure on their suppliers to cut corners and they in turn put pressure on the producers. The result is that everyone down the line exploits the people and the planet in the name of profit.

The challenge is to reverse that pressure by only buying products that you know are produced with care and attention. Labelling laws have been established to encourage that.

Here's a plan

Look out for the symbols that identify organic food such as Australian Certified Organic, suppliers that pay a fair price to farmers such as Fair Trade, and producers who adopt sustainable farming practices such as Utz. There are other schemes covering clothes, timber and paper, for example.

The Fair Trade logos on food that you buy indicate that the agricultural products meet certain standard environmental and humane values.

The Australian Certified Organic label indicates that the food is grown without pesticides and chemical fertilisers.

Reality check

Many food additives are traditional products. All numbered products have a large body of research available. Get yourself informed.

Certification, like many other forms of regulation, can have unintended consequences. Keep doing your research.

There is a difference between 'fair trade' and 'free trade'. Free trade agreements are usually structured to prevent countries from 'protecting' their markets by using tariffs.

Some foods certified as organic are grown on an industrial scale and may be environmentally harmful.

Utz is a different certification process that combines environmental sustainability with a fair deal for farmers.

Other certification marks and symbols simply let you know that the product was grown or produced in Australia and so has travelled less distance, and might keep the money you spend in the country longer.

The detailed ingredients and other information on the label are also useful, and the better you get to know them the more informed your shopping will be. Food acid 300, for example, means that Vitamin C has been added to the food.

Here are some common food additives that nutritionists consider reasonably good for you:

- **Beet red 162.** The 100s are colourings.
- **Acetic acid (vinegar) 260.** The 200s are preservatives.
- **Citric acid (330)** the 300s are antioxidants.
- **Pectin 440.** The 400s are thickeners and emulsifiers.
- **Magnesium sulphate (Epsom salts) 518.** The 500s are acidity regulators.

Costs

Fair trade food is usually in the midrange of product pricing — about 20% higher than the popular brands at the bottom of the range.

Fair trade coffee: $6.00/200g

Fair trade chocolate: $2.99/200g

Look it up
Fair trade free trade
Food additives
E codes food
Utz.org
Fta.org.au

Now try this!
5 Paying it forward
17 Get active
with your community

46. Where the herbs grow

Fresh herbs add zest and a rich and refreshing flavour to any food they garnish. There is nothing more satisfying than wandering around the patio with a pair of scissors picking the ingredients for a home-made pasta sauce.

Here's a plan

If you have a cupboard you can grow mushrooms; a window sill, you can grow sprouts; if you have a balcony you can grow any vegetable; and if you have a garden you are luckiest of all because you can grow a fruit tree.

Grow the herbs you use most often. That way you can pick them fresh every day. One of the advantages of most herbs is that they are pretty hardy: oregano, thyme, rosemary and sage are among the easiest plants to manage. They are easy to grow from seed, readily available as seedlings and do not require a huge amount of attention. Basil, parsley and coriander need a little more care.

The best way to start, if you are not an experienced gardener, is to buy plants already in their pots. This way you get to learn about caring for your little green mate without having to juggle potting mix recipes. Reuse the pots the next season for your new green pals.

Buy young plants at low cost, rather than fully grown ones that are already flowering

or fruiting. When you do get flowers and fruit they will last much longer as well.

Make sure you have some way of watering them, say a watering can or a large jug (a mug works).

Also, make sure that you are not watering the downstairs neighbours. Put every pot on a tray that holds the water. This keeps the plant moist for longer, too.

Photo by Marcus Spiske on Unsplash

HARD FACTS

HAVANA NOW GROWS **over 50%** **of its fresh food IN THE CITY ITSELF.**

Reality check

Like begets like and nature is bountiful. Put a pot plant on your patio and the leaf-loving critters will descend for lunch. Predators will turn up for dinner and voila, you live in a zoo.

If you don't have a green thumb, check out the tips in Indoor plants.

Consider purchasing native bush tucker. Learn what's edible and was grown in your local area before we arrived. It will promote healthier environments for our native fauna.

You can learn from plants. Work out by watching which plants like the sun and put them in the exposed positions, sheltering ones that like semi shade.

Spend some time watering your plants and picking off old leaves, bugs and other alien beings every week or couple of days. Plants do respond to tender loving care, whether you sing to them or not.

Growing food from scraps is a super cheap and funky method of propagation! Plant the bottom of lettuce heads, the top of carrots, ginger, garlic and potatoes that are sprouting. You get the pleasure of watching a fully grown plant appear from your cooking leftovers. Organic seem to work the best.

Costs

Young plants: $3+

Established pot plants: $10+

Designer pot: $35+

Look it up

Pot plants patio

Warrigal greens

Millennials plants

Havana urban farm

Now try this!

6 Indoor plants

26 Essential oils

47 Mung beans and love

86 Getting fed without giving a fig

Kitchen

••• WE NEED TO TALK ABOUT ...

47. Mung beans and love

Make healthy drinks and salads using sprouts grown on your windowsill from a handful of seeds. Save money, become independent and healthy for next to nothing.

The health benefits of eating fresh food are well understood. Juice bars do a roaring trade in wheat grass, bean shoots and other sprouts mixed with the regular line-up of fruits and roots on the fresh juice menu.

Fancy-pants sandwiches, fresh smoothies and sprout salads look exactly like the kind of rich hippy food that the average household simply cannot afford. In fact, sprouts cost next to nothing. A handful of seeds and some water are all it takes.

Here's a plan

Just add water to a seed and, hey presto, a young plant bursts forth: a package full of enzymes, sugars and vitamins, ready for you to enjoy.

Popular seeds for sprouting are mung beans, alfalfa, sunflower, fenugreek and wheatgrass.

Pop a handful of seeds in a saucer or small dish. Cover with water. Drain and replace the water every day. Give the seeds or sprouts a bit of a shake as you drain them. When they start to sprout, transfer them to a flat bowl or small plate covered with a damp cloth. Keep the cloth damp and toss the sprouts every day. Depending on the seed, you should have edible sprouts in five to eight days.

When they are the desired length, pop them into the fridge to stop them growing.

Some seeds, like wheatgrass, fenugreek and sunflowers, are better grown on potting mix or soil. Let them grow into little upright plants and mow them with a pair of scissors when it's time to eat.

Country girl in WA says: "There's nothing worse than trying to fill in that patch of lawn and waking up to all the new shoots being chowed on by 'roos. They're clearly the more delicious and nutritious option!"

Reality check

If you take a grain of wheat and grind it up, you get flour and can make bread. How can it be that the same grain of wheat, soaked in water and left to its own devices can increase its nutritive value?

The actual nutrient chemicals are not created by the sprouting process, but by the growth enzymes of the young plant.

A good deal of the nutritional value of most sprouts comes from the fact that they are young, soft and easily juiced and digested.

In hot weather you may need to water three times a day.

In humid weather, fermentation or mould may be a challenge.

Wheat grass, for example, is grown from a special strain of grass known as Red Wheatberry. This is different from powdered 'wheat grass'.

Costs

Sprouting kits are around $20

Seed is around $5/kg

Photo by devi-puspita-amartha-yahya- on Unsplash

Look it up

Sprout juicing

Sprouts nutrition

happyjuicer.com

sprout.net.au

Now try this!

6 Indoor plants

12 The nature of time

51 The power of the bean

60 Things that grow in the dark

48. Things we eat for lunch

Packing instead of buying your lunch not only gives you control over the environmental footprint of your food (and its packaging) but can save you around $10 a day. If you work full-time, that's $2,400 a year. Worth considering? I bet you wouldn't turn it down as a pay rise.

Here's a plan

Leftovers are the cheapest and yummiest lunch. No preparation, other than packing it, required. Lots of things taste better given a day or two in the fridge.

Putting away the leftovers offers alternative packaging opportunities. Silicon covers for bowls and saucepans can create airproof seals that keep the smell of your garlic-laden salad out of the strawberry shortcake. Beeswax wraps (cloth soaked in flexible but waterproof beeswax) can be used to cover goods or wrap firmer food directly.

If you are reheating your leftovers, most packaging is not oven-proof and some are not microwave-proof either. Silicon covers, most plastic food containers and most ceramic bowls are microwave-proof. Cover your bowl with a plate or an all-purpose cover you keep for the microwave.

Dried fruit, nuts, olives and other antipasto can be popped in a container, as can fresh celery, carrot, capsicum, apple and melon. Cut up whatever you have in the fridge and put it in a container for lunch. Put a little dip on the side and have carrot sticks with tzatziki. Yum!

By using the stuff you already have in the pantry and the fridge you are eating a classy upmarket lunch without buying anything special or using extra packaging.

Keep the packaging that you do have to buy. Paper bags from mushrooms, bread bags and takeaway containers can be repurposed to keep your lunch organised and fresh.

Photo by S Well on Unsplash

Reality check

Replacing single-use plastic with single-use paper or aluminium is not solving the problem. Reusable containers are the answer.

Who has time to pack lunch in the morning? The answer is preparation, preparation, preparation.

When you do the shopping, think about what you are going to take to lunch each day. Then consider the containers you will take it in. You don't want to waste packaging.

Grabbing a snack after work? Cheese and biscuits? Yay, I'll have a glass of wine with that. While I'm at it I might chuck some of that cheese in a container and some crackers in another. That will look great in my lunch box tomorrow.

Now try this!

7 Our high-speed lives

54 Baking bread

56 The packaging we purchase

Look it up

Own lunch frugal

Take away waste

Future food

Waste free lunch

eatability.com.au

A personal story

A busy mother, aka Container Queen, writes, "Good-quality plastic containers keep the food fresh and visible. My Little Giant has a huge appetite and so gets two lunch boxes with an assortment of fresh carrots, dried fruit and nuts, yoghurt, and leftovers or a sandwich. I treasure my containers, so my kids never leave the lunch box at school. Evah!"

Costs

For the price of a few containers you'll save thousands, literally.

HARD FACTS

AUSTRALIANS THROW OUT

10,000 tonnes

OF PLASTIC A DAY.

That's 400g each!

49. What's wrong with the supermarket

Photo by Hanson Lu- on Unsplash

The cheap food in your supermarket comes at a huge cost. Much of this cost saving is achieved by squeezing growers and suppliers, and passing on environmental costs to the broader community.

Supermarket-own brands are often half the price of competing products. The supermarket uses its monopoly power to drive its competitors out of business. Supermarkets pay farmers rock bottom prices, increase food miles, promote packaging and encourage car use.

The $1.00 milk deal made between the supermarkets and Murray Goulburn in 2013 demonstrates the problem. It drove Murray Goulburn to illegally change the price it paid farmers, and the dairy industry was brought to its knees. It continues to suffer, despite the supermarkets 'generously' giving farmers a drought bonus during 2018.

Another example is the compulsory quality-assurance scheme run by supermarkets that allows the supermarket to return fruit and vegetables that do not sell and get a full refund.

Farmer-friendly food cooperatives like Food Connect and the Open Food Network have emerged to address this problem.

Here's a plan

Instead of driving to the supermarket on your regular shop, stop and take stock of your fridge. Make a list of all the uneaten food you throw out to make room for the shopping.

Now, head to the local shops and buy ingredients for the next two meals as well as your weekly essentials.

Then, buy food as you need it each day or two for the week after that.

Keep track of expensive items. Also make a note of the items you could not get locally and what you ate instead.

After a full week or two, add up the savings from the food you did not have to throw away, the 'luxury' items and impulse purchases you normally make and the cost of driving to the supermarket.

Compare that to the items you had to pay more for.

Food cooperatives and bulk food stores have entered the digital age and now many bulk foods can be ordered online and delivered.

Costs

Individual items: up to 20% more.

Your shopping bill: up to 50% less.

Reality check

On average, supermarkets pay farmers about two thirds of market price for fresh fruit. In many cases this is below the farmer's cost.

More than half of family farms run at a loss and are supported by an external income.

There is no doubt that you will end up paying more for the same goods by shopping locally. You will end up buying less food that is of higher quality, though. The net impact on your heath will be positive.

Home delivery has its own footprint, so does driving to the shop.

Look it up

Food connect

Bulk food

Food cooperative

Supermarket farmers

#stupidmarkets

Food mile

Coles tasman scott

Organic vs regenerative

Now try this!

54 Bread baking

56 The packaging we purchase

67 Shop locally

50. Eating better meat

Despite advertisements showing green paddocks and sunshine, most meat is produced in factory farms where animals eat processed food laced with additives and antibiotics designed to make them grow fast and fend off disease. Organic butchers and local processors can help turn back the tide.

Two thirds of our beef and lamb in Australia is grass-fed, which is much less carbon and water intensive than animals raised in a feedlot. Because feedlot animals eat food grown under irrigation, they consume much more water and fertiliser per edible kilo than grass-fed animals. The transportation and processing, packaging and refrigeration all consume energy and resources. Industrial animal farming also raises many ethical issues. Nearly all our pork and chicken is grown in feedlots.

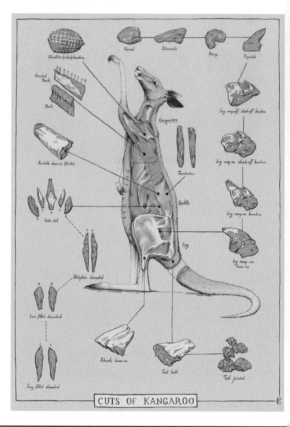

CUTS OF KANGAROO

Here's a plan

Eat less meat. From the point of view of our body's health, meat should be a supplement to, not the basis of, our diet. Eating less gives you the opportunity to seek out organic or specialist butchers with more interesting meat. That has the added benefit of promoting better meat production.

Use meat better. What about the bones? Collect them, throw them in a pot, cover with cold water and simmer for two hours. You have produced a fantastic base for all types of soups.

Eat different meat. Check the range of offal and unusual cuts at your local butcher. Check out butchers who specialise in Australian and game meats — kangaroo, rabbit, hare, duck and venison. Try kosher and halal butchers. You can find camel, goat and donkey as well as your Aussie standards.

Vegan hamburgers, synthetically grown in laboratory conditions, are now available.

PERSONAL WATER FOOTPRINT
LITRES PER DAY PER PERSON

Better meat

Household use

Reality check

Australian meat producers work closely with universities and scientists to establish sustainable meat production. That research indicates that Australian beef production uses much less than the commonly quoted 20,000L of water per kilogram of meat. They use the figure of 500L/kg for free range beef. This book uses the figure of 2,000L/kg for beef production on average, including processing.

Look it up
Halal butcher

Game meat

Beef emissions

veg-soc.org

Regenerative farming

waterfootprint.org

Now try this!
10 Ordering in food

47 Mung beans and love

54 Baking bread

HARD FACTS

WATER CONSUMPTION OF RED MEAT
Free range beef & lamb:
500L/kg WHILE ALIVE
Feedlot beef:
4,500L/kg WHILE ALIVE
Processing & packaging:
500L/kg

RED MEAT, CARBON FOOTPRINT
BEEF: 25kg CO_2e/kg

Lamb: 20kg CO_2e/kg

APPLE FOOTPRINT
Water: 700L/kg

CO_2e: 200g/kg

AUSTRALIANS EAT MORE THAN
100kg of meat each year.

Today, 1 in 8 Australians are NOW VEGETARIAN.
It was 1 in 10 a decade ago.

Kitchen

51 The power of the bean

The healthy and delicious Mediterranean diet is usually promoted as containing olives, fish, nuts, fresh vegetables and wine. The missing, secret ingredient? The bean. More properly called pulses, this group of high-protein foods includes peas, lentils and beans; the staple food of many cultures.

What would minestrone be without red beans, a plate of dips without hummus, an Indian feast without dahl, pea and ham soup without the peas? Lentils are the basis of many dishes from West Africa to Asia.

Their special magic is that they absorb nitrogen from the air through a symbiotic relationship with bacteria. As a result they enrich soil, instead of requiring fertiliser, and produce more protein. Mixed with nuts and other oil-bearing seeds, pulses provide the complete range of amino acids required by our bodies.

Here's a plan

Almost any stew you can make with meat, you can create with pulses. This super food comes in so many varieties you will never run short of recipes to follow or experiments to try.

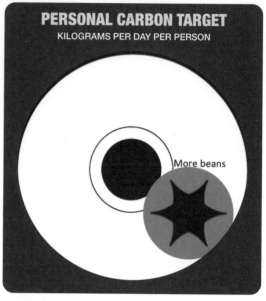

PERSONAL CARBON TARGET
KILOGRAMS PER DAY PER PERSON

More beans

Replacing half your meat with pulses will have a major impact

The trick with dried pulses is that you have to soak them before you use them and that means you have to plan ahead. If you can't find dry pulses where you shop, head to the local Indian, African or Asian supermarket. Soak them overnight, then drain and salt them before boiling them in fresh water.

Many pulses produce a brilliant stock when boiled that adds flavour to other dishes. The water in which chickpeas (garbanzo) are boiled has so much tasty protein it will set like

HARD FACTS | **A kilo of pulses produces 0.9kg of CO_2e to grow and process AND USES 70L OF WATER**

a jelly. Chickpea stock makes the best vegetable soups. Ever.

Some red beans and lima beans contain an enzyme (lectin) in the skin that is removed by soaking. Lectin is not good for you and you should not use their water for stock.

A personal story

The Urban Wolf notes, "Beans? You can't go past the broad ones. One of spring's best seasonal flavours. Try them cooked with finely cut strips of your home-cured bacon, diced onion, garlic and sour cream. They can handle the toughest frosts so can be grown in all areas of Australia."

Reality check

Buying pulses already cooked in tin cans might be convenient but it does not nurture your life or your planet. Look at the label to learn where they're coming from.

Beans mean gas. You will start tootin' more often — it's a sign that tum is happy, though.

Costs

You can make dahl with rice at 50c per person.

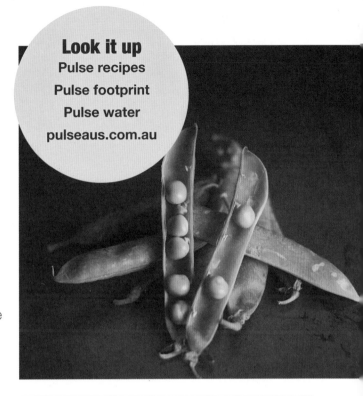

Look it up
Pulse recipes
Pulse footprint
Pulse water
pulseaus.com.au

Back in the day
As prisoner #AZ-85 Al Capone used a stock made from the shells of green peas to distil alcohol in the kitchens of Alcatraz.

Now try this!
11 A no-spend day
46 Where the herbs grow
59 Smoke your own
86 Getting fed without giving a fig

THAT COMPARES TO 2.7kg CO_2e AND 2,500L water for rice or 27kg CO_2e and 2,000L OF WATER FOR BEEF.

Vegan veteran, Leigh-Chantelle

Applying some self care:
Leigh-Chantelle

"Veganism is not just about a diet. It is an ethical way of living. It is important to do the best thing for our animal friends, the environment and other people. Being vegan is the best way for me to lead by example.

"I went vegetarian first when I realised the connection between the life that once was and the death that I was consuming. I was vegetarian for years before I went vegan because I didn't even know what veganism was. When I was at school there was one sentence in our home economics textbook highlighting the misconception that vegan diet lacks too many nutrients and minerals and is impractical.

"I've been vegan for 20-odd years now. It was harder at first, to get people to understand.

"Once you are interested and start learning about something new it starts spiralling. I started by agreeing that I don't want animals to be harmed, so I started with food, then you find out about soap, then places that sell shoes, then makeup.

"Now, people make a lot of decisions because they are mindful of the environment and animals. Because of that there are a lot more businesses, a lot more communities, and not-for-profits that are able to establish great alternatives for leather. Sources of leather-like products include mushrooms and seaweed. Universities are doing research into commercialising these products and into microbial plastics.

"I don't think that mass-industrialised factory farming provides any sort of connection to animals or the environment. That does not mean that mass production of fake meat or fake leather is the ideal alternative. Companies these days need to be ethical. Modern consumers demand that you are doing good for the world, and are not just trying to make money from the destruction of the environment and exploitation of people and other animals.

"One issue I have with veganism and the animal rights movement is that it hasn't changed enough. Systematic processes of production and consumption still dominate and we are just going along with. We are still mass-producing. We have not learned the essential lessons that are really important to move forward into the next stage of evolution."

Look it up
@leighchantelle
@TallulahEbbs

Tallulah

Fun creating new foods:
Tallulah Ebbs

Tallulah Ebbs lives in Gadigal country on the east coast of Australia, studies naturopathy and works at Alfalfa house, a community-owned, not-for-profit food cooperative with a zero-waste and farmer-direct emphasis. Alfalfa House is the oldest food cooperative in Sydney.

"Veganism has been a big journey for me. I was quite young when I went vegan 10 years ago. It wasn't very common at the time. I had been thinking about it and decided, 'if I don't do this now I will never do it'. Once I made the decision, it shifted a lot of things. I became aware of the nuances around choices we make every day, and the issues that inform them: animal rights, environmental issues, the ethics of industrialised agriculture. For example, palm oil is in a lot of food, including vegan food, and has a huge environmental impact because of the clearing of rainforests. Being vegan has helped bring my focus to the nature of these choices.

"It expanded my idea of ethics. Instead of mindlessly going about my consumption, not really caring about the decisions I make and the things I put into my body, it has expanded my mind, my awareness of how I make those decisions and the impact that I have.

"I am studying a Bachelor of Health Science in Naturopathy because it takes a holistic approach to health and that is part of the practice I want to develop in the world. In general, this Naturopathy degree focuses on nutrition and herbal medicine, complemented by courses in counselling and heavy sciences like anatomy and chemistry.

"I try to maximise my impact by inspiration, leading by example rather than lecturing. I try to be empathetic and open as I feel that is the best way to inspire others."

52. A vegan life

Live a life without harming animals. Veganism is the fastest growing segment of the food industry. The number of vegans in Australia has been doubling every three years. This has led to the appearance of vegan fast-food chains and vegan options in hamburger chains.

Cooking vegan is fun! Many people think that it's hard, time consuming and expensive to cook vegan food but the opposite is true. If you buy dry goods in bulk it's even more affordable.

Think of getting to know the ingredients like a flirtatious game. It might be a bit nerve racking at first (though it's still exciting) but the more you court the ingredients, the more comfortable you'll get.

Here's a plan

Check out the non-meat dishes on the menu when you eat out. Try falafels, dips, salads with peas, beans and pasta in them, dals, bean stews. Many cultures have signature vegan dishes because meat was traditionally scarce.

Explore recipes and ingredients of the dishes you like most. Make your own falafel balls, bean stews, dahl and hummus. Experiment with making your favourite stews and soups using beans, lentils, tofu and mushrooms. Start to explore the alternatives to meat.

Try to eat pulses with rice to make the meal a complete protein (all 9 essential amino acids) If you don't want to eat rice and beans together, you can eat them over the span of two days. Beans one day rice the next. That way you'll get all the amino acids in your diet that your body can't produce itself. Buckwheat and quinoa are both complete proteins

Find completely different foods that you enjoy. Eat fruit for breakfast instead of eggs. Eat salad as a main meal every now and then. Have nuts and dips instead of cheese or cold meats as a snack. Trying to substitute animal products in your diet is hard work and expensive. Forgetting about them and doing things differently is much more rewarding.

HARD FACTS

THERE ARE NOW 600,000 vegans in Australia. THIS COMPARES TO 2.5 million VEGETARIANS.

Reality check

It's expensive to replace animal products with niche vegan substitutes, but fun to try and make your own.

Make sure you are getting enough B12 by using a supplement or fortified vegan products. If you are concerned about nutrition you can see a nutritionist or naturopath to start a diet plan.

The largest vegetarian nation on earth, India, integrated the cow into the fabric of life. Female cows wandered freely, were worshiped and provided protein through milk, butter and cheese. Male cows were mostly castrated and provided the physical labour to operate mills, farm equipment and construction work.

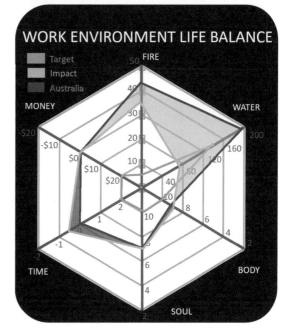

WORK ENVIRONMENT LIFE BALANCE

A small sacrifice in time creates significant benefits for your life and your planet

Costs

Vegan yoghurt: $12/L

Vegan mayonnaise: $20/L

Dairy yoghurt: $10/L

Egg mayonnaise: $12/L

Hummus: $10/L

Home-made hummus: $4/L

A personal story

Henrietta asks, "Why is so much foodstuff derived from female reproductive processes? Fruit, seeds, eggs, milk, nuts; it seems that we never really wean ourselves from the mother."

Back in the day

"I am oppressed with a dread of living forever. That is the only disadvantage of vegetarianism," George Bernard Shaw said in 1941 at age 85.

Now try this!

7 Get active
with your community

40 Hemp and bamboo

58 Salt and sugar

80 Be a sticky beak

Look it up

Plant based diet

Lab meat

Animal rights

peta.org.au

53. Feeding friends

Sharing a meal is a timeless act of community, friendship and caring. We love to show off and cook our favourite foods. To allow abundance become happiness; don't build a bigger fence, build a bigger table.

If we each stay at home cooking alone in our kitchens we are not only missing out on the social aspects of eating together, we are burning energy and effort inefficiently. If we shopped and cooked with each other, we would buy less and throw out less.

Here's a plan

You are going to cook anyway, so why not call a friend. It does not take much more effort to cook for two.

Other tips in this book encourage you to use fresh ingredients, grow your own herbs, prepare and preserve foods. Pick food from your garden, share your extra harvest with the neighbours and reap the rewards! Working with your food is an enjoyable way of connecting with your environment and the people around you.

Do it at work! Plan to take something to share to a meeting. Buy locally grown apples on your way to work in the morning. Make extra iced tea the night before and take a couple of litres to share in your break. Whether you are a good cook or not, there is always some way you can contribute.

Turn off the TV and have dinner at the table. Encourage the kid's friends to stay for dinner, walk or cycle them home and meet their parents.

Dream up your ideal dinner party. Start with the guest list, then, keeping in mind their food preferences, craft a menu that is made from sustainable, locally sourced food. Surprise a friend. Give them a call and tell them you are bringing round a home-cooked dinner.

Take around some ingredients and cook at their place! You are bound to learn something new. Sharing cultural idiosyncrasies through cooking, divulging secret family recipes and utilising specialised kitchen equipment is a

Photo by Matheus Frade on Unsplash

Reality check

Not everything can be sourced organically, grown locally or sustainably packaged. What is important is enjoying and sharing what you have while minimising the harmful, environmentally damaging products brought into your environment.

wonderful way to get a first-class cooking education without the hefty price tag.

A personal story

One of us remembers the search for an after-party, "We ended up in the Hills District and noticed there were no snacks and people looked hungry, so I got stuck into the eight-burner gas stove and made 24 plates of poached eggs on toast. Just as the revellers lined up for their plate, four big security guys arrived and rapidly escorted me from the party. I never got to eat the eggs."

Costs

Home-cooked food costs slightly less than pre-cooked and frozen food, but a great deal less than restaurant fare.

Cooking for four is much cheaper per person than cooking for one.

HARD FACTS

Up to 2 million OF US LIVE IN 1-person households. That's 1 in 10 people and 1 in 5 households. On average we each throw out almost 1kg of food every day.

Look it up
Simple fast recipe
Iced tea
Finger food ideas

Now try this!
3 Those packaged drinks
47 Mung beans and love
54 Baking bread

54. Baking bread

Photo by Kate Remmer on Unsplash

We cannot live on bread alone, but we can serve a wide variety of sandwiches and meals on toast. Making our own bread opens the door to converting our homes into hubs of production.

By making your own food, instead of taking it out of a packet, you extend that enjoyment of food beyond the eating to the cooking. Just as important, you avoid poor-quality ingredients, preservatives, and reduce the energy used to package, preserve and transport it. That's the essence of slow food.

Here's a plan

Start with a packet of baker's flour; it often contains a satchel of dry yeast and instructions for making a loaf of bread. That way you maximise your chances of success.

Let it take its time. Making a loaf of bread takes 8 to 12 hours, but only 15 minutes of that involves hands on work.

1. Mix the dough in the morning.
2. Knead it in the afternoon.
3. Bake at night or use your oven timer.

Bingo! Hand-crafted bread within your existing daily schedule.

Once you get the hang of it you can get creative. Nearly all cultures have some staple carbohydrate made from ground-up seeds mixed with water. Try different flours and adding different seeds to your bread to see what flavours and textures you enjoy.

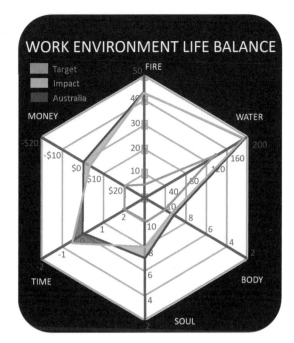

WORK ENVIRONMENT LIFE BALANCE

- Target
- Impact
- Australia

FIRE · WATER · BODY · SOUL · TIME · MONEY

Sharing the bread you make might be as important as making it

Different amounts of moisture affect the outcome. Wet doughs will create chewier loaves with big bubbles. Think of crumpets. Dry doughs will be more crumbly and will rise less. The results depend on the flour, the moisture of the dough, the humidity of the air, the temperature of your kitchen, the amount of time you let it rise, the amount of time you spend kneading it, the temperature of your oven, and the time you leave the dough to cook. Experiment. It's pretty hard to muck it up completely and you'll learn something every time.

Make two or three loaves instead of one and trade the extra with the neighbours. It takes the same time but produces additional results.

Reality check

Many modern apartments have limited kitchen facilities, because people eat out.

If that's your challenge, you can get a bread machine. Specific appliances, like rice cookers and juice extractors, will complement your limited kitchen facilities.

Look it up
Slow food
Slow cooking
Simple recipes

A personal story

Alette says: "My mum had a bread maker when I was growing up in the 90s. Waking up at 5:00am to smell fresh bread is still one of my most fond memories. I started learning to make my own bread when I started my sustainability journey. I have neither a bread maker nor a stand mixer. But, I got out of it some Michelle Obama-grade arms and some tasty loaves, and damn is it easier than the world seems to think."

Now try this!
3 Those packaged drinks
10 Ordering in food
53 Feeding friends
57 Barbecue fuel

55. Energy-efficient appliances

Whenever you have to replace a household appliance, make sure that you buy one that is energy and water efficient. Better yet, buy an efficient secondhand one. You'll save money and resources. Check that you really need the appliance: not buying one saves even more.

Household appliances are made of metal and plastic, both energy and resource-intensive materials. The resources and energy consumed in the manufacture of the appliance are difficult to recover, so replacing them less often is a significant saving. These appliances consume electricity every time we turn them on. And that clutter in our kitchen cupboards is a sign of our tendency to buy more gadgets than we need.

Here's a plan

Buying energy-efficient appliances, using appliances less and only buying the appliances we really need all reduce our environmental footprint.

Buy appliances that are energy efficient. Since most electrical energy produced in Australia is still generated by fossil fuel, the energy efficiency is directly related to the greenhouse gas emissions. Appliances are energy rated so we can quickly determine which ones use least electricity and so emit less greenhouse gas. Washing machines are also rated on their water use.

Energy-efficiency ratings are managed by the Australian Greenhouse Office. Called the Australian Appliance Energy Rating Scheme, it is a six-star system; the more stars the better. The labelling indicates the energy consumption of the product in numbers as does the number of star rating.

High-rating appliances tend to be better made and so also last longer. A stainless steel hot water service is usually guaranteed for 10 years, a vitreous tank for only two. Europe passed Right to Repair laws in 2019 which forces manufacturers to make appliances repairable to further reduce the amount of resources wasted by replacing appliances that break as soon as the warranty period is over.

Finding ways to do things without a dedicated appliance is an even more significant solution. You save the resources and energy used to manufacture them as well as the energy consumed by using

HARD FACTS — THE USE OF ENERGY-EFFICIENT APPLIANCES **can knock 3 tonnes** OFF YOUR TOTAL EMISSIONS.

Look it up

Energy rating

Water efficiency

greenhouse.gov.au

energystar.gov.au

savewater.com.au

A personal story

Alette says: "I moved into a tiny house that has an equally tiny kitchen. The only thing to cook on is a mini stove/oven on the counter. Because we only have one main power source, it easily trips out; we find using the washing machine and oven at the same time can be the biggest issue. Our solution was to whip out our butane-fired camping stove. It lives on the counter top alongside the electric oven, and it's preferred when we need to cook."

them. There are neat hand-powered alternatives for many appliances, some of them traditional, some of them using the latest innovations and materials.

Costs

Expect to pay 10% to 20% more for a very efficient appliance. Expect to pay less on your energy bill.

Now try this!

2 Turn down the air-con

35 The standby lightshow

43 Turn off the dishwasher

A MODERN REFRIGERATOR
uses about half the energy of a model
MORE THAN A DECADE OLD.

56. The packaging we purchase

Packaging keeps our food and goods clean and safe, so contributes to our quality of life. Unfortunately, it has taken over our bins and threatens to take over our planet. There are plenty of creative ways you can avoid excess packaging and still enjoy the products you need.

In 2019 many Australian states enacted bans on single-use plastic bags, but we still throw out tonnes of packaging that wraps our food, small items and parcels.

Whether you drop it in Pine River, Parramatta or Prahran, the plastic you throw away is extremely likely to end up in the ocean. Of the total amount of plastic produced, 10% ends up in the ocean; plastic dropped in the street will eventually get to the sea unless it is stopped by a council stormwater filter. If you do not put it in the bin, that's where it is headed. Because of the container deposit scheme and ban on single use plastics, Clean Up Australia reported a significant decline in the percentage of plastics in 2020. They picked up 16,500 tonnes of rubbish in one day in 2020, 5,000 tonnes of it plastic. The North Pacific Gyre is a highly visible island of billions of tonnes of plastic. The millions of dead birds and sea animals who ingest the micro-plastics are less visible.

Cling wrap is the ultimate disposable product. A simple roll of plastic, it is multipurpose, gets used once and is thrown away. The waste involved is alarming.

Lots of packaging combines plastic and cardboard or aluminium, making it harder to recycle.

Here's a plan

Become aware of the packaging and find alternatives. Shop at bulk food stores, support retailers that offer packaging alternatives. Follow the tips on reusable containers in Tip 48, *The things we eat for lunch*, and explore new forms of plastic in Tip 57, *Silicon and beyond*.

Buy meat from the butcher instead of the supermarket. Take your own containers, rather than use the butcher's plastic bags.

Buy fruit that is not in packets or individually wrapped, even if it means shopping at the farmer's market.

Take fine 'silk' bags, or reused paper (including mushroom) bags, that do not affect the weight of the fruit and veg, to the grocery store, rather than using the flimsy plastic bags they provide.

Household items, consumables and appliances actually need relatively little packaging. Select brands that use little packaging or use packaging manufactured from renewable sources instead of plastic: mushroom foam and bamboo wrap, for example.

The real test is to change your habits. Add 'Bag' to that checklist you run through as you walk out the door. You know the one. It goes like this, 'Key. Money. Phone. BAG'.

National Geographic has a comprehensive analysis of the North Pacific garbage patch

Look it up

Gyre rubbish

Turtles plastic

Cornstarch peanuts

Packaging embodied

boomerangalliance.org

sustainablepack.org

ecosilkbags.com.au

noplasticbags.org.au

tupperware.com.au

papermart.com.au

HARD FACTS

That 'reusable' shopping bag?

EMBEDDED ENERGY: 4.8MJ

Driving 120 metres: 4.8MJ

Aluminium = bottled energy
A packet of kitchen foil

≈ 6kg of CO_2e

Now try this!

3 Those packaged drinks

10 Ordering in food

48 The things we eat for lunch

65 The problem with recycling

67 Shop locally

90 Hand-made watering systems

Costs

A good 'silk' bag: $6

Reusable canvas bag: $5

Home-made shopping bag: $0

National Geographic has a comprehensive analysis of the North Pacific garbage patch

Reality check

It is increasingly difficult to get honey and peanut butter in glass. Hunt it down or find a bulk food store that will fill your own containers.

Some cling wraps contain phthalates. That is less common following a major publicity campaign a decade ago. The claims that they contain dioxins have been discredited.

Canned food is handy for long-term storage, but a lot of cheap canned food has been transported from around the world to alleviate a glut in the country of origin. Look for Australian brands like Ardmona SPC, which is once again in Australian ownership.

57 Silicon and beyond

The carbon chemistry at the heart of plastics has been based on cheap and plentiful petroleum. Those techniques are now being applied to biosynthetic oils (created by microbes) and to silicon, the most common element on earth.

We are carbon-based life forms.

We get our energy from the capacity of plants to combine carbon dioxide and water using the energy in sunlight to build complex carbohydrates. Fossil fuels capture energy trapped over billions of years and so burning them releases energy and carbon dioxide. We have used that energy to create the miraculous synthetic substances that surround us. The tragedy is that they consume a finite resource and release carbon dioxide.

Luckily for us, we have learned to harness the power of microbes to manipulate large carbon molecules and create modern plastics that do not rely on or release ancient sunlight. We have also used Silicon to create long-chain silicon compounds that are bendable (plastic) but heatproof, waterproof and airproof. These

Here's a plan

Look out for these plastics in the market.

Silicon plastics: Widely used to make cooking utensils, plastic containers and baking dishes. Strong, waterproof and airproof, a silicon cover can be used to seal a bowl and replace cling wrap or plastic bags. Silicon is also appearing in more industrial and mechanical environments as well.

Biodegradable textiles: Made from microbes rather than petroleum products, microbial plastics have begun to appear on the market. Algiknit is woven from a gel extracted from algae and dyed with natural products before being extruded into fibre.

Biopolymers: These products have begun to appear in medical settings, photovoltaic cells and inks, where specific properties justify their current expense. As biopolymers become more widely used their price will come down and their availability will lead to widespread use. Keep your eyes open for bandages, clothing and other everyday items made from biosynthetics.

Modern manufacturing approaches have given a new lease of life to ancient materials. The Zelfo sustainable packaging coming out of Germany was established experimentally in northern NSW to use locally grown plant fibres.

UP TO 90%
of the earth's crust is
MADE OF COMPOUNDS CONTAINING
silicon.
The melting
POINT OF SILICON IS
1410° CELSIUS,
WHEREAS ITS
boiling point is
2355° CELSIUS.

super plastics offer us all the benefits of plastic with much lower environmental cost.

We have also begun to revisit many ancient materials with new eyes; for example, using new manufacturing techniques to create new fabrics out of wool, or using the herd (pith) of hemp instead of gravel in concrete as the Romans did, creating lighter, stronger structures.

Costs

A biopolymer scarf is $US130.

Look it up

Biopolymer

Every day silicon

Zelfo

Hemp masonry

Polyfleece

polartec.com

repeatproducts.com.au

Now try this!

56 The packaging we purchase

90 Hand-made watering systems

75 Embrace embodied energy

The experts interviewed for this book point out that reversing the negative impact of industrialisation on your life and planet is not the job of individual consumers like you and me. We can contribute to the solution, but we cannot do it alone. We also know that we cannot wait for government and industry to solve it for us.

That makes it a pretty wicked problem to solve.

One way to pick apart the threads of the problem is to move away from seeing ourselves as consumers and begin identifying the opportunities available to produce things. By sharing the output of our production we build a resilient community and we lead by example to inspire others. The **hub of production** is an idea introduced at the beginning of this chapter. It comes from a woman named Cat Green.

Cat contributed a chapter called *Radical Homemaker* to a book titled *Fair Food*. At the time, she was writing her PhD on food sovereignty. Part of her radical home-making manifesto is that our idea of our homes has been constructed as a node of consumption and reinforced by advertising that encourages us to consume. Government rhetoric that we need to spend for the benefit of the economy feeds into that idea. Cat's simple assertion is that, instead, we need to transform our homes into hubs of production.

Right now, we buy stuff and consume it at home, alienating ourselves by consuming alone. If we make stuff to share, then we

Photo by Anshu A MVUs on Unsplash

put ourselves at the centre, or hub, of our network instead of at the edge. By making this move, we fill our lives with people and those people get something tangible from us that builds a relationship.

By engaging friends and neighbours in shelling the pigeon peas we grow on the spare block next door, we build community in ways that have worked for thousands of centuries. That community supports us in the present as well as the future. That network makes us resilient and helps us thrive instead of simply survive. When we read about international movements like Mondragon, ViaCempesina or Slow Food we see that the idea has real power.

Of course, the choices we make as a consumer can contribute to long-term sustainability, but we would have to buy a lot of hand-made soap to influence the footprint of soap manufacturing. By contrast, making the soap for other people spreads the word, increases the volume of hand-made soap and encourages soap manufacturers to respond to the market.

It is easier to say this than it is to do it, which is why the focus of this book is to help you create time in your already busy life to become a hub of production that will ultimately create time and independence for you, and nurture your life and planet.

Tip summary

One challenge with gardening is dealing with the harvest. You nurture your tomato plants through summer and then, all-of-a-sudden, you have baskets of tomatoes overflowing across the kitchen table and into the laundry. The first tomato is a delight. The first kilo of tomatoes feels like success. When the fruit flies start lurking over the 10 kilos of over-ripe tomatoes on the sideboard it all seems a little messy and difficult. The same goes for pears, plums, avocadoes and mangoes.

Basically, bacteria and larger bugs are the enemy that make your food go off.

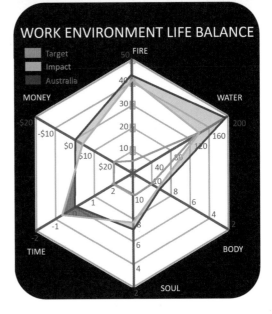

They can't live without air and water so you preserve your food by keeping one or the other away from your crop. You can dry food to get rid of the water or immerse it in oil, salt or sugar to keep away the air. You can get even smarter and create your own ecosystem in a jar that improves the nutritional value of your food, while keeping the nasties out.

That gives you a cellar full of goodies to give the neighbours when they pop in for a loaf of bread or the rellies at a family event. Most important, it saves you a trip to the shop every day for the year to come.

#	Tip	Page	🔥	💧	👫	👁	⏱	Ⓢ
58	Salt and sugar	152	✓	✓	✓	✓	✗✗	✓✓
59	Smoke your own	154	✗✗		✓	✓	✗✗	✓✓
60	Things that grow in the dark	158		✓	✓	✓✓	✓✓	✗✗✓✓
61	Things that grow in bottles	160		✓	✓	✓✓	✓	✗✗✓✓

58. Salt and sugar

An army marches on its stomach and that stomach was once filled with salted food. The nickname 'saltier' became the English word 'soldier'. Preserving food is the basis of civilisation, if that's what you call the Game of Thrones.

We head off to the shop to buy food when we want to eat and that puts us at the mercy of the market. If we could only grab the food when it was falling off the trees and put it away for later. Now there's an idea.

Here's a plan

Get food when it is plentiful, then clean and prepare your fruit, vegetables or meat so that you only keep the bits you want to eat.

Then boil it up with lots of salt or sugar and keep in a container without much air. Hey presto, you have invented corned beef, spam, jam, marmalade, apple jelly, ham and a million other traditional foods.

Preserving in solution

1. Sterilise your containers in boiling water or a hot oven.

2. Prepare your preserving solution by boiling water with sugar or salt in it.

3. Let the containers and the preserving solution cool so that you can handle them safely, but while they are still hot.

4. Place your prepared food into the containers.

Photo by Tim Toomey on Unsplash

Sauces, chutneys, purees, jams, jellies and marmalade

Once you start boiling food in salt and sugar, you can have real fun.

- If you cook your food long enough for it to fall apart then you have made a puree or a jam.

- Throw in a few flavourings (vinegar, spices) to make a chutney.

- Make the mixture nice and wet, run it through the food processor and call it sauce.

- Jelly, jams and marmalades are fruit cooked in sugar with special attention paid to whether there is enough pectin in the fruit (or added to it) to make juice set like a jelly.

5. Cover the food with the preserving solution, pushing it down to get rid of the air in the food but leaving an air pocket at the top of the container.

6. Place the lid on each container and seal while hot.

7. Boil the container in boiling water to drive out more air and create a vacuum seal.

Back in the day

Old mate writes, "My sisters and I used to hide under grandma's house and open bottles of preserved summer fruits as a stolen treat. Cling peaches in syrup was my personal favourite, though I remain partial to a stewed pear. Most unusual find? Some 50-year-old salted, green beans that turned to grey sludge when we opened them."

Reality check

Australia's suburbs are still full of fruit trees in older backyards, sometimes planted as street trees, that produce an abundance of food that needs to be put away. Picking and preserving that fruit is easy, communal and fun.

Costs

Damaged fruit, 10kg: $5

Sugar, 5kg: $5

Commercial jam, 10kg: $50

Now try this!
4 The snacks I love

46 Where the herbs grow

54 Baking bread

61 Things that grow in bottles

Look it up
Crop swap

Chutney

Permablitz

Fleet farming

59. Smoke your own

Food left near the fire gets old and leathery and lasts a long time. Smoking, drying, smothering food in salt, sugar or oil; all these methods eliminate water-borne bacteria from rotting our food.

Ten kilos of tomatoes can become a kitchen disaster if you don't have a plan. Ten kilos of kangaroo meat is going to make a big stink if you don't deal with it pronto. The trick is to get it out of the air and to eliminate as much water as possible.

Here's a plan

Spread it out in the sun. If it's mid-winter you might want to skip ahead, but most of us do our harvesting when there is a bit of sun around.

Whether it's tomatoes, apricots or kangaroo tail, the trick is to get the food into relatively small pieces and into the sun so that it starts to dry out.

If you live in the Mediterranean climates in the southern part of Australia, you can aim to dry it completely; the rest of us are stuck with semi-dried goods smothered in oil, sugar or salt. The nuclear option is that we use a food hydrator and suck that last bit of water out using solar-generated electric power.

Smoking is a neat alternative where you can apply heat and add a smoky flavour, without worrying about the daily weather report.

Preserving in oil

1. Sterilise your containers in a hot oven.

2. Let them cool without letting microbes into them so that you can handle them safely.

3. Place your semi-dried food into the containers as tightly as possible to minimise the oil required.

4. Pour in the oil, making sure all the air escapes from the food, but allowing a small air pocket at the top of the container.

5. Put the lid on and seal it.

6. Heat the container in boiling water or a hot oven to push out as much air as possible and create a vacuum seal.

Smoke, or dry, your own

1. Prepare the food as cleanly as possible to minimise damaged flesh that might be prone to infection.

2. Wash the food in vinegar, lemon juice or some other substance to disinfect it. Sultana grapes are often dipped in sulphur.

3. Place the food on trays so it can be arranged in the sun, or on dryer or smoker.

4. Check and turn every now and then to make sure it is not burning, being eaten by rats, or going mouldy.

If you are drying the food to a crisp, baggable product, have the air-tight plastic bags or glass jars ready in a warm, dry room and bag them up while they are still warm.

If you are salting or packing the food in sugar or putting the semi-dried food away in oil, do that when warm and seal as soon as you bed down the semi-dried food.

A personal story

The Urban Wolf writes, "How about a bit of pork on the fork? It's an oldie, but it's still a good option. I buy a certified organic pig with a colleague (66kg x $15), but the quality is fantastic! As a chef I know how to take it apart for roasts, cutlets, schnitzel, dice it for goulash and use the belly to cure bacon at home. As a German chef and smallgoods producer — no comments, please — I achieved the ultimate: no leftovers, not even trotters, ears and head."

Look it up
Home food smoking

Sausage making

Food dehydrator

Sundried fruit

Now try this!
46 Where the herbs grow

87 Food that grows on trees

98 Host a hive of bees

Enter the ... fermentiers

A gourmet tradition
The Urban Wolf

Wolfgang Kessler is a farmer in Victoria's South Gippsland producing smallgoods, preserves and Kombucha for the local community under the brand, Urban Wolf.

"The brand stands for responsible use of the land, taking care of the land and creating a local community of food producers."

When Your Life Your Planet spoke to Wolfgang he was poaching six kilograms of freshly made beef sausages in a stock made from the trimmings of the beef. He had to interrupt the call to take the sausages out of the stock so they could cool down before going into the smoker overnight.

"I am a German-trained chef and currently head of food hospitality at Holmesglen College, but I learned the values and love of food in rural Germany on the small plot where my family grew apples, pears, citrus, cabbages and exotic food, like tomatoes, in a greenhouse.

"Now I specialise in working with local farmers and the local butcher to create small goods, and to provide my range to members of my community; and also to share the wisdom of my uncle: 'If we could only grow what we need, we would solve many problems'.

Home made pastrami and roast garlic.
© 2020 Urban Wolf

"Unfortunately, the law in Victoria is very restrictive; we cannot sell any meat products where the animal was not killed in an abattoir. There is a real need for a cooperative abattoir to nurture that community food network."

Refreshing a traditional approach: Maya Krikke

Maya Krikke is the sole parent of a little boy and produces a probiotic drink called MYK's Kefir using whole fruit.

A lot of people associated kefir with milk-based products but I use water kefir grains, that consume the glucose in sugar, and then I do a secondary ferment with fruit. I also have a processed-sugar-free range based on honey.

"Water kefir originated from the cactus in the deserts of Mexico where people collected water in animal pouches and took home the granules that formed in the pouch to ferment with sugar. Those granules multiply, in the same way as a kombucha scoby or a ginger beer plant, and are then passed on to a new person to start making their own water kefir. Its scientific name is Tibicos.

"When I first started making it, my son and I did not like the taste very much, as it can taste quite bland and yeasty and we are very fussy. I kept experimenting with different sugars and whole fruit, and over three and a half years eventually found a taste that we both liked.

"I have since then studied science at University of Queensland (UQ) and realised that the pure fruit that I am using contains a lot of fibre, which are long-chain sugars and that results in a far more sophisticated drink. If you use cold-pressed fruit juice the Tidicos chews up all the short-chain sugars, and it tastes quite flat and bland. I use vanilla beans and pure fruit juice, and it tastes like the original fruit.

"From the beginning I have been using glass bottles because I am really against plastic. I offered people a 50c refund if they gave back the glass bottles and about 98% of people at the markets did.

"One challenge was that it was very hard to take that model to retail because retailers did not want to offer the refund. We found some outlets who would and got 4,500 bottles a year back, but that was only one in eight bottles that we were selling. As glass bottles are much more expensive, I could not expand the business because I could only afford to buy a certain amount of glass bottles.

"Then I got the chance to interview 250 students as part of an iLab at UQ and found that only 32% would return a bottle for money but 93% would bring it back if the money was donated for charity. That blew my mind, so we went from a 50c refund to donating 20c to domestic violence. In the first year we increased the return rate 50% to 60%. I raised $3,200 for domestic violence in one year.

"Then the Brisbane City Council stepped in and said you cannot reuse glass bottles because of the potential for contamination. Now we use a triple rinse, soak and scrub process, ending with a commercial sanitiser. As a result we cannot offer anything back on the bottle as all the funds are eaten up in the process of sterilising the bottle so we can satisfy the requirements.

"We have just passed a significant milestone of 50,000 bottles and the business is building steadily."

Look it up
www.mykskefir.com
www.ilovemymy.com

60. Things that grow in the dark

Photo by Jonathan Pielmayer- on Unsplash

Beer, cider, wine and whiskey are drinks made from fermented food. Bread, yoghurt, mustard, sauerkraut and kimchi are all foods that take advantage of the same process. Domesticated microbes are an essential part of human existence. Mushrooms are not microbes, but they grow in the dark too.

Preserving food by boiling it in salt and sugar is not the best way to extract the maximum nutrition. But we can harness natural processes to develop beneficial enzymes and improve the nutritional profile of our food. Some of these are so straightforward they have become everyday foodstuffs.

These are all ferments:

- Bread is fermented dough made from ground grain and water.

- Soya sauce, miso and Vegemite are all fermented foods.

- Sauerkraut not only tastes different from cabbage it is full of vitamins, enzymes and probiotics, and lasts for months (years if necessary).

- Kimchi is the signature accompaniment to Korean food.

- Black beans have a rich and warm flavour often enjoyed in stir-fried meals.

Here's a plan

1. Buy a cabbage.
2. Slice it up.
3. Sprinkle it with salt.
4. Wait a day and shake it up.
5. Repeat.
6. After four days it will have shrunken into a wet and sloppy mess of lactic acid. That's great.
7. Stuff the wet cabbage mix into air-tight jars with plenty of its liquid.
8. Keep the air away from the cabbage by putting some item into the jar that pushes the cabbage away from the air.
9. Wait for a few weeks.
10. Test by taste.

Congratulations, you have made your first sauerkraut.

Now you can expand with spices and different vegetables, adding olives, dried fish and other preserves to make your own signature dish.

Photo by Mockup Graphics on Unsplash

Reality check

Not everyone wants loosely controlled decay going on in the kitchen. Some people find it messy and smelly. You have to look after your ferment like you would a garden or a pet. And when you have a disaster it can be pretty awful.

Bad food stinks.

That is how our immunisation systems warns us. "Do not eat this rotten thing, it will kill you."

Costs

A cabbage in season: $1:00/kg

Sauerkraut: $6.00/kg

Look it up
Grow mushrooms

Kimchi

Probiotic

Burong

Now try this!
50 Eating better meat

86 Getting fed without giving a fig

94 Getting out into nature

61. Things that grow in bottles

Forget the kimchi and the sauerkraut, the real fun with fermenting starts with drinks. Cider and beer are easy backyard beverages; wine and whiskey want a wee bit o' work. But fermenting does not have to mean alcohol; kefir, kombucha and ginger beer are sober ferments.

We can reduce our food miles to zero by growing food at home. Growth can happen in a vat or bottle as well as in the garden. You reduce the packaging, eliminate unpleasant preservatives and build a resilient community by converting your garage into a hub of production.

Here's a plan

Fermentation is the conversion of a fresh food into a different form using the action of some mini-life form, like a yeast or a bacteria. That conversion often increases the nutritional value of the food as well as preserving it. It can also produce useful by-products, such as alcohol or glycerine.

- Beer is more fun to consume than boiled barley water, but it is essentially the same thing.
- Cider has the same relationship to apple juice and wine to grapes.
- Ginger beer, kefir and kombucha are easy to brew and are non-alcoholic
- Fermentation makes good stuff.

Start simply.

Try brewing some beer or ginger beer and see how you go. Ginger beer is easy enough to do with children and a great way to start your brewing journey.

You can get more detailed recipes online and find out about other ferments like kombucha, kefir or kava. Why do all these drinks start with a 'k'?

Join a local home brew group and taste test other's brews; get new ideas, equipment and share your war stories. These local networks form the backbone of the resilient communities that will help us thrive in the face of tough times.

Reality check

Cleanliness is the key. If you are not clean or you forget your ferment for too long, it might go haywire. You are providing nutrients and ideal breeding conditions for microbes. You want to create

HARD FACTS

Most ginger beer HAS A SMALL percentage of alcohol <3% proof

food, not biological weapons of mass destruction.

Lots of northern hemisphere ferments assume ambient temperatures of 25° or less. In many parts of Australia you will have to find a cool corner of the garage to act as your cellar. You can also explore ferments from warmer climates and leave the European traditions behind. Kava anyone?

Look it up

Kava

Kefir

Tibicos

Homebrew club

Now try this!

3 Those packaged drinks

13 Our alcohol consumption

7 Get active in your community

46 Where the herbs grow

Let's fix it

Drive less, drive slower.
Our obsession with time is
costing the earth.

62. Shank's pony

63. Drive like a smoothie

We need to talk about ... sharing and connecting

We've got too much stuff stored and we
hold it too tight.

64. Your zombie apocalypse kit

65. The problem with recycling

66. Holding a garage sale

67. Shop locally

68. The hidden treasure

69. Borrow the power tools

70. Repair café

71. Use public transport

72. Buying a bicycle

73. Cycle to work

74. Sharing the car

Plan ahead

Let's make long-term decisions
that drive down our footprint,

75. Embrace embodied energy

76. Buy good wood

77. Generate your own power

78. Alternative fuels

CHAPTER

05

GARAGE & SHED

The car, the bikes, a set of golf clubs, some ski gear, a kayak, the tools, work boots and a pile of stuff that's too good to throw away; our garages and sheds hold the things that do not fit in the house, are heavy, clunky, a bit grubby or are for the great indoors.

Many of those items involve travel. Personal travel and transport is responsible for one sixth of our overall emissions and uses about one quarter of the fossil fuels we burn. It's a serious contributor to our footprint. Taking stock of what's in the shed is a good place to start thinking about how we deal with that. It's also the place we store the tools we use to build and repair our properties and appliances.

Garage & Shed

The problem

The private car burns fossil fuels, it takes energy and resources to manufacture and it has spawned a drive-in culture of convenience that encourages consumption and inactivity, leading to obesity and diabetes. As a private convenience, it encourages us to build larger homes with internal garages, isolating ourselves from our neighbours and our communities, further cementing our roles as passive consumers. Cars are also expensive. Most of us go into debt to buy them, even though they will not increase in value, like a true investment does.

Really?

There are 1.4 billion cars in the world today with 75 million new cars produced each year. Those new cars consume about 80 million tonnes of steel and 14 million tonnes of plastic to build and produce 600 million tonnes of CO_2e. Australia buys more than one million new cars each year and has 20 million registered cars. The production of new cars for Australia is responsible for eight million tonnes of CO_2e each year. We emit 30 million tonnes of CO_2e each year driving them around.

On average we commute about 17 kilometres each way each day and drive about the same amount again to go shopping and socialising. In rural areas those figures double. Over 80% of us drive to work.

The greenhouse emissions from the operations of the transport sector in Australian total 100 million tonnes of CO_2e each year, about 70% of which we produce driving our cars. Transport produces about one quarter of Australia's total emissions, roughly the same as the proportion globally.

Let's fix it

Some of us have garages connected to our house. We go from an air-conditioned lounge room to an air-conditioned car and drive to an air-conditioned office/cinema/ restaurant. It is convenient; it is climate controlled and safe. It also has a huge environmental footprint and isolates us every step of the way.

We can make an immediate difference by leaving the car keys in the top drawer and heading out on a bike or on foot — 'Shank's pony' as Tip 62 calls it. That makes such a difference to our health, our engagement with the community and our awareness of the planet, as well as reducing our emissions, that we come back to it in different ways in different tips, throughout the chapter.

When we do drive, we can make a big difference, just by being aware of how heavy we are on the juice. These two simple tips make a small but positive difference to every aspect of our Work-environment-life balance, except on the clock.

#	Tip	Page	🔥	💧	🚹🚺	👁	⏱	Ⓢ
62	Shank's pony	166	✓✓		✓✓	✓	✗✗	✓✓
63	Drive like a smoothie	168	✓			✓	✗	✓

62. Shank's pony

Pick up your feet and walk. We came down from the trees and left our forest-dwelling cousins behind to walk upright on the plains. Walking is good for you and walking instead of driving is good for everything else. This is the no-cost, easiest, endlessly beneficial tip that just keeps on giving.

Our sedentary lifestyle is killing us. Obesity, heart disease and serious circulatory problems can all directly be ameliorated, improved and potentially cured by walking. More complex problems like diabetes, back pain, anxiety and depression benefit from regular exercise. Our car-based lifestyle is choking the planet.

There is absolutely no downside to getting off your backside and getting outside.

Here's a plan

Walking is good for just about every part of your body.

It clears your head, allows you to solve problems that have been bugging you, puts some air into your lungs and gets the blood flowing.

1. Take off the next hour.

2. Cancel your appointments.

3. Step outside and check out the weather.

4. Stop and look around until a destination comes to mind.

5. Walk there.

6. Do it now!

Walk somewhere you have not been before or been for years. Surprise yourself, take control of your circumstances and free yourself of dependence on an external source of energy.

- If you are in a book shop, buy this book first.
- If someone is waiting for you, take them walking too.
- If you are in a wheelchair, then roll. (I'm not here to perform miracles.)
- If the weather is terrible, forget it. (Even the best ideas have the occasional flaw.)

Instead of taking a morning walk and then getting ready for work and catching the bus, get ready for work first, then walk as much of the journey as you can. Same thing for those dashes up to the shop to get the bread, milk or memory sticks that you suddenly need.

Take the panic out of the situation, take the time to walk there and a world of benefits will be revealed. You might meet the neighbours; get the chance to talk to your housemate, lover or kids about things that you never quite get around to; and you do that exercise you can never find time for. Walking is great.

Back in the day

Our kids generally walk less than 500 metres anywhere. Our grandparents regularly walked five kilometres or more, every day. Their grandparents often ranged over 10 kilometres from home as children. We have trapped ourselves in a protective cocoon that is killing us.

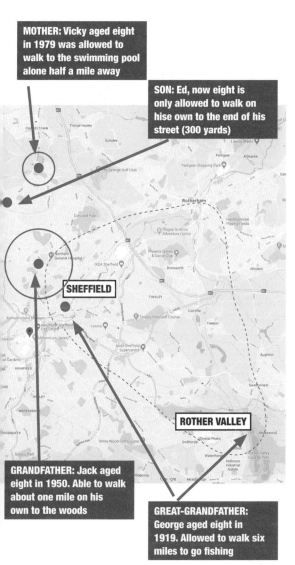

MOTHER: Vicky aged eight in 1979 was allowed to walk to the swimming pool alone half a mile away

SON: Ed, now eight is only allowed to walk on hise own to the end of his street (300 yards)

SHEFFIELD

ROTHER VALLEY

GRANDFATHER: Jack aged eight in 1950. Able to walk about one mile on his own to the woods

GREAT-GRANDFATHER: George aged eight in 1919. Allowed to walk six miles to go fishing

David Derbyshire created a sensation when he reported in the UK Daily Mail on the walking habits of four generations

Map data ©2020 Google

USE SHANKS' PONY

Look it up
Right to roam
Free range kids

WALK
when you can

AND EASE THE BURDEN WHICH WAR PUTS ON TRANSPORT

Now try this!

7 Our high-speed lives

12 The nature of time

17 Get active with your community

44 Pause before breakfast

63. Drive like a smoothie

Did you know that your petrol consumption is related to speed? How about the amount of air in your tyres? Turning off the engine if you are stopped for more than a minute also saves the juice. Driving smoothly is good for your pocket and your footprint.

We rush hither and thither to save precious minutes. Those extra bursts of speed cost the environment, even if you don't trip the speed camera. They have limited impact on the stopwatch anyway. Do the maths. Driving mindfully is good for our cars, our wallets and the environment.

Modern cars have onboard training software to make you a smoothy

Here's a plan

Check the manual of your car for the recommended tyre inflation. Pump the tyres to the upper limit of the recommendation. Don't go any higher as it will have a negative effect on the car's handling. The car rolls more easily on harder tyres and will save you fuel. Your ride will be a little bouncier, which is why you should not overdo it.

Set the cruise control lower. At 110km/h your car uses up to 25% more fuel than it would cruising at 90km/h. Cruise control reduces changes in speed, also saving fuel.

If you pull up at the lights just after they have gone red, turn off the engine. Letting it idle for more than 60 seconds uses more fuel than restarting it. Many modern cars do this automatically.

If you have a tachometer showing your engine's working speed, keep the engine revs to a minimum. Just don't press the accelerator so hard. It takes a little longer to take off, but your passengers will thank you for the calmer ride.

The traffic lights on most major roads are tuned for a 'green wave'. If you drive at the speed limit, adjusted for the average speed at peak hour, you are likely to get a run of green lights. Drive at any other speed and you are simply racing between red lights.

Forget the car next to you. This is not a race. The time saved by speeding in the city is almost imperceptible. You want to get there in a calm and relaxed manner, not as fast as possible. There is no chequered flag or golden cup of champagne if you shave a few minutes off the journey.

PERSONAL CARBON TARGET
KILOGRAMS PER DAY PER PERSON

Drive smoothly

A 10% reduction in your driving emissions saves fuel and money

A personal story

Old lead foot writes, "I find slowing down a real challenge. On my own, on a country road, I'm quite happy to tootle along at 10km below the speed limit. Put another car next to me and the 'horns of competition' rise to the challenge."

Look it up
Tyre pressure fuel
Idling fuel efficiency
Speed fuel consumption
nsca.org.au

Now try this!

7 Our high-speed lives
78 Alternative fuels
74 Sharing the car
71 Use public transport

HARD FACTS

IT TAKES
12% less petrol
TO TRAVEL ON AN OPEN ROAD AT
64km/h THAN IT DOES AT 80km/h

Fuel consumed each
MINUTE OF IDLING,
3L ENGINE: 30mL
5L ENGINE: 50mL

UP TO 40% OF
ROAD DEATHS INVOLVE A
SPEEDING CAR

CORRECT TYRE PRESSURE:
Fuel efficiency:
4% BETTER
TYRE LIFE:
10% longer
HANDLING: IMPROVED

We need to talk about ...

... sharing and connecting

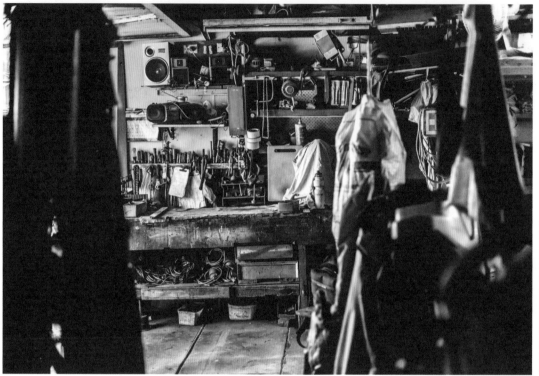

Photo by Jack Douglass on Unsplash

We put a lot of energy into protecting our privacy, personal space, ownership and individual rights. We like to have stuff and look after it, ourselves. To build communities that are more resilient and allow us to thrive without squandering resources and trashing the place, we need to loosen up a little and start to share.

If we believe that living our best life means exercising our individual right to take as much as we can get and it is up to everyone else to look after themselves, then we are unlikely to care too much about the environment, future generations or how the person who cleans our house feeds their children.

On the other hand, if we believe living our best life means taking responsibility for the impact of our actions on the rest of the world, then we will instinctively apply those principles wherever we can. The challenge is that we all have elements of both those extremes in different areas of our personality. We are also ignorant of how some of our actions affect others.

A quick look at the impact of any of these tips on the Personal carbon target makes it clear that it is impossible for you to solve the global climate crisis from your back deck. We need to coordinate our efforts and multiply the impact instead of each adding our own individual increment. It's just too little.

In the *Living Room* (Chapter 1) we identified the power of lobbying and media to get attention. In the *Garage* (this chapter) we are more interested in rolling up our sleeves and getting things done. The impact of rooftop solar panels is an example of how the collective impact of relatively small, practical solutions can drive major societal change.

Tip summary

Whether it is changing the way you travel, the places you shop, or how you handle your tools, there are opportunities to get out into the community and connect with the people in the neighbourhood.

The richer you make your life at home and in the immediate surroundings, the less time and effort you spend going out seeking satisfaction. The biggest challenge might be to see what is already sitting under our nose, the hidden treasures waiting for us in Tip 68.

Tip summary

#	Tip	Page	🔥	💧	👨	👩	👁	⏱	Ⓢ
64	Your zombie apocalypse kit	172					✓		X ✓✓✓
65	Let's nail this recycling	174	✓✓	✓				XX	✓
66	Holding a garage sale	178					✓	XX	✓✓
67	Shop locally	180	✓			✓	✓	X	XX
68	The hidden treasure	182	✓✓			✓		✓✓✓	✓✓✓
69	Borrow the power tools	183						X	✓✓
70	Repair café	188					✓	XX	✓✓
71	Use public transport	190	✓✓			✓	✓	XX	✓
72	Buying a bicycle	192						X	XXXX ✓✓✓
73	Cycle to work	194	✓✓			✓✓	✓	XX	✓✓
74	Sharing the car	196	✓✓				✓	✓X	✓✓✓

64. Zombie apocalypse kits

Photo by Pratik Gupta on Unsplash

Without getting too survivalist about it, you should be prepared for everything, from a public holiday to a major drama. Have a torch in the car, maybe a few tools. Why stop there? Be ready for the shopping, an impromptu picnic, a grazed knee or sliced finger. You might not have to face down zombies, but you certainly can expect the unexpected.

Modern cars are so reliable that many of us have barely looked under the hood, let alone opened the spare tyre well tucked under the luggage compartment. That is only one of the neat storage spaces in our cars, tucked away for easy access when we need them. And why leave it to passengers to fill those seat pockets and unnamed door compartments with discarded wrappers, unwanted receipts and broken accessories?

A personal story

A bookish lass reports, "My Mum kept a 'personal survival item' in the car to survive long waits outside sporting fields and school halls. It was a copy of Gone With the Wind that she claims to have read four times."

Here's a plan

It is quite useful to have jumper leads, a screwdriver and an adjustable spanner on hand in case someone, maybe even you, breaks down and needs a hand. It might be even more help, though, to have empty bags ready for a surprise shopping trip, or the bits you need for an adventure with the kids or impromptu picnic with a friend.

The name 'zombie apocalypse kit' is pinched from zeitgeist by a busy mother, who can host a picnic while waiting for an unexpected football game, a seed-saving expedition at the nature reserve or a glass of wine at a local lookout. Here's a basic list of its possible contents — a pale imitation of the original:

- Shopping bags to carry goods
- A first aid kit
- Fine bags to weigh fresh produce
- Keep cup (+1 for +1)

- Unbreakable wine glasses
- A foldable wheeled trolley
- A decent torch and some magnetic lamps that can be attached to the car
- Matches, lighter, a sheet of newspaper, a firelighter (carefully wrapped in plastic) and a candle
- A couple of litres of water
- A pocket knife and a picnic set of fork, spoon and flat plate
- Ziplock bags and a stack of small containers for unexpected bugs, seeds and food
- String, elastic bands, hair ties, a stretchable tie, rope
- Tea towel and other useful fabric
- Duct tape, blue tac, paper clips, hair clips and safety pins
- Jumper leads, straight and Philips head screwdrivers, pliers and adjustable spanner.

Reality check

Think about what you'd like to put in your own zombie apocalypse kit. Keep it neat, small and packed away. You don't want the contents walking off in people's pockets. Check it before a big trip — despite your best efforts it will be raided.

Look it up

Zombie apocalypse kit

Survivalist gear

Escape tool

Now try this!

36 A stitch in time

57 Silicon and beyond

79 Take only photos

84 Barbecue fuel

91 Where babies come from

65. The problem with recycling

Of course you recycle, you have a yellow bin. Right? We all know how well that is working. However, since reduce, reuse and repurpose are more effective than recycling, we need to manage and store the packaging we can't avoid.

We know that carting our rubbish off to a big hole in the ground is not sustainable, but 80% of our waste still goes to landfill. The problems include: organic waste creating methane, plastics lasting forever and batteries and other chemicals leaking toxins into the groundwater.

Since many Asian countries stopped accepting our 'recycling', local councils are stockpiling or dumping the contents of our yellow bins. One reason given for that international rejection was the contamination of our waste by thoughtless recyclers. We need to tighten up our act.

PERSONAL CARBON TARGET

Better recycling

Recycling half the plastic that goes to landfill reduces our CO$_2$e by 500g/d

Here's a plan

Set aside a corner of the garage or the shed where you are going to do this work. Make sure you clean it out regularly; this is not a hoarder's manual.

Get a bin, large box or tough bag for the containers that earn a deposit. Appoint one person as the beneficiary of the returns. Recan is one example of a commercial service; most neighbourhoods have individuals who collect them on rubbish day; some councils have a special purple bin.

Identify the reusable items and stack them where they can be topped up or taken away. Identify where they are going and set up a regular system for getting rid of them. Egg cartons to the neighbour with chooks, half-litre bottles to the beekeeper, plastic trays to the seedling grower up the road.

Batteries, phones, e-waste and scrap metal all attract enough return to support special dealers who will take the goods off your hands. You might get something for the most valuable items, say copper or lead, but you are doing this to nurture your life and your planet, not for the filthy lucre. Aren't you?

Wood, clothing, furniture and old appliances are destined for your local waste transfer depot at the moment. The good stuff will end up in the Tip Shop and the rest might get mined for its resources.

Reality check

No-one wants to handle biowaste. Do not put used tissues, facewipes, napkins, food containers, plates or cutlery in the yellow bin! If you wouldn't want to handle something from your neighbour's bin a week after they disposed of it, do not put it in yours.

Look it up

Bottle strip cutter
Cassava starch bags
Zero waste
recyclingnearyou.com.au
boomerangalliance.org

1
PETE

Now try this!

3 Those packaged drinks
48 The things we eat for lunch
56 The packaging we purchase
90 Hand-made watering systems

HARD FACTS

Most homes will generate **2kg of garbage and 500g** OF RECYCLABLES TODAY. **The average** garbage bin contains **14.4% paper** and 11.7% containers.

In 2016-17, Australia generated **67 million** tonnes (Mt) **of waste per year,** sending 55% (37Mt) **TO RECYCLING,** 3% to energy recovery (2Mt) **and 40% (27Mt) to disposal.**

Municipal waste (from households and council operations) **makes up about 21%** OF AUSTRALIA'S ANNUAL WASTE **generation and 17%** OF NATIONAL RECYCLING.

Enter the ... recyclers

'Woke' to recycling:
Claire Tracey

Claire Tracey is an artist who works with waste to raise awareness of the problems presented by waste and our attitudes toward it.

She started using 'found' plastic-bottles to make large scale artworks in 2010. One of her first public works was a solar light for an underpass on the Maribyrnong River in the Moonee Ponds area.

"I collected bottles from the creek and used them to make a solar light for the underpass. A solar panel powered LED globes within the artwork. Part of the brief was to make the area safer because the existing lighting was regularly broken. Interestingly, the art was made from waste bottles that have very little value and so it was not a target for vandals and lasted a long time."

She also made a 15-metre dragon out of recycled plastic bottles collected by people attending the Chinese Australian Museum during the Year of the Dragon and mounted the artwork onto the side of the building.

"I was pleased that the community participation became a treasured part of the

outcome that complemented the enormous dragon."

A large crazy monkey outside the National Library was the most popular of that series or awareness-raising works.

In 2018, Claire decided to stop using plastic.

"Partly thanks to the container deposit scheme, the awareness of the harm done by plastic has increased to the point where the urgency of that particular message was reduced. Perhaps more subtly, though, I realised that I was perpetuating the idea of recycling and that is not a positive message.

Claire is now looking at other types of waste generated in urban spaces and how that can be used in art. She is specifically exploring the use of plastics in relation to Covid19 and the broader topic of plastic and hygiene.

"So many people finish drinking out of a bottle and put the lid back on. God knows where it ends up, in landfill or a river, but we know that the virus lives on well in plastic. We might be burying a toxic time capsule for the future."

Look it up
Claire Tracey Art
envorinex.com

Making recycling real:
Jenny Brown

A manufacturer of plastic goods for industrial applications since 2003, Ms Brown has been waging war on waste by recycling as much plastic as possible and producing goods made from 100% reclaimed waste in the bulk of her products.

Envorinex is based in northern Tasmania and employs around 12 full-time staff on two different production lines, reclaiming and processing waste and producing a range of products from railings for roads, non-slip mats for oil rigs, through to simple clips and accessories for a range of applications.

"Plastic can be reused hundreds of times and last for centuries if it is properly processed," she said, "the important thing is to get it right the first time."

She said that the enemy of recycling is contamination. Envorinex deals exclusively with industrial and agricultural waste because domestic waste is so contaminated that it is extremely difficult to recycle.

"This is why the waste from Australia and other rich countries has been rejected by China, India and Malaysia. They simply cannot process it," she said.

66. Holding a garage sale

Having someone pay you money to take your stuff away is a win all round. They get a cheap thingummy, you get some money and the waste stream gets nothing. Just the way we like it.

The reason there is so much waste is that we keep buying new stuff. One way to reduce the amount of new stuff you buy is to buy old stuff instead. Instead of throwing away stuff you don't need anymore, sell it instead.

The great thing about a garage sale is that there is no middle person taking a cut; you can look your customer in the eye as you name your price. You can also invite the neighbours round to sell their stuff and make it a community-building, reuse fest.

Traditionally held on a Saturday morning, you might generate the funds to go to the races in the afternoon or out to dinner in the evening.

Here's a plan

Pick a weekend six or more weeks into the future when you know you and your friends will be around, and you don't mind spending the day trapped at home.

Set aside some space where you can start collecting things you don't need any more.

Invite your friends to add their stuff to the pile, or to bring it on the day and help you sell it.

Fix and clean the items that look a little old and tired.

Visit a few garage sales in your neighbourhood to get a feel for prices and the popularity of various goods.

Check out the socials for your neighbourhood, community noticeboards at shopping centres, libraries and other locations so you can advertise your event.

Make sure you have plenty of cash for change and a 'bum' bag or cash tin to keep it in and investigate the best way to take card payments. Most stationery stores have eftpos systems that plug into your phone and turn it into a cash point.

For the big day: get your stuff ready the evening before. Put out a sign giving the starting time and then start on time.

Make sure you have shelter from the sun or rain.

Back in the day

One of us lived in Alice Springs for a while. "Everyone left town before summer, so everything was for sale at bargain-basement prices. They called them lawn sales even though there was no grass. The locals scooped up the bargains and sold them to the southerners moving into town in the New Year."

Reality check

You might find it easier to give things away than sell them. There are freecycle networks that make it easy to give things away. Many charities are overloaded with donations and reluctant to take on the health challenges of cleaning old furnishings.

Photo by Charisse Kenion on Unsplash

Look it up

Hold garage sale

Freecycle

Opportunity shop

Now try this!

11 A no-spend day

38 Secondhand clothes

53 Feeding friends

72 Buying a bicycle

90 Hand-made watering systems

67. Shop locally

Photo by NeONBRAND on Unsplash

Looking after your local businesses is important because it supports your community and that comes straight back to you. Every dollar you spend locally supports local business. If you spend it with a national or international business it disappears immediately.

Local shops employ local workers and provide services that you can enjoy with your neighbours. The high-street strip of shops is getting a new lease of life as large malls crumble under pressure from an oversupply, changing demographics and pressure from online shopping. The coronavirus crisis accelerated the tensions between mall owners and retailers.

Here's a plan

Buy the ingredients for dinner at the local shops (the grocer, the butcher) on your way home from work. Your food will be fresher, you will get to know your community and you'll use less energy. Yum.

Local shops have specialised to survive the competition from malls and online shopping. They provide specialised services and a shopping experience. Part of that experience is friendly service by local people.

 **HARD FACTS** | **THE ITEMS BOUGHT IN THE AVERAGE WEEKLY SUPERMARKET SHOP IN AUSTRALIA have collectively travelled 70,000KM**

Shop locally and you will reduce the pollution that comes from shopping, reduce the environmental impact of the food you purchase and contribute the maximum you can to the local economy.

Shop with friends and neighbours: offer a lift to an elderly or less able person or to pick up a few items for them. One of the stresses of modern life is that we don't spend enough time with our friends. Mental health problems are exploding because we feel stressed, lonely and anxious. If only we could make more time in our lives to socialise we would be happier and healthier.

When you shop together you learn about new foods, new ways of cooking and different cultural values. Expand your horizons by staying in your suburb.

Do it on foot

Any opportunity you take to walk (or cycle) to the shops makes a contribution to the environment. Shop regularly to reduce the amount you carry. That means you will not be carrying a full trolley of shopping at one time. Get a decent carrier for your bike or, fashion forbid, a shopping jeep. Alternatively, get a pram and pretend you traded the kids for food.

Reality check

The impact of each dollar 'circulating' in the community is overstated. Every time it changes hands, a large chunk is sent to suppliers outside the community. There is a multiplier effect; every dollar you spend locally multiplies the local economy about 1.3 times, rather than the 4 to 7 times often quoted.

There is a reason that globalisation dominates commerce: it makes things cheaper. It will cost 10 to 50% more to shop locally.

Look it up
Food miles
Local produce shopping
Dead mall
sustainabletable.org.au
urbanecology.org.au

Now try this!
38 Secondhand clothes
49 Skip the supermarket
53 Feeding friends
72 Buying a bicycle!

On average, each item HAS TRAVELLED AROUND

1,000KM

Food cooperatives sourcing LOCALLY WORK REALLY HARD TO GET ALL THEIR PRODUCE

WITHIN 100KM

68. The hidden treasure

You live in the best spot in the world. There is magic, just around the corner, which you have not discovered yet. Cancel that holiday away and holiday at home.

Because overseas flights were stopped in 2020 many of us booked domestic holidays instead, often travelling by road rather than air to minimise the risk of infection. Extend the concept further: actually explore the neighbourhood where you live instead of seeking 'greener pastures' elsewhere.

Here's a plan

Find a fiction book set in the city, town or suburb in which you live. Or get hold of a local history from the local library, council or historical society.

Whizz through it, identify the highlights closest to you and plan a walking tour from your house to see them first-hand. Tell your friends. Invite them to join you. Plan a picnic.

Contact the local historic society, walking group, school, birdwatching association, cycling group ... and tell them what you are up to. Someone will want to join in or will have a suggestion.

Here's some more

Talk to the oldest person in your street. Get them talking about their experiences in the neighbourhood and their favourite places. Get instructions from them so you could actually find the site. Social distancing permitting, see if they want to join you in the exploration. You might find a deserted underground railway station, and old bomb shelter, a drainage system that has never carried any water, an exclusive spa retreat that is hidden away behind high fences.

How would you ever know if you do not take the trouble to find out?

If you have the urge to get out of the immediate locality, take a train trip as far as you can or a wildlife tour in a neighbouring town. Exploring means doing the unusual, and the really unusual is more likely to be over the back fence than it is in a standard tourist destination.

A personal story

The author reminisces, "I spent the weekend with my lover in the Melbourne suburb of Richmond, exploring the landscape mapped out in the novel *The Cartographer*. Not only was it a wildly romantic weekend, we met lots of local characters, none of whom had read the novel, but all with interesting yarns."

A Richmond landmark much loved by the locals who worked there
©2020 Headland Properties

Reality check

The ecological benefits of any particular expedition are minimal. It is the absence of transport that saves on emissions. The long-term benefits of living locally, discovering new picnic spots, community gardens and other activities that you do not have to drive to are immeasurable.

Look it up

Open gardens

20 minute neighbourhoods

Historical walks

auswalk.com.au

Now try this!

17 Get active
with your community

61 Shank's pony

82 The dog walks with you

69. Borrow the power tools

Chain saws, hedge trimmers, lawn mowers and vacuum cleaners consume energy, make noise but do the job. Use them sparingly, preferring manual tools instead. When you really need them, get them from a tool library.

Appliances to make our morning coffee or warm our feet before bed proliferate. We fork out another hundred hard-earned dollars so the latest gizmo can save us one and a half minutes of unnecessary effort, which we spend on our derrieres complaining that we don't get enough exercise.

Leaf blowers cross the line. Pick up a broom and move those lawn clippings along. Get real, good planetary citizens. Let the Zen calm of sweeping transport you into the zone enjoyed only by the universe's best sweeper, you.

A personal story

The Brisbane Tool Library works like a book library but people can borrow hand and power tools, sporting equipment, party equipment; all those things that we own but usually only use occasionally.

Members can sign up through the website or in store and then borrow four items for up to two weeks. Membership is $75 a year or $60 concession. The benefits to members include reducing their ecological footprint, and saving money and storage space. Members can borrow expensive items like jackhammers and large items like kayaks.

Here's a plan

Feel the balance of the broom handle, the action of the bristles; watch the swirl of fluff over the scurrying of grit. Get the brush and dustpan, pick up your sweepings and put them in the compost.

Enjoy the serotonin rush of a job well done. Love yourself a little for taking care of one corner of your life, quietly and considerately. Apply this lesson to all the weekly chores. In fact, they are chores no more. They are mediative healing experiences in which you lovingly tend a disordered chaotic scenario back to vigour.

Then, when you need that extra grunt of a power tool, find the local tool library and borrow one. If you don't have a tool library in your area, hire the tool instead. Either way, you pay a fraction of the price of owning one, share the resources around and still get the job done. Tool libraries and sharing sheds have the advantage of being community-owned assets.

The Gold Coast Tool Library gets creative with power tools ©toollibrary.org.au

HARD FACTS

HAND-HELD POWER TOOLS
produce about

1kg of CO$_2$e an hour

Look it up
Tool library
Thesharingmap.com.au
brisbanetoollibrary.org
brunswicktoollibarary.org
innerwesttoollibrary.com.au
toollibrary.org.au
Leaf blower warming
Lu Tze Discworld

Now try this!
7 Our high-speed lives
18 Hire a human
30 Oil and vinegar
75 Embrace embodied energy

Enter the ... librarians

Practical de-growth:
Sabrina Chakori

Sabrina Chakori is an advocate of degrowth

The Brisbane Tool Library operates from the State Library of Queensland and has 350 members and 60 volunteers, with 20 volunteers active in any week.

"Our skilled team looks after all the tools and camping gear, tests and tags them so they are safe to use and checks them over every time they are brought back.

"We have an inventory of 1,500 or 2,000 items for loan, and a much larger number waiting until we have time to check them. We collect the tools from the Brisbane Recovery Centres and from the community.

"As a society, we talk a lot about waste as being compost or broken things, but we have seen that waste exists in the form of tools and appliances in perfect condition. Anything that needs repair we send to another social enterprise, Substation 33, and they handle the e-waste.

"The idea is to recreate a community-driven sharing economy and re-imagine how resources are used and shared. We try to re-create the commons, in which users have rights without needing to own the objects. This replaces the need for 'things', with social structures of sharing and human relationships.

"I am of the generation that already inherited the sick planet, I was born in 1992, the year of the first climate conference in Brazil. Since then nothing has changed. In fact, it has become worse. We tell consumers they have to live in a 100% sustainable way, but the reality is we also need a systemic change. We need a contraction of the economy to downscale consumption and production.

"We live on a planet with limited resources, but the current model abuses and ignores this limitation. For this reason we're pushing for a new economic system and not just new sustainability policies.

The Brisbane Tool Library acts at different levels. At the micro level we change individual behaviour. At the meso level we create communities, which is why it is important to have a physical space; our gentrified cities create alienation and encourage an individualistic mode of consumption. At the macro level we encourage people to consider economic degrowth as the inspiration for a new sustainable society. Imagine if we measured economic prosperity in in terms social and ecological wellbeing.

Look it up
brisbanetoollibrary.org
toollibrary.org.au

Community startup:
David Paynter

Founder David Paynter has always been passionate about reducing waste and finding a way to transition our cities to a more sustainable way of living,

"I was frustrated to see so many of the products we buy made to be disposable. I would visit the tip and see all the items that are being trashed and look at them with despair — if only there was a way to recover and share them. Do we need to, or even want to own all these items we rarely use?

"From this the Gold Coast Tool Library was born and incorporated in 2019. Our small but passionate volunteer team are currently in the start-up phase, building systems and processes, recruiting volunteers and collecting donations.

The Gold Coast library is engaging locals

70. Repair café

Photo by Philip Swinburn on Unsplash

Paddling against the torrent of disposable goods is the modern tinker, the 'I-Can-Fix-It' who can and does. They extend the life of apparently broken appliances, restore bicycles from hard rubbish collections and make old furniture new again. Take your first steps toward joining the ranks.

Tools and appliances are designed to be disposable. Cheaply made, they have taught us to be lazy. We don't bother to repair things, we toss them out. A tragic waste of resources and energy; there is a great deal of merit in finding ways to reverse the tide.

Here's a plan

Set up a workspace with a decent light and a place to keep your tools tidy and within reach. Find some way to separate the fine, clean work required for electronics, fabrics and fiddly things from the grunt work of sharpening axes and removing rust and grease off mechanical parts. (Especially if you are working on the dining table!) A canvas-backed blanket that goes soft-side down on the dining table provides a decent firm surface to work on without risking the varnish.

Start with some easy tasks and learn the art of failing fast. If you can't fix it with the stuff on hand, then throw it out. You were saving it from the bin anyway. If you don't, unfinished projects will proliferate. I promise.

The easiest jobs are cleaning and refurbishing hand tools and reconnecting loose or broken electrical leads. An $800 cordless vacuum cleaner sitting in the rubbish collection with a loose wire on the charger? Thank-you very much. That'll make a nice gift.

Cleaning deserves preparation and care. Look after your own tools. Discover traditional cleaners like linseed oil and turpentine. Get expert with hand tools like the wire brush or a fine set of files that can be used for cleaning jewellery, saw sharpening or repairing bolts.

The maker among us loves to create something from nothing with whatever material comes to hand. Such tinkers might focus on electronics, electric motors, petrol engines, wind-powered devices or wooden toys that move. Others focus on the more esoteric: lightning generators, DIY genetic engineering or extra-terrestrial music.

If you know a maker but are not that way inclined yourself, take them a problem, present them with a challenge and inspire them to make you something you cannot otherwise own. That way you harness their energy and inspired tinkering for your own benefit.

Look it up
Repair café
Reverse garbage
Test and tag
Tip shop

Reality check
Electricians are licensed for good reason. Repairing loose wires is rewarding but strays very close to the danger zone that is mains voltage electricity. A 240V jolt can give you a decent whack that will have you sitting on your rear end wondering what hit you. If you don't know the difference between neutral and earth, get a basic education before you electrocute yourself or the neighbours.

HARD FACTS

Pricing can discourage repair
SHOVEL WITH HANDLE: $25
SHOVEL HANDLE: $25

Now try this!
25 Those dripping taps
36 A stitch in time
55 Energy-efficient appliances
64 Your zombie apocalypse kit
69 Borrow power tools
90 Hand-made watering systems

71. Use public transport

In theory it's great. In Australia it's pretty awful except for some inner city areas. But public transport still offers huge advantages over driving, despite being crowded, slow and expensive. You can read, write, work or relax while someone else transports you around. You don't have to worry about parking at the other end.

Driving cars is responsible for about 19% of Australian greenhouse gas emissions and commuting is responsible for just over two thirds of that. The daily commute adds about two hours to everyone's work day and costs 10s of billions of dollars in productivity. If we could organise our transport effectively, that downtime could be minimised and travel time could become productive.

The biggest challenge for public transport users in most Australian cities is the limited connecting services. Successive governments have implemented user-pays pricing which has driven prices up and patronage down, pushing more people onto the roads, making the situation worse.

The road networks are hard surfaces that prevent water soaking into the ground. In Australian cities, around 12% of the surface area is paved. Reducing the number of roads would make our cities greener and cooler, and would regenerate our waterways.

Here's a plan

Yes, public transport can be frustrating, but then so is the traffic. Give it a go. Take a good book, power up the tablet, listen to the radio. Study or do some paperwork. Public transport makes a huge dent in air pollution. On the whole, it runs on time. Public transport might be slower than driving on a good day, but road congestion is more common than transport network failures.

This is one case where there is a severe limit to what we can do as individuals. We really need to lobby our governments and insist that ongoing investments in road infrastructure are not the future. We know that it is possible, because every now and then governments excel themselves, usually for major sporting events, and the transport system works like a dream.

Photo by CHUTTERSNAP on Unsplash

PERSONAL CARBON TARGET

Using
public
transport

Using public transport to commute saves 3.2kg CO$_2$e/day

HARD FACTS

GRAMS OF CO$_2$e GENERATED PER PASSENGER km

Car driver: 172
BUS PASSENGER: 104
TRAIN PASSENGER 45
PLANE PASSENGER: 200

In our major cities
1 IN 5 CHILDREN
HAS ASTHMA

1 IN 7 CASES
OF ASTHMA IS DUE TO
road transport

Reality check
Owning a car and catching public transport does not save you heaps of money. But if you get rid of the car you can save around $100 - 200 per week. If you pay for parking, add those savings in as well.

Look it up
Driving car megajoules
Public transport advocacy
Action for air
Asthma rates Australia

Now try this!
7 Our high-speed lives
72 Buying a bicycle
74 Sharing the car

72. Buying a bicycle

Photo by Christin Hume on Unsplash

Riding a bicycle combines many of the benefits of walking with the speed of driving. You get to whizz to the shops without blowing out your footprint and exercise at the same time.

Here's a plan

If you do not have a bike, identify your budget and act accordingly.

IF YOU HAVE NO MONEY

Keep an eye out for discarded bikes or bikes at tip shops and lost property sales. Look out for bike pumps, lights and other bits and pieces at garage sales and junk markets. When you find one, clean up your bike, identify broken parts and explore options for replacement parts. If the tyres are going flat, you need to pay $20 for an inner tube. There is no way around that one.

IF YOU CAN SPEND HUNDREDS

Explore the bike stores to understand the market and then look for a good secondhand bike. You could also start with a reasonable-quality bike that is cheap because it needs repairs and pay the local bike shop to fix it up for you.

IF YOU CAN SPEND THOUSANDS

Do your homework, then waltz into the bike shop and buy exactly what you want.

IF YOU HAVE A BIKE ALREADY

Check the tyres before you ride.

Check your lights when you come home. Charge them if they need it.

Give the whole cycle a reasonable once over every 10 rides or so. Keep some oil handy to keep the chain running smoothly and to dab on any squeaks. Identify any rattles and tighten up that loose bolt.

If you don't know much about fixing bikes, find a volunteer bike group, local council workshops or check the resources in Look it up in this tip.

Back in the day

It was the rubber tyre and the ball bearing that made the bicycle popular. Until the invention of the tyre, early bicycles were known as bone shakers.

Reality check

The cost of bicycles spans an enormous range. Avoid cheap bicycles from toy shops or department stores. A bike from a bike shop comes with a guarantee and a regular service.

Unlike cars, bikes are usually lighter than their rider. Almost all your energy goes into moving yourself along. That's efficient.

Look it up

back3bikes

bikes4life

secondchancecycles

Bicycles for humanity

australiancyclist.com.au

bfa.asn.au

HARD FACTS

Bicycles are hot.

VEHICLE SALES IN AUSTRALIA

Bicycles:

1.2 million

CARS:

1.0 MILLION

BIKES OUTSOLD

cars each year since 2000

Now try this!

7 Our high-speed lives

61 Shank's pony

94 Get out into nature

73. Cycle to work

Free transport, no traffic jams and a workout. All at once, with almost no running costs. A bicycle is an all-round investment in nurturing your planet that will pay you back in all areas of your life.

The bicycle is faster than the car in most cities over distances less than 10 kilometres. It keeps you fit and reduces pollution as well as saving time. Serious bicycle paths are now part of most urban plans.

The bicycle is the most energy-efficient machine yet devised for road transport. Primarily because of its light weight, most of the energy applied to the pedal is used to actually transport the rider.

Here's a plan

Ride to your workplace on the weekend to time yourself and explore the best route. Identify the sections where you have to get off the bike path and into traffic, and make sure you are comfortable navigating them.

Chat to colleagues who ride and find out about the 'end of journey' facilities for bicycle security, showers and lockers.

Start with a day where you do not have meetings first or last thing so you have a bit of a buffer in case something goes wrong.

Be prepared for peak bike hour. Those bike lanes get pretty intense with everyone hurrying to work.

Check out your bike properly and make sure you carry a basic repair kit and tools.

Reality check

You will go faster than the traffic in peak hour but, on average, riding generally takes longer door to door than driving.

You cannot read, write and work while you ride. You do get to exercise, socialise and to experience the landscape.

Roads are designed for cars with bike lanes often added as an afterthought. You may mingle with fast and furious traffic.

HARD FACTS

About 1 in 6 Australians RIDE A BIKE EVERY WEEK, ALTHOUGH ONLY **1 in 70 use it to get to work.**

Look it up
Bicycle transport
Bike lanes
australiancyclist.com.au
bfa.asn.au

Now try this!
61 Shop locally
71 Use public transport
78 Alternative fuels

Watch out for drivers suddenly opening doors. Hit the person, not the car beside you. Save your life.

Riding can be hard work. It makes you sweat. If your workplace has showers you can use them to freshen up when you get to work, otherwise you may need to use a local gym or baths. You might need to avoid riding to work meetings in summer.

Cycling is more efficient and healthier than commuting

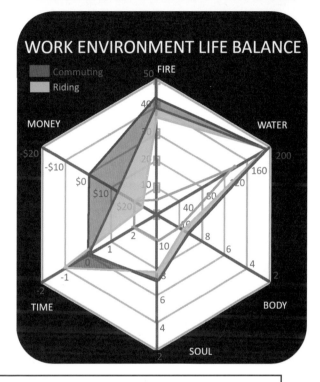

WORK ENVIRONMENT LIFE BALANCE

A personal story

The publisher recounts, "I tried riding 13km along a busy road to work, but quickly gave up; to preserve my life expectancy. I later noticed a creek-side bike path that I have explored to form the basis of a 16km route that avoids most roads. I'm back on the bike."

Compare this to cities like AMSTERDAM WHERE OVER half of all trips made are on a pushbike.

COPENHAGEN IS THE OTHER standout cycle-crazy city, WITH 1 IN 3 TRIPS MADE ON A BIKE.

74. Sharing the car

Don't go alone, ring up a mate. Find someone who needs a lift or pick up a hitchhiker. Lend your car to someone else. Your car could start earning its keep.

Rideshare services and scooter hire services are changing the model of car ownership in Australia. Inner-city developers are converting the car parking spaces required by regulation into zones that can be used as car parks, storage spaces or exercise areas. Apartment owners are simply not buying cars.

You can harness this shift in attitudes to share your car and so reduce your impact on your planet.

Here's a plan

Car-pool with colleagues or neighbours. Chat to other people who use a car to commute. Get a lift with them, offer them petrol money. Offer to return the favour.

Do the same thing socially. Take some friends to dinner by picking them up instead of meeting them at the restaurant.

Look at car-pooling apps or groups. Think about car-pooling a road trip instead of flying.

Look at car-sharing apps. Many councils now offer special parking zones for share cars, making it easier to find a park close to your destination. Car Next Door, GoGet, PopCar and Flexicar all operate in many Australian capitals. Traditional rental cars cater for different sections of the market. They still provide a car-share service, but the company owns the car instead of a private individual.

Of course, if you share a car with your friends and neighbours you do not pay the app company anything. Car-pooling arrangements work well for major events where lots of people travel to the same destination.

Reality check

The Australian Tax Office has advised that it is planning to tax income from car-sharing apps.

Cars weigh over one tonne, that's 10 times the weight of one big passenger. At least nine tenths of the energy being spent is being wasted. So putting an extra 100kg person in the car takes about 900kg off the road! As well as petrol and air pollution, this saves wear and tear on roads, lost time through congestion and reduces the overheads of maintaining a major road network.

Many councils offer free parking for shared cars

HARD FACTS

THE MORNING COMMUTE
6 million drive
HALF A MILLION GET A LIFT
less than one million use
PUBLIC TRANSPORT

GLOBAL CAR SHARING THROUGH APPS
120,000 PEOPLE
8,000 cars
CAR RUNNING COSTS:
$≈200 A WEEK

A personal story

In Cuba, if a traffic policeman sees a car with an empty seat, they may pull them over to the side of the road until a hitchhiker can be found to fill the space.

Look it up
Car pool

Car share

carnextdoor.com.au

goget.com.au

flexicar.com.au

coseats.com

Now try this!
Now try this!

61 Shank's pony

71 Use public transport

75 Embrace embodied energy

Plan ahead

While we are in the garage, let's do some long-term planning for our sustainable future. I'm talking about building materials, I'm talking about your new car, I'm talking about your power supply.

When we planned ahead for the bathroom (Chapter 2), we had a look at our total water footprint and saw that it was much larger than our daily water target at home. The amount of water that goes into making our food or producing our plastic drink bottles is not immediately obvious to us: it is embedded into the food or the bottle and has become embodied in it. The terms 'embodied' and 'embedded energy' have become almost interchangeable.

When we discussed the impact of driving compared to public transport or cycling earlier in this chapter, we looked at the emissions involved in driving the car. But what about the emissions involved in making it?

When we buy a car, for our personal use, we are responsible for all those emissions embodied in the car. One tonne of steel alone is responsible for two tonnes of carbon dioxide or its equivalent in other greenhouse gases. Then there are the other materials: the upholstery, the trim, the airbags and the structural plastics. On top of that is the manufacturing and the transport. The footprint of a car is between five and 15 tonnes of CO_2e before you start driving it.

When we share a car, or ride on a bus, we are only responsible for a minute fraction of the emissions that went into making it because we are sharing them with all the other people that use that vehicle over its entire life.

Photo by Anshu A MVUs on Unsplash

Calculating the emissions involved in a material or a product over its lifetime become very important when we make major purchases or build things that last a long time. We refer to these calculations a few times as we Plan ahead in this chapter.

Tip summary

This section deals with energy. It starts off with a focus on the concept of embodied energy and then looks at that wonderful resource that captures carbon out of the air, using solar power, to create a building material. Trees! You've got to hug them.

After our house, the next biggest purchase that most of us make is a car. Despite car sharing and ride sharing, the vast majority (about 85%) of us, still own a car. Given the role of road transport in Australia's emissions, the type of car we buy is a very important purchasing decision.

And still, today in 2020, over 65% of our electricity is generated by burning coal. Renewables are growing fast, despite government interference in the market

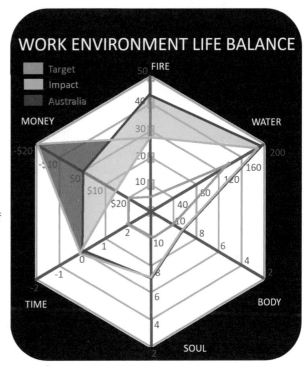

to protect the fossil fuel sector of the economy. That change has been driven, to a significant extent, by roof-top solar. The generation of power, distributed across suburban streets of our cities, has changed the profile of the electricity supply and the price of the panels that generate it. It is an example of consumer-driven change to inspire us all.

#	Tip	Page	🔥	💧	👨👩	👁	⏱	Ⓢ
75	Embrace embodied energy	200					X	
59	Buy good wood	202	✓✓	✓✓				XX
60	Generate your own power	204	✓✓✓	✓				XXXX ✓✓✓
61	Alternative fuels	208	✓✓✓					XXXXX ✓✓✓

75. Embrace embodied energy

The embodied energy of a manufactured object is the amount of energy required to make it. This should be taken into account when making major purchases. To measure the impact on climate change we need to estimate the emissions associated with that energy.

The challenge is that this information is not always readily available.

Here's a plan

Buy things that last a long time and can be repaired. The less often you have to buy an item, the less energy you will consume over time. Here are some general principles:

- Lighter products that contain less material will generally contain less energy.

- Goods or packaging made from renewable materials like paper do not consume resources that are finite.

- Goods made from recycled materials save on the energy required to extract the raw materials but embed the energy used to recycle them.

- Locally manufactured goods do not contain the energy required to transport them.

- Look for metal tools and appliances that are screwed together, rather than plastic ones that have been heat-moulded. This is because they can be taken apart and repaired.

Photo by Lenny Kuhne on Unsplash

Reality check

When calculating the carbon footprint of the embodied energy of common items, there are often one or two materials or processes that dominate the calculation. Focusing on these big contributors is a simple way to get a conservative estimate of the carbon footprint of the embodied energy.

Flying fresh food across the world, for example, far outweighs the contribution of growing it.

Mike Berners-Lee in the UK calculates that the total emissions produced in manufacturing an average car are around 10 tonne of CO_2e. That's about five times the steel it contains.

Steel and concrete are literally the building blocks of the modern city. They need to be used for projects that will last for centuries, if not millennia. Unfortunately, we seem hell-bent on rebuilding the city every 50 years or so.

Look it up
Embedded energy
Lifecycle emissions
Concrete emissions
greenvehicleguide.gov.au

Now try this!
50 Eat better meat
56 The packaging we purchase
78 Alternative fuels

HARD FACTS

Construction waste:
53% OF THE WASTE
IS SENT TO LANDFILL.
30% of concrete
is recycled.
60% OF STEEL
REMOVED FROM BUILDINGS
IS RECYCLED.

CONSTRUCTION WASTE
FROM THE AVERAGE HOME:
4 and 5 tonnes
while building it.
200+ TONNES
IN ITS DEMOLITION.

CO_2e PER kg
AIR FREIGHT:
750g CO_2e PER 1,000km
Steel production:
2kg CO_2
CONCRETE PRODUCTION:
400g CO_2

76. Buy good wood

Wood is renewable, natural and pleasant to live with. Trees capture carbon and when we build with timber, you lock it up permanently. That's great, but it is important that our timber buildings are not responsible for the destruction of precious tropical rainforest.

The versatility of wood makes it a very useful building material. Lots of furniture is made from wood. We have also seen a resurgence of wood in multi-storey buildings such as 25 King in Brisbane and Forte in Melbourne. Best of all it's a renewable resource. If you are planning to buy wooden furnishings or fittings or build with timber, then you are familiar with the benefits.

The problem is that lots of wood on the market today is ripped out of old-growth tropical rainforests. This is a significant contributor to global warming. It takes from decades to centuries to grow a tree that produces tonnes of building materials. Our challenge is to ensure that our timber is sustainably sourced.

Here's a plan

Whether you are buying wooden furniture or building a house you can make sure the timber you buy is not from tropical forests by checking its credentials using one of the certification systems.

Look for the FSC or Responsible Wood label. Organisations like the Responsible Wood and the Forest Stewardship Council help you determine how to best preserve this invaluable resource. These labelling schemes set out to establish that the wood is grown sustainably and that all steps in the process from tree to timber are ethical.

In addition to the certification programs it is worth knowing where the timber comes from. Locally sourced timber is not only labelled so that you can confirm that it has been produced ethically, it has consumed less resources because it has not been transported around the world.

Reality check

There have been disputes between certification bodies about the merits of different certification schemes. You will need to satisfy yourself about the certificate your timber carries. The links in *Look it up* contain details about this debate.

25 King in Brisbane is Australia's tallest wooden building ©Aurecon

HARD FACTS

SELECTIVE LOGGING IN rainforests causes 6%

OF THE DAMAGE OF CLEAR FELLING

Destruction of TROPICAL RAINFOREST IS RESPONSIBLE FOR 10% OF GLOBAL EMISSIONS

AUSTRALIA HAS LOST 44% of its open forests DUE TO AGRICULTURAL expansion, primarily in Queensland, and 25% OF ITS RAINFOREST. WE ARE STILL LOGGING OLD-GROWTH FORESTS IN TASMANIA.

Look it up

Sustainable forestry

Responsible wood

FSC Watch

Timber certification

Chain of custody

Fsc.org

Now try this!

17 Get active with your community

20 Invest ethically

40 Hemp and bamboo

77. Generate your own power

Hook up solar panels, a biogas plant or a windmill and connect them to the grid. Add a battery and store the electricity you need at night. You pump green power into the system and protect yourself against major blackouts.

Generating electricity is responsible for 34% of Australia's greenhouse gas emissions. Roof-top solar now accounts for 13% of total electricity production. However, 65% of energy is still produced by burning fossil fuels.

You can wait for the government, pay for green power or generate it yourself.

Here's a plan

Solar panels are by far the easiest solution.

Check your electricity bills. Work out how much electricity you use and separate the charges for the electricity and the daily supply charge. That enables you to calculate how many panels you need and how long it will take to pay for them. Many electricity companies have an online calculator on their website to help you do this calculation. You can divide your quarterly kWh by 7hrs x 91 days to get a rough estimate of the number of kW your panels should provide.

Get a number of quotes and compare the separate guarantees and costs for the panels, the inverter and the installation. You should get a 10-year warranty on the panels, the same on your inverter and a 5-year warranty on the workmanship.

Do research into the government rebates available on buying the panels that have almost certainly been included in the quoted price. The solar feed-in tariffs for the power you sell to your electricity provider will influence your payback period, not the cost of the panels.

Batteries will reduce your bill even further (they store your daytime power instead of you selling it to your retailer and then buying it back at night), but they are still expensive and may not pay for themselves within warranty.

If you are not good with numbers, get someone — not the salesperson — to help you compare the quotes and decipher the offerings.

Find out about community solar. You might be better to invest your money in a community

HARD FACTS

Roof-top solar is now responsible FOR GENERATING 13% OF AUSTRALIA'S ELECTRICITY

Look it up

Home biogas

Waterlily turbine

Water rotor

Whirlpool turbine

Reverse metering

Buy back electricity

PERSONAL CARBON TARGET

KILOGRAMS PER DAY PER PERSON

Generate your own power

solar farm that supplies green power to you more efficiently than putting it on your roof. Some communities do put the panels on your roof then act as the retailer, investing the profits in the community, maybe putting panels on community buildings.

Home biogas plants, water and wind turbines are also available.

Costs

A 6.6kW system retails for around $9,500.

You get a government rebate of over $3,500, so pay less than $6,000.

Now try this!

8 Buy green power

14 Meet your heater

16 Insulate your home

32 Solar hot water

55 Energy-efficient appliances

101 Intelligent design

Reality check

Don't wait for battery prices to drop before buying panels. You can still buy the battery when prices drop.

Solar panels are inefficient compared to large-scale solar and wind, but they're more efficient, cheaper and have a lower footprint than coal or gas.

Electricity companies now add
$100 PER QUARTER
SUPPLY CHARGES TO COVER DECLINING REVENUES

Renewables on the Road: Erich Schultz and family

Inspiration through innovation: Erich Schulz

Erich Schulz is a medical doctor, passionate environmentalist and electric vehicle owner.

"The genius of Elon Musk is to create an electric car that is sleek, fast and totally desirable. He has smashed the golf buggy reputation and built a car that is delightful to drive and wins drag races. It has allowed me to have conversations with many of my conservative medical colleagues that then leads to discussions about climate change that simply would not happen otherwise.

"I bought the cheapest model I could. It has one motor, a range of 400km, and can deliver about 75kWh of power. Charging on an ordinary power point overnight adds 150km to my range for the next day. I only ever use a fraction of that around town. At a super-charging station it takes 20 minutes to get 250km worth of charge.

"I recently went on a road trip, partly to test the Tesla and partly to get the teenagers into the car so I could engage them. The rhythm of the trip was 'drive for two hours, stop for 20 minutes and have a coffee.' Five of us drove 1,000km and it was an extremely comfortable trip, with all the electronics and creature comforts you could ask for.

"In the past people had 'range anxiety' worrying about the distance they could travel. Hybrid cars are a transition solution, designed

Musician and electrician, Mal Mackenzie combines both loves as head electrician at music festivals

to address that. Because the new electric cars are lighter and more efficient and because charging stations are more common, that is no longer an issue.

"As a medical professional I have first-hand experience of getting people to lose weight, stop smoking, drink less, exercise more and eat healthy foods — simple stuff that would literally save their lives, but people cannot and will not do it. As humans we are just not built to sacrifice things that we enjoy for long-term benefit.

"What that means is that there is no point for dedicated, caring people to be yelling at the rest of humanity to 'come and think about the future like I do'. You have to recognise where people are at and help them take the next step. There is not going to be a revolution based on pushing bikes uphill and eating mung beans."

Applying common sense:
Malcolm Mackenzie

Mal is a fully licensed electrician and electrical contractor who has owned and operated a machinery repair and sales business and now runs an electrical contracting company. He has over 40 years' experience in the electrical trade.

He worked with the author on the popular radio program The Generator from 2005 until 2010, analysing energy policy, and bringing practical and business nous to many interviews and news stories.

Mal developed an Australian-made portable solar pack for camping (before cheap imports made it uncompetitive) as well as one of the first free-standing containerised solar power generators for small, remote holiday homes.

He has also developed a simple audio player for people with limited sight or dementia.

Garage

78. Alternative fuels

Tesla appeals to upmarket driving with style and an enviable reputation at drag racing

Tesla has made the electric car attractive through high-speed performance and sleek design. Hybrid cars have been the darling of car fleet owners for over a decade now. Existing cars can use biofuels such as ethanol to migrate away from burning fossil fuels

The petrol engine has enabled billions of middle-class citizens the world over to own their own vehicle and drive at speed in comfort for distances that would have been unthinkable in the past. The cost has been a huge boost in the blanket of carbon dioxide warming the planet. A huge 24% of global emissions are from transport and about 40% of that is from private cars.

The problem with petrol is that it releases carbon dioxide that was trapped billions of years ago. We have burned half the planet's oil reserves in less than 150 years and will burn the other half in less than 50. That's billions of years of CO_2 released in two centuries.

The lowest price of electric cars is now around $50,000 — below the luxury car price but still at the high end of the average family car. Australia's charging network has 800 charging stations, which is well behind international standards and a fraction of the nation's 6,000 petrol stations.

Here's a plan

If you are in the market for a new car and plan on spending more than $30,000, have a look at a hybrid version of your favourite model. The purchase prices are similar and the cost of ownership is a fraction of the petrol model. You can charge the car from a power point at home and if you use renewable electricity your fuel emissions are zero.

Keep an eye out for new sources of fuel available at the standard fuel pump. At the moment that is primarily ethanol, though there are some biodiesel providers in most states.

Alternative fuels are made from sugar and other crops that capture CO_2 as they grow. They still require energy to process and they create CO_2 when you burn them. In addition, they use precious farmland and water and displace the growing of food.

Waste biomass already exists, so energy derived from it is 'free' but there is not enough waste biomass to meet our energy needs. Algae are the most likely, long-term source of energy from biofuels.

One of the technologies being widely explored and promoted is hydrogen, but its practical use is still a long way into the future. Hydrogen is not a source of energy, because it has to be manufactured. It is a way of storing energy and so works more like a battery. Its advantage is that it can be transported, pumped and burned like fossil fuels, and so can take advantage of existing manufacturing and delivery infrastructure.

Photo by John Cameron on Unsplash

TESLA VEHICLE CHARGING

Look it up
Hydrogen unpacked
Hybrid car
Tesla races
Biodiesel supplier
greenvehicleguide.gov.au

Now try this!
61 Shank's pony
71 Use public transport
72 Buying a bicycle
74 Share the car

Let's fix it

Walk around the block, take in the sights. Get into the zone.

79. Take only photos, leave only footprints
80. Be a sticky beak
81. Water in the evening
82. The dog walks with you

We need to talk about ... playing nicely

It's lovely to enjoy nature.
Let's give it a chance to look after us.

83. Going on a picnic
84. Barbecue fuel
85. Your inner pyromaniac
86. Getting fed without giving a fig
87. Food that grows on trees
88. Nature on the strip
89. Planting a local
90. Hand-made watering systems
91. Where babies come from
92. The dinosaur family
93 Feeding the chooks
94. Helping out nature
95. Our community garden

Plan ahead

Build for the long term.
Future-proof your home.

96. Fertilise naturally
97. Don't fence me in
98. Host a hive of bees
99. Put some water in your tank
100. Double glaze
101. Intelligent design

CHAPTER

06

OUTSIDE

The sound of the lawn mower still dominates Saturdays in many suburbs, despite the gradual disappearance of the once-traditional backyard. Whether you live in an urban apartment or on a semi-rural property, getting outside the house is a significant part of balancing your life and engaging with your planet. Food, sunshine, friends and action — sounds like a party.

Outside

The problem

Although we spend most of our time inside, the connections that we make with the natural systems that support us all occur outside. The connections we make with each other are more grounded in nature and the activities we do outside are good for our physical and our mental health. Sweetie, we need to get out more.

How we'll fix it

The hanging gardens of Babylon were one of the seven wonders of the classical world. Since the first cities were built, the notion of nurturing a little piece of nature for pleasure has been central to the concept of urban planning. In Persian, the word Pardis means both garden and paradise, and the formal Paradise Garden remains a feature of modern Iran.

Exposure to nature is now a recognised form of stress relief with formal forest-basking events held in highly urbanised countries and syndromes such as nature deprivation disorder being recognised in human-resource literature.

As well as being therapeutic in their lovely splendour, gardens have an important role in creating a sustainable food-supply future.

Plants interrupt the hard surface of the city, cooling them down by breaking up the head island effect.

Shading the western and northern walls of your house will shave three to five degrees off the internal temperature, depending how hot your summers are.

Plants also allow water to penetrate into the earth, replenishing the water table and reducing direct runoff (and thus the pollution carried by stormwater) into the rivers on which most of our cities are built. The Smart Cities project specifically targets increased groundwater as a contributor to healthy waterways.

Gardens also provide a source of food and other organic material that complements the existing food distribution networks. Growing food reduces the use of fertilisers, pesticides, farm machinery, transport, packaging, processing and storage used to get food to your table.

Tip summary

As an entrée to enhancing your connection with your planet, it's worth just taking the time to get outside. Walk around the block, take in the sights and look for signs of a sustainable, resilient community. Get into the zone.

The tips in this section take it one step further, providing you with some exercises for active learning as you rediscover the joy of breathing in the air and the ambience of your surrounds. Make sure you don't trash the place; look a little deeper into the neighbour's plant profile, nurture the plants in yours and keep Fido from getting too interested in the affairs of others. There's a little time involved but the impact on your health and wellbeing will be immediate.

Photo by Pedro Ramos on Unsplash

#	Tip	Page	🔥	💧	🚹🚺	👁	⏱	Ⓢ
79	Take only photos, leave only footprints	214			✓		✓	✓
80	Be a sticky beak	215				✓	✗✗	
81	Let's water carefully	216		✓				
82	The dog walks with you	218			✓			

79. Take only photos, leave only footprints

Get out into nature without trashing it with these two simple rules. Leave it the way you found it and don't leave anything behind. Simple.

When you get out into nature, the last thing you want to confront is a pile of someone else's garbage. Nor do you want to find damaged plants, muddy creeks or damage caused by thoughtless fires.

Don't dig it up, or pull off flowers, nuts, leaves and seedlings.

Don't throw away your food scraps, carefully folded paper wrappings or the terrible packaging that your friends may have brought to your environmentally thoughtful walk. Take it all home. Even better, persuade your friends take their rubbish home too.

That includes rope. When you tie something to a tree, anchor a boat on a seagrass bed, or pull off a branch to swish away the flies, it is easy to think that one little bit won't hurt. The problem is that 3.5 million of us use national parks an average of three times a year and 10 million little bits do hurt.

If you are going somewhere you have not been before, download or print a map so that you can check it in areas that might not have reception. Check that you are dressed for the proposed activity and take lots of water.

Photo by Bee Balogun on Unsplash

Look it up
Leave footprints
take photos
Environmental walk
Lnt.org
kab.org.au
ecotourism.org.au

Now try this!
61 Shank's pony
68 The hidden treasure
83 Going on a picnic

80. Be a sticky beak

That old lady up the street with the rambling garden would love to chat. Ask for a cutting; offer her something you've grown — next thing, you'll be gardening together.

If you are new to gardening, there is nothing like an experienced mentor to guide you through nature's pitfalls.

There are almost certainly people in your neighbourhood who have time to stop and give you a bit of advice about the yellow leaves on your lemon tree, or dieback on the silverbeet. Besides, they know the vagaries of the local climate and the bugs that descend on your garden out of the blue.

If you are an old hand with a green thumb, you might not need Mrs Kafoop's advice, but you may well be able to use her potting shed, heritage seed collection or even a sunny corner where you could plant those spare tomato seedlings.

By working with the people in your community, you expand the area under cultivation, extend your local food network and increase the capacity of your community to feed itself.

Look it up
Garden sharing
Community garden
School gardens
communitygarden.org.au
100 mile diet

Now try this!
6 Indoor plants
46 Where the herbs grow
47 Mung beans and love
61 Shank's pony

81. Let's water carefully

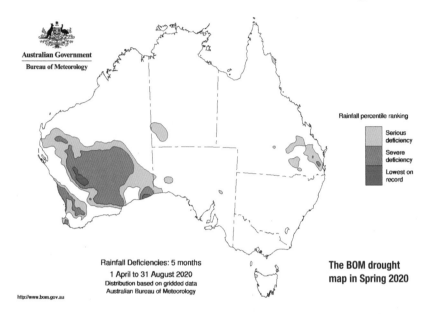

Rainfall percentile ranking

Serious deficiency

Severe deficiency

Lowest on record

Rainfall Deficiencies: 5 months
1 April to 31 August 2020
Distribution based on gridded data
Australian Bureau of Meteorology

http://www.bom.gov.au

The BOM drought map in Spring 2020

The driest continent on earth invests huge amounts of water in keeping lawns green and rose bushes blooming. The recent hottest summers on record remind us to use water carefully. Watering our gardens in the evening is one way that we can respect the power of the sun and keep our plants alive.

Despite occasional deluges across many parts of Australia, much of the country remains drought declared. The intense heat of the weeks between Christmas and the return to school will continue to play havoc with many plants in our gardens, especially those of European origins.

The danger is that we waste water trying to keep them alive only to watch them frizzle to nothing on a particularly hot day.

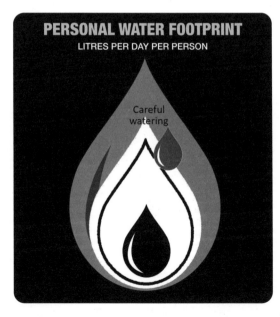

PERSONAL WATER FOOTPRINT
LITRES PER DAY PER PERSON

Careful watering

Careful watering may save 20% of your gardening water

Here's a plan

The water in the ground is the water that feeds our plants and rivers. By watering in the evening, we give it time to soak in before the sun sucks it up into the sky and away. Use a full stream of water at the base of each plant to let it soak in, rather than spraying water all over the garden. Watering a quarter of the garden for one hour at a time is more effective than whizzing over the whole place in the same time.

Even though most of us live in cities, understanding the way that water works is an important part of successfully keeping our green space alive. Trees and plants suck water out of the ground to grow. The effect is to cool the air by releasing moisture into it. That's why it's always cooler near trees than it is in the open. That's also why it is much better to wash cars and other things on the lawn than it is on the footpath. Getting as much water as possible into the ground nurtures our planet so it can nurture us.

Water restrictions will continue to apply to many areas across Australia, even if they are not currently drought declared. Most of us live in capital cities and can currently water whenever we like. When restrictions come in, they limit the times that we can water to the cool periods in the morning and the evening. Now you understand why. If you can do it in the evening, that helps.

HARD FACTS

FINES EXCEED

$200

for breaking level 3
RESIDENTIAL WATER
RESTRICTIONS.

Reality check

Some parts of Australia are humid. In warm, humid weather, you may be better off watering in the morning because mildews and fungi might get hold overnight.

Look it up
Evening watering
Deep watering

Now try this!
31 Process greywater
89 Planting a local
91 Where babies come from

82. The dog walks with you

When you say to Rover, "Off you go, little fella," his instinct is to chase anything that moves. Keep him inside at night.

Loyal and loving, the pet pooch is a primordial part of the human psyche. From the Neanderthal hearth to the most modern palliative-care facility, *Canis lupus familiaris* has an important role to play.

Nevertheless, when he runs free, he lives up to his middle name, lupus — Latin for wolf. If Fido's nose leads him to a ground-dwelling mama bird raising a brood of chicks, then bye bye, baby bird. This chikadee is fricasee and Fido's smiling happily.

Here's a plan

Train your dog to stay in the open; "On the beach", "On the grass", "Walk with me", "Here Snoopy" or the somewhat stricter "Heel". Don't let Rover out at night. Have your dog desexed.

Reality check

Dogs run in packs and a pack of dogs can do a lot of damage in a few hours, then be calmly back on the family mat in the morning. Packs of dogs have killed possums in the inner-city of most capitals, knocked down old ladies in the suburbs, and terrorised wildlife in parks and suburban bushland.

Many councils have specified 'Dog exercise areas'. Dogs are not allowed within 20 metres of children's play equipment in many inner-city councils.

You can keep a watchful eye on Fido's faeces and fangs to avoid council fines, but sex is an urge that will drive the most placid pooch to scale the fence and head off for a night on the town.

Dogs who haven't been desexed have 4,000 unwanted pups every week in Australia and around 850 of those are destroyed. Don't add to the canine carnage; send Snoopy in for the snip.

HARD FACTS

DOGS IN AUSTRALIA:
2.3 million
DAILY FEED: $12 MILLION

A personal story

I pose a canine quandary: "We pick up dog droppings to avoid overloading the waterways with phosphates and the nasty diseases it can carry. However, we are manufacturing plastic bags to do it. There has to be a better way. What is it?"

Look it up

Wild dogs city

RSPCA euthanasia

Stray dogs roam

PetRegister.com.au

Rspca.org.au

Petnet.com.au

Now try this!

19 That doggie in the window

34 What the cat does at night

62 Shank's pony

Daily vet bill: $6 million
UNWANTED DOGS DESTROYED DAILY:
AROUND 120

We need to talk about ...

... playing nicely

Photo by Federico Garcia on Unsplash

It's lovely to enjoy nature. It's great to reap the benefits. While we're at it, let's give it a chance to look after us and make sure we leave something for everyone else who follows in our footsteps.

Australia is blessed with a large land area and a small population, so we have a greater capacity to enjoy nature than many other parts of the world.

Despite the devastating effect that two centuries of colonisation has had on the landscape and the First Nations people who sustainably managed it for the best part of 1,000 centuries, we are still blessed with a wide range of environments, rare plants and animals that can teach us a lot about how nature works.

We really are a lucky country, and if we awaken to the opportunity we can harness it and thrive.

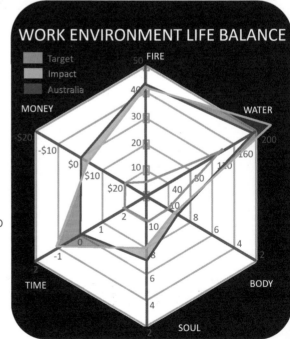

WORK ENVIRONMENT LIFE BALANCE

Target
Impact
Australia

FIRE
MONEY
WATER
TIME
BODY
SOUL

Tip summary

Some of us are more 'outside people' than others. Plants, animals, food and fire have varying amounts of appeal. This chapter aims to spark your interest in the outdoors and connect with your planet to bring balance into your life. When we are aware of the natural systems that support us, we are also aware of the threats to those systems.

Plants offer shade, the coolness provided by evaporation, a rich variety of smells and a big chunk of the food we eat.

Getting to know our local plants can be pleasant, rewarding and might feed us every now and then.

Animals have a cute factor, as well as balancing the local ecosystem. Companion animals, the local wildlife and the animals we keep to provide food are all part of the natural systems that support us.

Fire is fun, but something we need to treat carefully. Especially now that we know the CO_2 it produces will warm up the planet for future generations.

Tip summary

#	Tip	Page	🔥	💧	👫	👁	⏰	💲
83	Going on a picnic	222		✓	✓	✗		✗✗✓
84	Barbecue fuel	224	✓✓					
85	Your inner pyromaniac	226	✓✓					
86	Getting fed without giving a fig	228		✓	✓✗	✓	✗	✓✓
87	Food that grows on trees	230	✓	✓	✓	✓	✗	✓✓
88	Nature on the strip	232	✓	✓✗		✓	✗	
89	Planting a local	234	✓	✓			✗	
90	Hand-made watering systems	236		✓	✓✓	✓	✓	✓
91	Where babies come from	238				✓	✗	✓
92	The dinosaur family	240				✓		
93	Feeding the chooks	242	✓	✗	✓	✓	✗✗	✓
94	Helping out nature	244			✓	✓✓	✗✗	
95	Our community garden	246	✓	✓✗	✓	✓✓	✗✗	✓✓

83. Going on a picnic

Sharing food, having fun with friends and nature bathing all in one afternoon? No wonder the French Impressionists kept painting picnics.

A picnic's a great way to share food, swap recipes and local knowledge while enjoying your local treasures. Sometimes we forget how simple it is to throw a few things into a basket, grab a blanket and head off to the local park.

Here's a plan

You need a picnic basket. A cardboard box works almost as well, but you do need something firm to pack your food securely that is easy to carry. If you are walking you might use backpacks.

You need food. Salads and cheese are great for picnics, as are cold roast meat or veggies or other leftovers. You can just make sandwiches if you do not want to dish up food while you're out.

Avoid waste; put everything you are going to eat into reusable containers. Grab the nuts and dried fruits for your trail mix from the bulk jars in the pantry, select fresh fruit, fill everyone's water bottles and put the hot drinks in a vacuum flask. See if you can source the edible cutlery made from baked grains. Find out about portable smokeless stoves.

Picnic rugs have become an art form. ©2020 Wandering Folk

You don't want grass stains on your picnic finery, so remember to take a picnic rug or chairs to sit on, and try to choose a spot with some sort of shelter. Just remember that picnic gear gets heavy. It is not just the food, it is the hardware. Learn to live with less, or take the shopping jeep you bought for shopping on foot.

The more you do it, the smoother this process gets.

Invite friends who live nearby to a picnic you can both walk to. Share the food you've cooked, your great bargains from local shops and your planet-saving adventures.

By walking, or riding your bike to the picnic, you are not only reducing the pollution and the fuel used to drive, you are reinforcing the new habit of getting around by using as little energy as possible.

There's another advantage. You're getting to know your local area better. You are engaging with the local environment and community. Who knows, your save-the-planet picnic might inspire the family on the next picnic table.

Now try this!
53 Feeding friends
54 Baking bread
61 Shank's pony
68 Hidden treasures

Look it up
Woodslane walks
Biolite stove
Picnic recipes
Wandering folk

Reality check

You might find the notion of a picnic dull, daggy, naff, twee or boring; well, you'll be surprised how far a little imagination will take you. Give it a theme; make music. Whatever it takes to get your too cool for Monét friends out into nature.

Although we are not a nation of litter bugs, the amount of rubbish we produce away from home is still quite incredible. Over 16,000 tonnes of rubbish was picked up on Clean Up Australia Day 2020, one third of it plastic. And that is just the stuff that escapes into the environment.

Just because a picnic is outdoors does not make it sustainable. If you fill your picnic basket with European cheeses, smoked salmon and spring water bottled in Hawaii, the energy content of your food will far outweigh the energy you may have used cooking and eating at home.

84. Barbecue fuel

Kenyan social enterprise, Sanivation is making fuel from human waste

Before you throw another shrimp on the barbie, check your fuel. Charcoal is good, electricity and gas can be renewable, but coal is a disaster. Check out the new solar barbecues.

To eat outdoors is to fully immerse yourself in nature. To add fire to the equation anchors the occasion. The smell of smoke, the sizzle of food meeting hot oil, the sound of barbecue tools scraping those caramelised juices off hot metal ... it is hard not to salivate.

The tradition of outdoor cooking as a social occasion is common from Morocco to Fiji.

Of course, burning stuff warms the planet. Try to use renewable energy: electricity, charcoal, wood, solar or biogas. An international agency has developed charcoal balls made from waste.

Here's a plan

Don't throw away your existing barbecue. That is a waste of the energy it took to make it. Adjust your fuel instead.

If it uses heat beads (coal), try burning wood or charcoal instead. You'll have less ash at the end and might enjoy the taste of your food more, too.

Gas produces less carbon dioxide than coal to create the same amount of heat. There is a downside, though. Most gas is extracted from fossil fuels, so it is still non-renewable energy.

Don't leave it burning after you've cooked either. Kettle barbecues can be shut down almost as effectively as electric ones. The point is, you are using a precious resource, so be sensible.

Check out the rapidly evolving solar barbecues in a camping shop, barbecue shop or environmental store. They produce an incredible amount of heat but cook a little differently to a fire under a grill.

Early models worked better on food in pots than food laid out on a tray. The pot captured the concentrated sunlight, whereas the open food had to be moved in and out of the hot spot. New systems are emerging all the time.

HARD FACTS

FOREST LOST IN AUSTRALIA SINCE COLONISATION:

Rainforest, **25%**

Open forest, **44%**

Woodland, **32%**

Mallee forest, **30%**

Reality check

The cost to the environment, as with most human activity, is the use of energy. Burning coal, nearly pure carbon (C), adds two oxygen atoms (O_2) to every carbon atom, creating carbon dioxide (CO_2) — more than three times the weight of the original fuel. So, half a bag of heat beads produces almost five kilograms of CO_2. Using an electric griller for an hour produces less than half that.

Arguably, burning wood is carbon neutral if you grow new trees to replace what you burn.

Look it up
Solar barbecue

Biogas

solarcooking.org

Now try this!

10 Ordering in food

14 Meet your heater

50 Eating better meat

83 Going on a picnic

85. Your inner pyromaniac

Everyone loves a bonfire, but make sure you're not burning smelly old rubbish. Check your wood for paint, preservatives or plastic attachments. Do not burn the old sofa.

Don't burn your rubbish. It releases the maximum amount of pollution, right where you live. Compost it, recycle it or, if you have to, pop it into the bin. Just don't buy that brand of goods next time.

Most Australian cities have pretty tight restrictions on backyard burning, for good reason. The smoke haze that lingers over many cities is significantly worsened when lots of people stoke the fire pit. Most cities allow you to have a cooking fire and those restrictions allow enough flexibility for a little fun.

Many of us get out of town to let the inner pyromaniac loose, but that needs care and common sense as well.

Here's a plan

The cooler climes of the southern half of our island continent nourish deciduous trees. Lovely looking leaves in autumn form carpets of colour that annoy neat and tidy gardeners.

Do not burn those wayward leaves. Compost them instead. Of course, there are millions of them, all the more compost for your well-established and very grand grounds. The rhododendrons and hydrangeas will love them.

Warmer parts lack the lurid display of autumn leaves but produce plenty of dry sticks in hot times to take the nip out of a winter evening. In the inland a drop of 20°C when the sun goes down is commonplace and there is no better cure than a raging fire to regain the midday warmth.

Collect your timber sensibly. Do not steal the homes of birds, reptiles and small creatures that inhabit hollow logs and dead trees. Collect timber that has fallen in the last few years and is old enough to burn well. Do not take anything out of the forest in national parks or nature reserves designed to protect wildlife.

Everyone with a backyard collects a pile of sticks from trees and shrubs, old brooms and wooden things that break. Keep a stick pile; once a year jump on it and move it. That pile of organic matter sequesters carbon in your soil while aerating it and providing nutrients.

Photo by Jared Berg on Unsplash

Reality check

Burning wood is not environmentally sound — we justify it because we love it on the basis that there are many trees and we are sparsely populated. Try to be considerate about the wood you burn.

Back in the day

Old mate remembers, "My grandfather piled up whole trees for Guy Fawkes Night and we'd blow up an effigy of the conspirator with a pound of gunpowder for a head. Now that's what I call a fire."

Look it up
Burn rubbish fines
Firewood collection permit
Air quality smoke

HARD FACTS

MOST COUNCILS BAN THE
burning of rubbish
AND IMPOSE FINES OF
$500 OR MORE
FOR DOING SO.

Now try this!
56 The packaging we purchase
76 Buy good wood
84 Barbecue fuel

86. Getting fed without giving a fig

Not everyone's a gardener, but that does not mean we can't all grow some food. Grow stuff that is pest resistant and doesn't need tender loving care. Find food growing in the wild. Plant it where it will look after itself. Create edible landscapes.

Rosemary, oregano and thyme grow wild across Mediterranean hillsides, and that suits our climate too. Most of the food we eat has a wild cousin that needs no tender loving care. We can re-wild our gardens by encouraging those wild things at home.

Here's a plan

First step is separating the beneficial wild things from the toxic.

One corner of your backyard is greener than the rest. Identify the food in that patch by searching for the names rattled off below, or search for <edible weeds>. Pull out the baddies and eat the goodies. Yeehah, you're already gardening.

Leafy and upright plants include sorrel, mustard, stinging nettle, dandelions or amaranth. Sprawling wild greens include chickweed, gotu kola, oregano, thyme and mint. Succulents like aloe vera and portulaca are commonplace. Bushes like rosemary, pigeon peas, tulsi, coffee and curry plants grow wild.

Photo by NordWood Themes on Unsplash

Reality check

Henrietta writes, "I was leading a summer camp in the USA and had to do a crash course in local plants. It is a major booboo to take your happy hikers into a patch of poison ivy, or worse."

Old gardens often have a lemon tree, other citrus, plums, crab apples, quinces, papaya, mangoes and guava that produce fruit every year, are pest resistant and easy to cook once you know how. Many vines bear fruit as they sprawl over sheds, old frames or the back deck. Passionfruit and grapes are tough. Madeira vine and choko are invincible, though not desirable to every palate.

Have a chat to your local elders or see if the community centre has a guide to your local bush tucker. Many cities have foraging walks.

Now you can start planting. Put some of the favourite food you have discovered in the second lushest part of the garden.

Before planting the big stuff, map the shadows. Don't let your big trees and bushes steal the sunshine of the little ones. There's more on trees in the next tip.

As you map out your no-fuss food forest, think of yourself. Plant the things you need every day close to the door, put the animals and fruit trees out the back. Voila, you have a garden that will produce food even if you don't **give a fig**.

Back in the day

One deadly mistake you do not want to make is to eat hemlock. It looks like wild carrot but is poisonous enough to have been used to execute Socrates.

Look it up
Permaculture zones
Edible weeds
Bush tucker
Urban foraging
Edible landscapes
Guerrilla gardening
Johnny appleseed

Now try this!
88 Nature on the strip
91 Where babies come from
95 Our community garden

87. Food that grows on trees

Food trees are easy to look after. Gardening problems solved. Look around your suburb. You will see plums, citrus trees and other local varieties of fruit everywhere. Join the movement. Grow your own.

The urban lifestyle is fast, crowded and dominated by hard surfaces and sharp corners. It can be challenging to inject the organic into our urban lives, especially if you live in an apartment, rent or relocate on a regular basis.

A fruit tree is a marvellous thing. Prune (trim) and feed it in autumn, weed it in spring, water it in summer and harvest a crop of delicious, nutritious home-grown fruit as summer ends. The seasons might vary depending where you live.

Discover what fruit grows in your area. Walk your neighbourhood, spy on your neighbours. Talk to them; every gardener loves to share a chat, maybe even some fruit or cuttings.

Keep track of where the morning and afternoon sun shines in both winter and summer. Put the fruit trees and big plants on the southern fence so they do not shade your leafy greens.

If you do not have a backyard, read up on community gardens in Tip 95 or go guerrilla gardening. Find a patch of land that gets a bit of sunshine, some regular rainfall or runoff, and is close enough to home to keep an eye on it.

Dig a hole, put some fertiliser in it, then plant and water your tree. You can borrow a shovel and buy the fertiliser when you buy the tree. If you do not have a hose, get a bucket. If you are not planting at home, borrow a barrow and a big bucket so you can cart all this to your tree's new home.

Once a fruit tree gets going you can feed it once a year, prune it every two or three years, water it in really hot weather and wait for it to produce. Don't wait for the fruit to

HARD FACTS

Fruit trees
COST BETWEEN
$20 and $100.
Fruit trees generally start producing within
4 years.
DWARF FRUIT TREES will produce enough FRUIT FOR A FAMILY.

leap out at you announcing that it is ready to eat. Keep a close eye on it and pick it just before it is perfectly ripe. Preserve your spare fruit using the tips 58 to 61.

Reality check

Birds, bats, beetles and other b-words like the look of your favourite fruit just as much as you do. Gird your loins and get ready to fight for your food. Try to fight the good fight without poisons and other weapons of mass destruction. We are trying to nurture our planet, remember?

Trees are fantastic foragers. They send roots out to find water and nutrients. You may want to separate your veggie patch from the orchard and use raised beds or wicking beds.

Many nurseries sell a range of highly toxic pesticides to keep the bugs off your fruit. Explore natural pest management and make your own sprays.

Photo by Merve Sehirli Nasir on Unsplash

Look it up
Espalier
Pruning fruit trees
Natural pest management

Now try this!
6 Indoor plants
31 Process greywater
44 Pause before breakfast

88. Nature on the strip

Steve Murphy of recreatingthecountry.com.au uses local grassland plants to enliven his street

The nature strip. One of Australia's most cynical misnomers. Since when did 60 square metres of buffalo grass, mowed fortnightly, become 'nature'? In Alice Springs, it's gravel.

The space between our houses and the street is pretty intensely used. Utilities like water, gas, electricity and internet connections run through channels, under or beside the footpath on which we walk.

In leafy suburbs, large trees well-maintained by local councils create a cool, green landscape that contribute significantly to property values. Other suburbs are dominated by broken shopping trolleys,

derelict real estate signs alleviated by the occasional patch of well-tended flowers.

We can find ways to maximise the opportunity to green our environment with food plants and dramatic shows of colour, and create shade and a pleasant micro-climate at the same time.

Here's a plan

Identify a plant that is doing well in your garden that you are happy to see more of. Pick a corner of your nature strip that is not driven or walked over regularly and get the shovel. The dirt might be hard, so dig deep and add a lot of organic matter into

the hole before you plant. Dig up one of the plants from your garden and move it to your new spot. Water well and watch.

The point of using an existing plant like that is you know it will actually grow and it costs you nothing in case someone protests, rips it out or calls the style police to discuss your taste in tubers.

If you want to plant trees, dial before you dig so you know you are not planting on a gas pipeline. Check out where the powerlines are and the height of your planned street tree. Find a food tree that does well in your area and does not need a lot of care. Source a seedling and plant it.

Look up <Miyawaki forest> forest and plant a mini forest outside your front fence.

A personal story

Inner-city Brisbane has a number of major roads lined with Tamarind trees. Every summer, Indian families work the street, picking the tamarind pods to make the paste used in so many chutneys and curries.

Reality check

Check that the food plant you are about to install is not a noxious weed or the sworn enemy of your local Landcare group. Coffee and Brazilian cherry are great street trees that provide food but spread quickly and are often unwelcome.

Council may want you to register what you are planting. Talk to the neighbours. Councils generally respond to complaints. Avoid grumpy neighbours and stay under the radar.

Look it up
Nature strip planting
Regulations planting
Miyawaki forest

Now try this!
46 Where the kitchen herbs grow
92 The dinosaur family
91 Where babies come from

89. Planting a local

Plants that have flourished in your area for millennia support local insects, birds and animals. Even taking climate change into account, they are adapted to local conditions and more likely to flourish. Identify local plants and plant them in preference to imported competitors.

The loss of biodiversity is a major contributor to ecosystem collapse. You might wonder how much different a few backyard plants can make, but once you have watched the local birds and insects take advantage of your hard work you will see that every plant makes a difference.

Here's a plan

Chat to the locals. See if there is an indigenous community centre or an elder who is willing to share their traditional knowledge. You can ask them about food plants in your area. Chat to gardening groups and older neighbours. Even older white fellas have useful knowledge of local plants. The closest botanical gardens might offer some clues, too. Look for a nursery specialising in indigenous or native plants.

Take walks in local nature reserves and keep your eye out for open days in people's gardens. Ask locals about the plants in their gardens.

The advantage of planting species local to your area is they don't need too much tender loving care. They were growing there before your house was built, after all. That means they are used to the weather and bugs. Best of all, the local birds and bees are used to them.

Less watering, less weeding and more local fauna visiting your garden: natives have a lot to offer.

When you see a plant you like, ask about it. If it is native to your area, great. If it's not, make sure you're not planting a noxious weed, before you put one in the ground.

While you are wandering, look for unused land where you can plant — roadsides, vacant land, bits of land lost between developments. That extends your garden and improves the neighbourhood. Contact local Landcare or bush regeneration groups so you do not undermine their efforts.

HARD FACTS | **More than 60 Australian plant species ARE NOW THOUGHT TO BE EXTINCT AND OVER 1180 ARE THREATENED**

The waratah is a showy native and the emblem of NSW

Look it up

Sustainable house day

Endemic plants

Exotic weeds

Water Australian natives

anbg.gov.au

weedinfo.com.au

Reality check

The most significant advantage of natives is that they generally use less water. Nurturing local plants maintains biodiversity by keeping active specimens alive. The energy and resources used to maintain your garden are considerably less.

Just because a plant is common in your area does not mean it is native. Most weeds are imported, some of them from other parts of Australia.

Costs

Native plants in tubes: <$5

Native plant of the week, in a 20cm pot: $20

Back in the day

In the 1970s it was so fashionable to plant natives that many people planted forests around their house.

Now try this!

6 Indoor plants

17 Get active
with your community

46 Where the herbs grow

ON AVERAGE, NATIVE PLANTS USED IN GARDENS need about 15mm of water each week, ABOUT HALF THAT OF SIMILAR EXOTIC SPECIES.

90. Hand-made watering systems

You can poke holes in a hose, pepper the place with PET bottles, put the bathwater onto the berry patch or just place old food barrels around the garden. Find ways to store water for a not-so-rainy day.

The dry years and water restrictions that follow them are getting closer together. Keeping the garden alive is a luxury in the heat of the new Australian summer. Having plenty of water on hand in the garden for those dry times is one way to get through the furnace months.

Here's a plan

Chop the bottom off a PET bottle, or any old bottle you can chop, and pop it into the ground next to a thirsty plant. It will work as a funnel and allow you to water directly under your mulch. It gets the water underground quicker, preventing it from evaporating, and encourages your plants to send their roots down where it is cooler and the moisture stays longer.

Instead of chopping it, just fill the bottle with water and shove the pointy end into the dirt. Even without the lid, this works as a slow-release watering device, trickle feeding the plant over a couple of days.

Larger containers are even more effective. Food barrels of 10, 20 and 100s of litres can be used to catch water when it rains and let it go in the garden when you need it.

Old hoses that have holes in them can be drilled at regular intervals to create a drip or sprinkler system. Sprinkling spreads the water round, but drip systems deep-water small areas. Either way you need to leave them on long enough to soak the ground and then let it dry out in between watering. Otherwise plants do not develop properly and become dependent on a regular H_2O fix.

Wicking systems

A wicking bed is a waterproof container that can be used to make an efficiently watered garden. By holding a large quantity of water in the bottom of the container and using rocks or other obstacles to keep the soil and the roots of the plants out of the water, you can create a self-watering garden that only needs to be topped up when the weather is dry.

IBC food containers that hold 1000 litres of liquid can be cut in half and used to create two wicking beds.

Different types of gravel, rocks or mesh can be used to separate the water from the garden itself. The details will depend on your local weather, soil and the plants you want to grow. The best method is to play and learn.

Marcellahella posted this bottle and wick system to instructables.com

Photo by NEONBRAND on Unsplash

Look it up
Wicking gardens
PET bottles reuse
Water saving devices
napcor.com
waterrocket.uh-lab.de

Now try this!
3 Those packaged drinks
31 Process greywater
81 Let's water carefully

91. Where babies come from

Photo by Daniel Öberg on Unsplash

Sexual reproduction creates biodiversity by shuffling genes from both parents. Collecting seeds nurtures nature by maintaining that diversity in your backyard. Seed sharing spreads it round.

Collecting seeds is the basis of agriculture. The seed is nature's package of nutrients for the newborn plant; a miracle that literally needs just a drop of water to be revealed.

Agribusiness employs industrial-scale farming using monocultures of genetically engineered crops that depend on fertilisers and pesticides. Holistic, intensive farming empowers local communities and maintains biodiversity. It uses the same amount of land, significantly less fertiliser and pesticide, and a great deal more human effort. You cannot sit in the air-conditioned comfort of a laser-guided harvester while you are picking pumpkins in the local community garden. You can chat with your neighbour, though.

Here's a plan

Let the second-best plant in your crop go to seed and collect those seeds for the next crop. Who can resist eating the best one?

Keep your seed dry. Moisture will encourage mould and other microbes, or might encourage it to sprout when you least expect it.

Trade, or give away, some of your seeds at the local seed-savers group. Share the joy and discover new varieties.

The way to separate seeds from plants varies widely.

For large seed heads, like sunflowers, bang the seed on the side of a bucket and then scrape the seed off by hand. Most grasses are best laid out on a flat blanket or board and whipped vigorously (threshed). The seeds of many herbs, like Basil, can be stripped from the plant manually and then the seed separated in a bowl by blowing off the loose plant material (winnowed).

The seeds of fruit, like tomatoes, can be separated while wet, by washing, or after drying. Do not get too enthusiastic about washing your seed. If you dry the seeds in their natural, slimy coating, they will have extra nutrients and natural enzymes when they sprout.

Reality check
In the last 20 years, global seed companies have begun registering patents for genetically modified seed and suing farmers whose crops incorporate their genes.

Many seeds that you purchase in packets are hybrids. Like mules, a hybrid of a horse and a donkey, these hybrids may not be fertile, or may produce unreliable seed.

'Heritage varieties', old-fashioned plants that have fallen out of favour, are not hybridised and are available in many hardware stores and nurseries.

HARD FACTS

GENETICALLY MODIFIED FOOD PRESENT IN 70% OF PACKAGED FOOD

94% Soybeans (US)

90% Corn (US)

20% Canola (Rape) (Aus)

Look it up
Seed saver
Future food
Heritage variety
seedsavers.net
futureoffood.org

Now try this!
46 Where the herbs grow
80 Be a sticky beak

92. The dinosaur family

Photo by Kerin Gedge on Unsplash

Birds and reptiles fail the cute-and-furry test wired into you, me and other mammals. No big round eyes and mother's milk for these babies; it's all about eggs, scratchy feet and feathers or scales.

It's not surprising then to find out that both birds and reptiles are in the family tree of dinosaurs. The dinosaurs are descendants of reptiles, and one group of dinosaurs, the two-legged theropods, evolved into birds.

Despite their distinctly non-mammalian features, the members of the dinosaur family are very useful and entertaining to have around the house. Birds whistle while they work and offer all the drama and comedy of a soap opera. Lizards are a little less showy, tending to warm themselves in the sun

Reality check

Without calculating the footprint of feeding individual animals, let's agree that their presence is an indicator of a naturally harmonious environment.

Purists say don't feed the birds at all; at least learn who eats what.

Make sure that you are not simply procuring dinner for your favoured feline.

If birds are fighting with or flying into windows, screen them somehow.

rather than leaping about noisily at dawn. Compared to mammalian invaders, these dinosaur relatives eat less of our fruit and vegetables and more of the annoying insects that prey upon our plants. We like that.

Here's a plan

We can encourage these creatures into our gardens with native plants that provide food and shelter, bird baths, nesting boxes, food enclosures and piles of sticks: you might attract a breeding pair.

Even if your front garden is a basic square of buffalo grass with one oleander tree, you can bring a little nature into your life by simply adding a bird bath.

Some birds eat insects, others pollinate plants while getting at the nectar in the flowers. Plant trees and shrubs that offer birds places to sit, hide and nest.

It doesn't have to be a fancy work of art with cherubs spouting water and terracotta grape vines curling up the stem. A takeaway food container on a stool with four centimetres of water in the bottom and a brick to stand on will do. Your lizards will love a saucer under the garden tap. Just make sure you tip it out and add fresh water every week or two to stop the mosquitoes breeding.

Nesting boxes, or instructions for making them, are often available through local councils and wildlife groups.

Feeding systems need a little care and planning, otherwise you might attract unwanted bandits rather than desirable locals. Don't find yourself enslaved to a scourge of mynahs.

Look it up

Suburban birdwatching

Ausbird.com

www.followthatbird.com.au

Now try this!

6 Indoor plants

19 That doggy in the window

34 What the cat does each night

46 Where the herbs grow

93. Feeding the chooks

The humble hen is an ecological powerhouse. She eats your table scraps, makes eggs and, if you want it, meat. A boon for the garden, *Gallus domesticus* is a useful bird.

We love protein and that's what animals produce. Chooks eat food scraps, garden pests and produce eggs and meat with a minimum of fuss. People also eat rabbits, pigeons, quail and guinea pigs that are easily kept on rooftops and balconies, providing meat in the middle of the city at very, very low cost.

Here's a plan

If you have a small shed or a large aviary convert it into a chook shed and put a fence around it so your chooks get a little sun. Or, you can buy a mobile hen house and move it around.

Get feeders and watering systems so you only have to check your chooks twice a week. You will probably collect the eggs every day, but you might want a weekend away now and then.

Give them branches, broom sticks or an old ladder to sleep on. They perch at night. Also make sure there is a choice of nesting boxes.

Letting the chooks into your garden will keep down the pests and fertilise the plants. Just make sure you fence them out of the seedlings, and keep an eye on what they are digging up and tearing down.

Chooks moult at least once a year so don't panic if one or two start losing their feathers. It might take a month before they come back to full health.

To make sure the animals, and your family, stay healthy, keep the water and food containers clean, throw plenty of straw

Reality check

Immunised day-old chickens cost $10 each. You will feed each chicken something like $60 worth of feed each year. In return, one chicken will provide you with around 240 eggs, so at $0.25 per egg, you are getting top-range eggs for bargain egg prices. You can buy a roast chook for about $10, so it is the eggs not the meat that make them valuable.

A chicken will start laying at about six months old. A 'point of lay' chicken (or a pullet) will cost between $30 and $50. You save yourself six months food and the effort of raising them.

Rodents love chook food: keep your food in mouse-proof containers; avoid spilling food when feeding your chickens.

Photo by William Moreland on Unsplash

around and clean out their enclosure seasonally. Also keep an eye out for pests or diseases. Simple cures like diatomaceous earth will keep mites under control.

A personal story

Old mate advises, "Get your chickens from a registered breeder. There is nothing more depressing than raising chickens only to find out they have Marek's disease and need to be killed, buried and your entire chook house disinfected."

Costs

Day old chicken: $10

Layer: $40

Annual feed: $60

Eggs per year: 240

Cost per egg: 25c

HARD FACTS

THERE ARE

24 billion chooks

IN THE WORLD TODAY.

Look it up

Gallus domesticus

Keeping chooks

poultryhub.org

rentachook.com.au

Now try this!

6 Indoor plants

19 That doggy in the window

34 What the cat does each night

44 Pause before breakfast

50 Eating better meat

94. Helping out nature

Exploring the neighbourhood with your eyes open reveals damage that needs attention. Plants, animals and waterways sometimes need a helping hand. Get involved in cleaning, healing and regenerating your planet.

If you love animals but want to nurture your planet, it might be worth caring for animals from the wild. Some of us prefer to play with plants, repairing riparian vegetation that provides cool, clean water for aquatic life, or simply creating green space for human enjoyment.

As we poke around behind the façade of our manicured landscape, we will inevitably discover some nasties: overflow from septic tanks, industrial pollution, rubbish dumped illegally in a dead-end street.

Taking action means knowing where to turn for help.

Here's a plan

Don't go it alone; find an organisation near home.

Wildlife rescue organisations, like WIRES, are complemented by groups supporting specific species by planting habitat or eliminating feral predators. Working with these groups brings home the damage caused by our domestic pets: parrots with broken wings, mauled lizards and so on. Barbed wire tears muscles, skin and tendons. Animals can break bones trying to escape. Many wounds become flyblown.

Structured approaches are available through Landcare groups, bush regeneration groups or community groups formed around a particular project, such as cleaning plastic out of creeks so it does not end up in the ocean. You will also learn about the plants and animals endemic or indigenous to your backyard.

Many of these organisations have field days where you can get stuck into a project and work out if it is for you.

Reporting bad environmental behaviour can get complicated. Generally, local councils are responsible for illegal dumping of rubbish and state environmental authorities have the power to deal with industrial

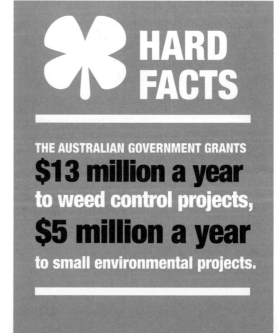

HARD FACTS

THE AUSTRALIAN GOVERNMENT GRANTS
$13 million a year
to weed control projects,
$5 million a year
to small environmental projects.

pollution. Damage to forests and other protected areas should be reported to the organisation responsible for the land. You might face a challenge when the owner of the land is the culprit. A local environmental group or environmental officer in a community group or council may have resources to help rectify the crime.

Councils are taking action against illegal tree clearing for private views
©2020 TropicNow, Renee Cluff

Back in the day

Property owners in scenic locations have been known to improve their view by 'trimming' the local greenery. Local councils have occasionally responded by erecting giant billboards emblazoned with a message along the lines of, "Trees that once grew here were removed illegally by vandals who have not owned up to their crime."

A personal story

Sometimes things that look shocking are quite natural. I saw thousands of crabs on a beach frothing and foaming after heavy rain. Thinking they were poisoned by a pollutant I rang the EPA, only to find out that they had been flushed out of the river and were dying because of the salt water. It is a regular event that helps sea birds get fat for the breeding season.

Look it up

Wildlife care

Bat care groups

Animal shelter

edo.org.au

Pollution enforcement

wires.org.au

landcareaustralia.org.au

npi.gov.au

australianwildlife.com.au

fauna.org.au

animalsaustralia.org

Now try this!

17 Get active with your community

61 Shank's pony

80 Be a sticky beak

92 The dinosaur family

Outside

95. Our community garden

Photo by Markus Spiske on Unsplash

Put some energy into the community and get a public garden in the ground. Grow food together, party together and build a community that can sustain itself.

Fresh food production is reasonably efficient. The carbon and water footprint of food you grow is similar to that of a farmer. So is the price. Given that kids don't eat their greens and look down their nose at anything grown in your garden, why would anyone want to grow their own food?

Even more weird, why would people want to do it as a group, when it involves wrangling with committees, arguments about who stole my sunshine or, worse, silverbeet?

Food that you grow is more nutritious, can be grown without industrial fertiliser or pesticides and does not require transport. A community garden allows people to contribute different skills and strengths, providing the resources to develop an orchard and grow staples like grain and pulses that do not make sense in a backyard.

Plus, you get to boast to someone who cares about the size of your pumpkins.

HARD FACTS

Food bill as percentage of income
AUSTRALIA 1920: one quarter

Australia 1960: one sixth

Australia now: one tenth

DEVELOPING COUNTRIES NOW:

one half

Look it up
Community gardens
Power of Community
Communitygarden.org.au
comfoods.org.au

Now try this!
16 Getting active
with your community
44 Pause before breakfast
45 What's on the label
53 Feeding friends
59 Smoke your own

Here's a plan

Australia's cities are blessed with a wide range of community gardens. Large well-established projects include Ceres and the Nunnery in Melbourne, Apace in Perth, Glover's Garden in Sydney and Northey Street in Brisbane. Council websites are one source of information about community gardens in your area.

If there is not one in your area, you could learn a lot about starting and running a community garden by visiting one of these sites. Of course, the first step, obtaining the land, is the most difficult.

If you're lucky enough to live near an existing garden, all you have to do is roll up and volunteer to help. You often need to go onto a waiting list or earn the right to have your own plot.

A personal story

A contributor who knows writes, "In Cuba in 1993, the collapse of the USSR suddenly switched off the oil. Cuban agriculture collapsed and there were food riots in the streets.

"Two Australians in Havana, where I grew up, taught permaculture and helped people set up community gardens in the city. Over 80% cent of Cuba's food is now organically grown. Most of it in the city.

Back in the day
In Europe, common land was an asset available to the broader community.

In Australia we do not have a strong tradition of communal food production.

If we work with nature to harness the natural cycles of wind, rain, growth and decay we can live in harmony while expending very little effort. After all, that is what people did for millennia before the growth of empires demanded exploitation.

If we combine that ability to live harmoniously with the best science and technology, we can live in relative luxury without extracting those resources at sword point, gun point or the expense of future generations.

Building a house that will not fall down for a thousand years is one step in that direction, learning how to generate our own electricity and collect our own water are somewhat easier. The tips in this book are the first tentative steps in this direction.

It will not be easy. Civilisation has been built by the game of empires for over four millennia. We assume that exploiting others is the only way that we can obtain wealth. Some of us measure our wealth by comparing ourselves with others.

We need to find new paradigms that build for the long term and allow nature to nurture us, rather than inflicting harm. The widespread idea that we need to choose between the economy and ecology is an indicator of how deeply this world view has been embedded in our thinking.

We could get philosophical and religious about it (and quote **Genesis 26**) or we could be completely practical.

We live on a finite planet and so have finite resources; we cannot continue to grow forever. At some point, we will reach the limits and need to find a way of life that does not depend on exponential growth. Again, we do not need to get religious or apocalyptic to identify some indicators that we might be quite close to that limit, now.

Understanding that long-term plans should encompass centuries rather than years is probably a good place to start.

Photo by Saj Shafique on Unsplash

Tip summary

You can future-proof your home by building in the systems now that will support you free of charge over decades. Secure your food supply, your water supply and control the climate inside your home by building the infrastructure that harnesses natural forces and does not require any energy.

Plan ahead sections in previous chapters have encouraged you to insulate the house, generate your own power, recycle as much of your greywater as it is safe to and establish some domestic infrastructure that has long-term benefits.

Now it's time to fill in a few gaps by adding some insects to the menagerie of animals supplementing your food supply, recycling nutrients, collecting rainwater and taking steps to control your indoor climate without expending any energy.

It is these long-term projects that will really nurture your planet and, in turn, your life.

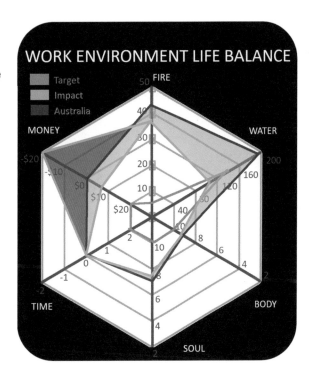

WORK ENVIRONMENT LIFE BALANCE

#	Tip	Page	🔥	💧	🧑🧒	👁	⏱	Ⓢ
96	Fertilise naturally	250	✓✓		✓			XX
97	Don't fence me in	252				✓		✓✓✓
98	Host a hive of bees	256			✓	✓		XXX ✓✓✓
99	Put some water in your tank	258			✓✓✓			XXXX ✓✓
100	Double glaze	260	✓✓		✓			✓✓
101	Intelligent design	262	✓✓✓	✓✓	✓✓			XXXXX ✓✓✓✓

96. Fertilise naturally

Gardens need food, too. In plant speak, that means poo. Don't steal their sunshine, add plenty of water and they'll grow like billyo.

The soil is the home of your plants and the ecosystems that support them. Blanketing your garden with a mulch of grass clippings, dry leaves, woodchips or bark protects the soil, and provides protection for the earthworms and other critters in the ecosystem that nurtures your plants.

Here's a plan

You can capture nutrients from waste food and garden waste. Worms, chooks and other animals can speed up the process of turning it into plant-ready nutrients, but so can the microbes in a compost.

Compost

Trees drop leaves; the grass gets mown; weeds get pulled up; there is a lot of plant matter to process.

You can turn it into compost in a couple of weeks or months. A good compost heap has a mix of green leaves, brown sticks and dried leaves, food scraps and fallen fruit. A good compost heap will get hot when you first pile it up; this speeds up the composting process and kills any weed seeds.

Animal manure

You can buy animal manure from hardware stores or more cheaply from roadside stalls in semi-rural areas. Horse and cow manure are full of plant fibre and are easy to handle. You can compost it with your own garden waste. Chicken poo has a lot of phosphorus and urea and not all plants love it, especially before it is well rotted down.

Poo from your dog and cat is not very pleasant to handle and better in the bin.

Photo by Neslihan Gunaydin on Unsplash

Worms

Worms eat food faster than microbes, producing liquid fertiliser which is more nutritious than compost. They don't like onions and citrus peels, though.

You can build a worm farm yourself with an old wheelie bin, or you can buy one off the shelf. There is a stack of flat boxes or trays, with a reservoir to catch the worm 'juice' at the bottom and a tap to drain it off. Mix it with four parts water to feed your garden and pot plants.

Compost worms are specialist animals. You can get red wrigglers, red worms and tiger worms at most hardware stores. Ordinary earthworms don't flourish in a worm farm nor compost worms in the garden.

Look it up
Great compost
Worm farm
Compost tea
permacultureaustralia.org.au
compostrevolution.com.au

Reality check

Commercial fertilisers come from two main sources. Most nitrogen fertilisers, ammonium nitrate, for example, are manufactured from natural gas. Those 'fossilised farts' are chemically processed into salts which are easily taken up by plants.

The other primary source is from mining bird poo from South Pacific islands, like Nauru, or bat guano.

Costs

Worms are cheap, easy to look after and incredibly productive. Worm farms can cost from $70 to $400 or you can build one yourself.

Commercial fertiliser costs $10 to $20 a 20kg bag.

Now try this!
6 Indoor plants
31 Process greywater
46 Where the herbs grow
51 The power of the bean

HARD FACTS

After one century of phosphate mining
80% of Nauru is a barren wasteland.
THE VAST MAJORITY OF THAT PHOSPHATE HAS BEEN USED IN AUSTRALIA.

97. Don't fence me in

We talk about building community but live in individual houses; isolated from our neighbours, sometimes afraid to greet them, reluctant to borrow a cup of milk. It might be time to let down our guard.

Two men with hammers took away my childhood views today.

We chatted as they fenced me in:

Yarns of tennis across low fences, shared barbecues, pet escapees.

Joy and pain, shared memories of neighbourhood.

The suburb where I live.

"It's all going mate," the young one laughed,

"behind a tonne of Colorbond and palings."

The jokes were short, the view went fast.

Their friendly faces and hi-vis went too

Behind the rapidly advancing wall.

We protect our personal privacy as a precious asset, quite upset if someone or something invades our space. At the same time, we wonder why we are anxious, depressed and lonely; why there is an epidemic of mental illness, self-harm and suicide.

Building bigger tables instead of higher fences might help commence the healing.

Here's a plan

Instead of starting unannounced on major structural renovations, start by chatting with the neighbours. Take them food. Leave a pot plant on the door with a note. Just start sharing the stuff that emerges from your 'hub of production'.

We have to build interest and motivation before we can build trust, and we certainly cannot build community without establishing the trust first.

Offer to look after animals and plants for the neighbours, ask them to do simple things for you. Asking for help is a great way to build rapport.

Once you have rapport, find ways to connect across the fence. If the fence is low

HARD FACTS

Mosquitoes love solid fences. The lack of breeze at a low level makes LIFE EASIER FOR THEM.

Low fences are a passing memory

Look it up
New urbanism
Urban renaissance
Bigger table higher fence

Now try this!
17 Get active with your community
61 Shank's pony
80 Be a sticky beak
66 Holding a garage salel

enough, put a chair on either side to use as a stile. Once you have crossed that barrier, the rest will come naturally.

The aim is to build community rather than get too hung up on the security infrastructure of your property.

Reality check

I shared the full version of the poem that starts this tip with the fellas building the fence. They were quite angry.

"I've been building fences for 15 years and you are the first person who has ever complained," was among the milder comments.

I was pleased to think that poetry still has immediacy and power, and then a close friend pointed out that she relies on her high fences for security; an important reason quite specific to her circumstances.

Back in the day

Villages on five continents for 3,000 years have all been designed with a fence around the outside. We've run them through the middle of our community.

Enter the ... apiarists

Reaping the bounty:
Suburbeea Honey

Suburbeea Honey is run from home by Darrin and Fiona Milnes in suburban of Brisbane and sells honey and beeswax products like lip balm, furniture polish and wax wraps in the community and at local markets.

"We started beekeeping seven years ago when we found a beehive in a hedge at our house. We smelled the honey and got a bit closer to find a well-established hive in a hedge that was hanging over the fence and needed to be removed.

"A local beekeeper came to help us box it up. He was in a full suit with hood and gloves. We were in normal clothes with a hood. At one stage the branch broke and there were 40,000 bees in the air around us. We did not get stung.

"He suggested that we might get 40kg of honey from the hive, and our eyes lit up, 'What are we going to do with all that honey?' In the first year we got 250kg. The vacuum cleaner was sitting on top of four 25kg buckets, every corner of the house had a bucket; we ran out of friends and family who needed honey.

"It has been a pretty steep learning curve. One year I was pregnant and could not fit into the suit and we had to rope in all these newbies who were comfortable to work in a suit and near bees.

"That year was amazing because we watched them all Winter, building the hive, setting up the breeding combs and then suddenly in Spring we could not believe our eyes. Everything

Darrin 'smoking' his bees to settle them down

was happening so fast: bringing in nectar and pollen, a lot of babies being born, new storage combs. There is a lot going on in the hive.

"We did a bee-keeping course and learned that two hives is better that one and then that turned into three and one year we had 600kg of honey hence the reason you might run into us at local markets. There is an increasing awareness of the benefits of natural, raw honey. People are asking if we use heat in the process so clearly they are being educated.

"When we are taking the honey out, we keep the capping wax and any deformed or old frames, and render that to get out the dirt and clean it up. We sell the raw wax to people making mouth pieces for didgeridoos, polish or soaps. We make lip-balm and wax wraps to replace wax paper or cling wrap.

"We connect with other local businesses. Alison from Giggle Suds uses our wax and honey, plus a lot of local products, gum leaves, and the chocolate chilli stout from the local Ballistic brewery. The brewery used some of our honey with cinnamon in a one-off beer, called 'Grandfather-oaked beer'."

Education is a primary driver for The Australian Native Bee Company

Steve Maginnity, **Australian Native Bee Company**

"I was a high school teacher; I purchased some hives for the school and then went to a European bee course, only to be told we could not keep the hives on the school grounds for health and safety reasons: European bees are the most common cause of anaphylaxis in Australia.

"I started thinking about alternatives and found that native bees were active as pollinators on the macadamia farms in this area and produced a small amount of honey, which has strong local flavours. Then my research indicated that they are stingless, not just that they don't sting, they can't sting, and I thought, 'Well, these are ideal for school.'

"The focus of the business has shifted away from education to pollination. Nut and berry farmers and horticulturists need bees on site to pollinate their crops. Climate change and fires have combined with disease and pesticide to damage European bee numbers, so native bees have a significant advantage. Berry farmers now require as many bees as I can provide."

Look it up
@suburbeeahoney
tanbc.com.au

98. Host a hive of bees

The humble bee pollinates your flowering plants, collecting pollen and nectar to feed a vibrant hive that is a well-organised and fascinating community. Bees are a social insect with different roles and clear communication protocols to describe the whereabouts of food and potential threats. They also produce sweet, wonderful tasting honey that is an added treat.

Bees play a critical role in pollinating the plants that feed us and cleanse the air and water on which we depend. The 2007 film, *Bee Movie*, plus documentaries and news stories have raised our awareness of the challenges faced by the global population of these little critters.

Native bees produce much less honey but do not sting

Here's a plan

Host a hive of bees in your backyard. Your plants will get pollinated, you will have front row seats to view the fascinating world of social insects and, if you are interested, can harvest kilograms of sweet, raw honey that tastes great and is good for you.

Native bees pollinate local plants, are stingless and require relatively little care. They do not produce a lot of honey, though.

European bees produce tens of kilograms of honey every year and need to be managed properly. If left alone they might be prone to predators or disease, or they might flourish and swarm, creating new, wild hives around your neighbourhood

that need to be managed. Their sting is potentially dangerous, causing allergies in certain people, especially those that have been stung a lot.

You need a hive (box) for the bees to live in, with some frames on which they can build their comb (sheets of wax cells to store honey and raise the young). Many suppliers will sell a hive ready made with bees inside it; you just need to set it up in a shady spot where the temperature remains between 18° and 33°C.

If you are raising European bees for honey you will need protective equipment and smokers to manage the hives, and knives, extractors and containers to process

Look it up

Beekeeping

Bee death

Raw honey

Beeswax

Now try this!

4 The snacks I love

17 Get active
with your community

28 Lotions and potions

56 The packaging we purchase

and store the honey. Indicative costs are given here.

You can start small, just with a box and some frames then join a club or find a local beekeeper to help you manage from there.

Costs

Flat pack box: $20+

A full suit: $150+

Smoker: $25

Extractor: $300

Reality check

European bees need to be checked once or twice a month during winter, and the hives need to be robbed regularly during spring and summer so the bees do not swarm.

There is a reasonable amount of physical labour involved in handling 40kg of honey.

Bee stings can cause anaphylactic shock in people with allergies. Talk to your neighbours before installing a hive and when you are robbing it.

Benefits

400kg honey: $6,000

HARD FACTS

Boxes in a bee hive:

3 or 4

HONEY PER BOX:

40kg twice a year

Two hives

ARE MORE STABLE THAN ONE

HONEY PRODUCED:

400kg a year

99. Put some water in your tank

Our bodies are around 60% water. Water is the stuff of life. The network that gets water to our kitchen tap is complex and energy intensive. Why not catch the water that falls out of the sky?

One of the privileges of living in a wealthy country like Australia is that we turn on the tap and clean, healthy drinking water comes out of it, reliably and cheaply. We pay a couple of dollars for every thousand litres we use. At a couple of dollars for a thousand litres, water is so cheap we generally think of it as being free.

If the electricity goes off, though, so does the water. Backup generators keep it coming for short periods of time but many regional towns were without water after the 2020 fires. Older European cities lose an extraordinary amount of water in their leaky water supply. To reduce the losses, some turn off the water supply at night. The affluent have their own water reserve on the roof.

Here's a plan

You already have the water catchment area — that's your roof — and the plumbing system to direct the water to one place — that's the guttering on your roof. All you need is the storage.

Slimline tanks are now designed to fit beside houses on small blocks, and underground storage has become popular to save space.

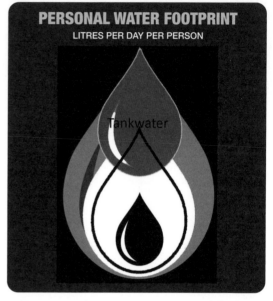

PERSONAL WATER FOOTPRINT
LITRES PER DAY PER PERSON

Tankwater

A 5kL tank could provide a family's bathroom and toilet water for three weeks

Photo by Casey Schackow on Unsplash

Polyethylene tanks are light, cheap and stable. They are resistant to corrosion but will degrade in sunlight and have a life expectancy of around 10 years.

Steel tanks, which do not degrade in sunlight, have a similar cost and weight profile, but are more prone to corrosion from water and salts.

Concrete tanks are expected to last 25 years, but are heavy and expensive to transport and install.

Keeping the water underground has many advantages, especially in suburban backyards where space is a valuable commodity. Prefabricated concrete tanks are relatively easy to install underground and become practically permanent.

If you live near running water you can try one of the new water-powered Barsha pumps. Just remember, there are regulations about taking water from local creeks and rivers.

Reality check

Some people are concerned about the chemicals used to treat our water, primarily chlorine to kill the bugs and fluoride to complement dental health. As far as we are aware, there is no serious scientific evidence that indicates we are killing ourselves with these chemicals, but you can avoid those concerns completely by capturing your own rainwater. Don't forget, the authorities treat tap water for a reason; a lot of dangerous microbes live in water. There are risks either way.

Costs

Cost and life expectancy of 5kL tank

Plastic: $1,200 10y

Steel: $1,500 20y

Concrete: $3,000 25y

In-ground: +$10,000 100+y

A personal story

A fruit farmer in Shepparton was furious that he had to plough his crop into the ground because of changes to the irrigation infrastructure. "Give a city dweller a kilolitre of water and it will turn into sewage, give me a kilolitre of water and I'll turn it into food."

Look it up
Tank life expectancy
Underground water storage
Domestic water
Barsha pumps

Now try this!
31 Process grey water
32 Solar hot water
81 Let's water carefully
90 Hand-made watering systems

100. Double glaze

Cold countries in Europe and North America use shutters and double glazing to prevent heat escaping through windows. It also keeps the heat out in summer. As our summers get more intense, double glazing becomes essential.

Windows are responsible for over 30% of the heat lost in most homes. The single panes of glass common to most Australian homes prevent air moving out of the room, but radiate most of the heat that falls on them. Curtains help, but a layer of air trapped between two sheets of glass is best.

Here's a plan

If you are renovating, installing double-glazed windows makes perfect sense. For a little extra expense you can solve a major insulation challenge, while enjoying the style of window you prefer. Of course, you would insulate your home at the same time.

Photo by Guillaume Issaly on Unsplash

If you are building or buying a new home, insist on it being properly insulated with double-glazed windows. If possible you should make sure the home is positioned to let the winter sun warm up the living spaces while being protected from the summer heat. The additional money you spend on building will come flooding back to you in low energy bills and a comfortable lifestyle.

It is always cheaper to get something right at the beginning than fixing it later. Retrofitting double-glazed windows is

Reality check

A Windows Energy Rating System (WERS) has been developed to provide a simple star-rating system for standard window units.

To use the WERS you identify your climate and the appropriate ratings for windows, then match the available windows against the selected rating.

The higher the rating, the more the window acts like an insulated wall.

often quite expensive and sometimes impractical. There are now retrofit double-glazing systems on the market. They may not be available from your local providers.

There are alternatives to double glazing that achieve similar effects in situations where double glazing is impractical. They are known as secondary glazing or glazing films, and work by trapping air between the existing window and the pane of glass or membrane that is installed. The impact varies widely and is not rated on most government websites, but some companies advertise very positive reviews.

Tinted, toned or coated glass can reduce the amount of the sun's heat flowing into the room but, for safety reasons, it is recommended that windows are not more than 20% reflective. These approaches work by limiting the sunlight transmitted through the glass and have almost no insulating ability.

Look it up
Secondary glazing
Solar Heat Gain
Visible Transmittance
U-value
Wers.net
Awa.org.au
Efficientwindows.org

Now try this!
2 Turn down the air-con
9 Control the airflow
16 Insulate your home

HARD FACTS

REPLACING SINGLE-FLOAT glass windows with double-glazed windows CAN HALVE YOUR HEATING BILL.

While they cost more, they pay for themselves over time **and continue saving YOU AS MUCH AS 25% on your energy CONSUMPTION AND BILLS.**

In the southern half of Australia, **double glazing is used to KEEP WARMTH inside more than half the time.**

The price of a double-glazed window will depend on its quality, **BUT YOU CAN EXPECT TO pay at least 25% to 35% more** than for single-glazed windows.

101. Intelligent design

Good design supports the needs of those who use it and minimises the energy required to implement and maintain the design as well as to make use of it. These general principles apply to urban planning, architecture, interior design, permaculture and the design of the products we use.

In general, we live in a world designed to maximise short-term profit rather than long-term stability. In our homes, that is reflected in the energy we consume in heating and cooling, the disposable nature of our appliances and clothing, and the lack of serious opportunities to recycle our waste. Applying intelligent design to these problems can contribute to a more pleasant environment that requires little maintenance and nurtures our planet and our life.

Here's a plan

If you are renovating or planning to build a new home, find out about passive cooling and heating. Build the southern walls to be solid and limit the flow of heat through the walls, arrange the windows on the northern and western walls to allow in the winter sun and keep out the heat of summer. Create courtyards that hold cool air in summer and allow winter sun into the home.

Use the interior walls to best manage the airflow within the home, making it easier to heat living areas in winter and cool the upper areas of the house in summer.

Reality check

Good design costs money. One reason many of our homes rely on air-conditioning is that it is cheap to build houses from flimsy materials, without large roofs that provide shade. Over a lifetime, though, good design pays for itself. The challenge for most of us is funding that long-term investment.

Manage the flow of water through the home to minimise the water that runs off the property and so nurture your plants and regenerate the ground water. Explore the possibility of a composting toilet.

Design the relationship between the kitchen and the garden to maximise the flow of food from the garden to the table, and waste food to the garden. Find out more about permaculture in planning your garden, water and waste strategy.

Talk to your neighbours about sharing infrastructure like water tanks, fruit trees, chook yards, workshops and laundries. The ownership of items that we each use a little is a major contributor to over-consumption.

Open your home to neighbourhood events like Sustainable Homes Day and Open Gardens that encourage the sharing of ideas and resources.

Back in the day

The Great Plains Shelterbelt was a US New Deal project of the 1930s designed to restore the desert and prevent the excesses of the Dust Bowl and the Great Depression. It created work for people planting native trees in large swales to capture water and nutrients, rebuild forest and restore waterways.

Look it up

Urbanism

Passive design

Design futures

Nightingale project

Walkable neighbourhood

Compost toilet

Suburban self-sufficiency

Now try this!

2 Turn down the air-con

9 Control the airflow

16 Insulate your home

31 Process greywater

46 Where the herbs grow

74 Sharing the car

86 Getting fed
without giving a fig

ANTIKY

07

THERA

An ancient Greek analogue computer, made of brass, the Antikythera could display astronomical observations and calculate the dates of future Olympic games. It is properly described as a celestial calculator. The tips in this book represent the visual interface of the Antikythera. This section, by comparison, exposes the workings; the calculations behind the figures; the visualisations given throughout the book; the assumptions and sources behind the terms.

Ρ	**Glossary**
Σ	**Ready reckoner**
Τ	**Personal carbon target**
Υ	**Personal water target**
Φ	**Work-environment-life balance (WELB)**

P

GLOSSARY

Carbon dioxide

Caused by breathing or burning carbon, carbon dioxide, CO_2 combines two oxygen molecules with every carbon molecule, releasing energy. Carbon dioxide is 3.2 times heavier than the carbon burned to produce it. It also takes up more space than the carbon burned to create it. Compressed into a liquid it takes up 4.4 times the space, frozen as a solid it takes up 3 times the volume. This fundamental physics challenges the notion of carbon capture and storage.

Carbon dioxide equivalent

Defined in detail on page 4 in the introduction to this book, carbon dioxide equivalent, CO_2e, is the amount of carbon dioxide that would have the equivalent warming effect as a particular volume of greenhouse gas. One tonne (t) of methane, for example, is equivalent to 25t of carbon dioxide. One tonne of waste food produces 20t of methane, so we would say that one tonne of food waste produces 500t CO_2e.

Carbon footprint

The idea of an environmental footprint is based on the notion that we leave a mark on the environment wherever we go. The more lightly we travel, the less visible our footprints are. Our carbon footprint, then, is the total amount of carbon dioxide we produce in a particular time period. Just by walking around breathing, we produce about 1kg per day. In 2019, Australians each produced about 46kg/d.

Carbon offset

When we fly, our trip creates about 100g of carbon dioxide or its equivalent in greenhouse gases for every passenger for every kilometre. We can tick a box when we book our ticket to offset those emissions for a few dollars. The idea is that our offset fee is used to plant a tree or build a wind generator that will 'remove' the carbon we have emitted. But that only works if the offsets actually take carbon dioxide out of the air, like trees do, and as long as we do not use it as an excuse to keep making unnecessary emissions. It is also important that we account for the cost of nurturing the tree to full size, not just planting it.

Cheap energy

Not a formal term but used in this book to refer to the vast amount of power released from fossil fuels that could be simply dug up and burned. The Great Acceleration in wealth, health, population and destruction of the environment that has taken place over the 20th century is almost completely due to the availability of cheap energy.

Cradle to grave

When we use a toaster, it consumes about 2kW of electricity to heat your bread, emitting about 22g CO_2e/minute. It also took a lot of energy to make your toaster and it is responsible for more energy consumption when we throw it in the bin. The total energy consumed over its lifetime is the cradle-to-grave footprint of that toaster.

Embedded energy
(see Embodied energy)

Embodied energy

The average adult eats 2700 kilocalories of food a day. That is the energy available in that food for the body to convert into useful work. (See Energy, below). It takes a lot more energy than that, though, to create the food, process it, refrigerate it, transport it and cook it before it appears on our plate.

That total amount of energy expended on getting the

food to the table is called the embedded (or embodied) energy. Theoretically, we can calculate the embodied energy of anything. Practically it is quite difficult. It is an important concept in this book because we want to make decisions that reduce the harm we do to the environment and that means reducing the embedded energy we consume.

Energy

When we are full of beans we say we have lots of energy. Energy is the capacity to do useful work.

The amount of energy expended to accelerate a car to 60km/h, for example, or to raise the temperature of a litre of water by 1°C. Energy has its own units — joules (J), calories, megajoules and kilocalories (kilocalories, or food calories, is generally written as 'Calories'). We 'burn' that energy at different rates, depending how hard we are working. A sedentary but awake human burns 140 Calories an hour, an athlete in top-flight burns 400. Those figures can be given in metric as 588J and 1,680J.

One joule of energy per second provides one watt of power. A joule can also be called a watt second. The common name for 3,600 million joules is a megawatt hour or 1MWh. That is the standard way of measuring the generation of electrical energy at a power station.

Fire and flooding rains

Dorothea MacKellar's *My Country* is a poem best known for its second stanza, which begins "I

love a sunburnt country" and ends "a land of droughts and flooding rains". In January 2020, huge fires burned one million hectares of forest up and down the east coast of Australia. The fires remained out of control until intense rain events dropped hundreds of millimetres of rain causing dramatic flooding. Despite the flooding rains, large sections of the country remain in drought.

Genesis 26

The first page of the Christian bible quotes God, "let [man] have dominion over the fish of the sea, and over the fowl of the air, and over every creeping thing that creepeth upon the earth."— Genesis 26. Genesis is taken from the Torah and similar sentiments are expressed in verses 30 to 35 of Chapter 2 in the Quran. Theologians argue over the significance of this, suffice to say that many people believe they have a God-given right to exploit natural systems.

Give a fig

The expression is handy for those occasions where the f-bomb is inappropriate but comes about because of our schizophrenic attitude to the humble fruit of the Ficus carica. Fresh figs have long been the property of royalty. Dried figs, on the other hand, have been commonplace rations for workers. Today's prices?

Fresh figs: $30/kg or @ $2.50

Dry figs: $10/kg or @ 12c

We currently give 20 dried figs for a fresh'n.

Green power

The term is generally used for electricity supplied by a retailer who promises that it has been sourced from renewable generation. Some providers still include electricity for which carbon offsets have been purchased. (See also carbon offset and renewable energy.)

Heat pump

A refrigerator is a heat pump. It uses the compression and expansion of gas to transfer heat from inside the fridge to the outside, allowing us to freeze or chill the contents. Modern hot water services perform the opposite function to heat up the water. Reverse cycle air-conditioners can switch between modes.

Hub of production

A full explanation appears on page 150 in *Plan ahead* of Chapter 4, *Kitchen*. The concept is essentially that we should not perceive ourselves as consumers but as producers. This simple shift in thinking empowers us to be independent of the global financial and consumption networks.

Modular lighting systems

Up until a decade ago, lighting systems were literally built into the walls of the house, or retrofitted at great expense by draping wires into wall cavities, or burying them in hard surfaces, such as plaster over brick. Wireless induction and LED lighting have allowed immense flexibility and creative approaches to lighting spaces.

Glossary

Systems range from solar-powered fairy lights through to sophisticated interactive lighting.

Nett energy benefit

When I chop down a tree and burn it to heat water, the nett energy benefit is the energy used to heat the water minus the energy that I expended in collecting and chopping the firewood. I get much greater benefit if I burn petrol because it takes very little energy to collect and transport it.

The nett energy benefit from the tree can be calculated by estimating the potential energy in the wood of the tree, minus the energy spent in collecting and processing it, minus the energy that goes up the chimney when I burn it.

The nett energy benefit from a solar panel is the energy captured by the solar panel from the sun (20% of one kilowatt hour, per square metre times the size of the panels times the hours of its lifetime – 15 years), minus the embedded energy in the panel, the battery, the inverter, and the wiring.

Petroleum has been the most efficient fuel ever found. Less than 5% of the energy in the fuel has been consumed by the time we put it in our tank.

What that means is that it is going to get more and more expensive to extract energy in the future. Nearly all economic models use 20th century energy prices to model the future. Gas fracking,

shale oil and biofuels all require significant amounts of energy to produce. Currently, about 6% of global emissions come from the capture of energy. Depending on the nature of future energy investments, that figure will rise markedly over coming decades.

Personal carbon target

See section T (tau) in this Antikythera.

Personal water target

See section Y (upsilon) in this Antikythera.

PET

Polyethylene Terephthalate (sometimes PETE) is a hard, easily recycled plastic used to make drink bottles, containers, and fibres for strapping and webbing. It is generally identified by the number '1' in the standard recycling logo. See Tip 65 in Chapter 5, *Garage*.

Power

The scientific term 'power' is used to measure the amount of energy expended in a specific time. Your speaker, for example, might consume 8 watts, which means it uses that much electrical power to generate the loudest volume it is capable of. If you played it at half volume for an hour, you would consume 4 watt hours of energy. Every second it is on it is using 4 joules of energy. See also *energy*.

Purchasing power parity

To help us understand the reality of people living in other parts of the world, the concept of purchasing power parity (PPP) compares the price of a 'basket of goods' in two different currencies. Comparing the cost of a week's food in two different currencies exposes the relative cost of living. A weird side-effect is that when we talk about the global poverty line as $1.50 a day PPP, we mean what it would be like if you had $US1.50 to live on in the USA. That's tough. Many of us incorrectly assume that living on $1.50 a day is easier in poor countries because of the lower price of food.

Renewable energy

When we generate energy by burning coal or gas, we use a resource that has taken billions of years to create. When we burn wood or charcoal, we use a resource that has taken decades to create. When we convert the energy from sunlight or wind into usable electricity then we are capturing energy that is new. That same amount of energy is available again tomorrow, we cannot use it up.

If we store renewable energy by using it to pump water up hill, by creating hydrogen from water, or by melting salt that retains its heat for days, then we are storing renewable energy. Hydrogen has an advantage over the other alternatives because it can be bottled and transported, and it can be used in internal combustion engines.

Salts

Salts are simple compounds that generally dissolve in water and are only used in relatively small quantities by living things. The most common salt, sodium chloride, is known as sea salt, or table salt. A small quantity of salt is essential for our wellbeing, but high quantities of salt kill life, and so we 'salt' our food to preserve it. Salts are generally the result of a reaction between an acid and a metal and so some salts corrode many metal items, like steel water tanks and plumbing.

Saponin

A group of plant-based chemicals that generate foam or suds in water and have similar cleaning properties to soap, without the harsh chemical history and resource usage.

Sugars

Sugars are relatively simple carbohydrate molecules that form the basic building blocks of life. They are created by plants using photosynthesis to combine carbon dioxide and water and make sugars. Sugars store energy which is then released when the molecule is digested by an enzyme or microbe. Yeasts convert sugar into alcohol or glycerine, for example. Larger and more complex molecules are built

up to create proteins, for example, by adding other elements in more complex structures.

Like salts, sugars can be used to preserve food, by binding all the available water and oxygen and preventing living things from living in the food and spoiling it. Similarly, sugars are essential for life but are harmful in excess.

Telecommuting

The idea of working remotely emerged as computer networks became widespread around 1990. Human resource and industrial relation issues slowed down its implementation until Covid19 enforced working-from-home as standard. The evolution of formal structures to support telecommuting are still yet to evolve but, now we are all doing it, they will.

Tiny house

The tiny house movement has emerged from the intersection of the requirement for affordable housing, the desire to reduce our environmental footprint, and the availability of mobile housing for worksites based on shipping containers. There is a rapidly evolving body of lived experience and literature emerging from the people driving this movement.

Total water footprint

See section Y (upsilon) in this Antikythera.

Triple bottom line

The bottom line is traditionally used in accounting to measure the profit; that is, the amount of money left over after all the expenses have been deducted from the total revenue (the top line).

The triple bottom line is a concept used to measure the benefit or deficit to the environment and society by the activities of the company. Despite being discussed quite regularly it has not been incorporated into the fundamentals of mainstream business activity. The concept of B Corps has probably come closest.

Two-tonne lifestyle

If we are to reduce our carbon footprint sufficiently to keep global warming within two degrees Celsius, we essentially have to drop our personal emissions to around 2 tonnes (t) of carbon dioxide equivalent a year, that is 5.3kg per day. We currently emit around 17t a year and so this is an incredible change of lifestyle.

Work-environment-life balance (WELB)

See section Φ (phi) in this Antikythera.

READY
RECKONER

This section defines the typical or average Australian home and the calculations used to measure our footprint. There were 25.6 million living in Australia in March 2020 according to the Australian Bureau of Statistics (ABS). We lived in 11 million households with an average household size of 2.4 people. The average Australian home has three bedrooms and sits on 474m2 of land.

Averages do not describe everyone, we are not all typical, but they do provide a starting point for talking generally about society. If we understand what the average emissions are per person, we can start to see how significant our own personal emissions are, and what the impact is of the decisions we make.

Emissions

Climate chaos, water scarcity, biodiversity loss, food sovereignty, global slavery, economic uncertainty; we have selected climate as the initial axis for focusing our attention.

The Australian government's Department of Industry, Science, Energy and Resources (DISER) Quarterly Greenhouse Gas Inventory reports the total Australian emissions in the year to March 2020 as 529Mt.

That same report indicates that the portion of that due to consumption in Australia (as opposed to exports) is 435Mt = 17 tonnes per person per year. This is the figure used in international reporting captured by sites such as CarbonWatch and adopted to create the **Personal carbon target**, described in section T below.

CarbonWatch reports that Australian per capita emissions have been above 16t/y = 44kg/d since 1989. They peaked at 20t/y in 2004 and were 16.96t/y in 2017, almost the same as reported by DISER in the year to March 2020.

By comparison, the world's per capita emissions reached 4.5t/y in 1979 and have slowly crept up to 4.8t/y after peaking at 4.9t/y in 2014.

The May 2020 Greenhouse Inventory from DISER is based on 2018 figures and it divides national emissions from consumption into

- Agriculture 20%
- Mining 18%
- Utilities: electricity, waste and water 35%
- Manufacturing 11%

- Services, including construction and transport 12%
- Residential 13%
- Timber −8%

This is a different arrangement than used in the Quarterly Inventory because it distributes energy, transport, waste and lost emissions across the sectors, including households.

That is more useful for our purposes and so these percentages have been used to calculate the contributions of sectors like agriculture.

The share of Australia's emissions produced by goods which end up being consumed by households is 319Mt (60% of the total and 73% of the 'consumption' emissions). That includes the indirect emissions from food and other products consumed in households. It is quite different than the emissions actually produced in the household.

Energy

Globally, energy is responsible for 73% of emissions, 24% in industry, 16% in transport and 18% in buildings. Significantly, 8% of fuel combustion is not accounted for and 6% is consumed in the production of energy, according to CarbonWatch. That loss is used to calculate the **net energy benefit**, which defines the effectiveness of any source of energy.

In most accounting, the energy emissions are distributed among the sectors where they are employed.

In Australia, the energy and water sector are responsible for a combined 35% of total emissions.

The primary source of figures regarding energy production and consumption is the Department of Industry, Science, Energy and Resources (DISER) Australian Energy Statistics website and the reports and summaries provided there.

Those two sets of figures are used to break down Australia's energy consumption by sector.

Electricity generation by fuel type is of key interest as it allows us to calculate the impact of reducing our electricity consumption. That varies by state, but we have applied the national average.

In 2019, Australia consumed 265PWh of electricity; that is 9.8MWh per capita over the year or 27kWh per day. We each consume about 16kWh per day at home, the other 11kWh per day is used by industry and commerce on our behalf.

That electricity is generated by fuels that have quite different greenhouse gas emissions. The share for each fuel and its emissions per MWh of electricity are:

21% renewable (0 direct emissions)

56% by coal @ $1tCO_2e/MWh$

20% by gas @ $500kgCO_2e/MWh$

On average, we emit $660kgCO_2e$ for every MWh of electricity produced. Calculations in this book assume $0.66kgCO_2e$ for every kWh of electricity.

Electricity consumption in the home is based on the 16kWh/d figure given above and shared as follows, based on a 2014 CSIRO study of energy consumption. It is consistent with recent international studies: 16kWh/d = $10.6kg\ CO_2e/d$ which is 23% of our personal footprint. Notice that other forms of energy are used to heat water and our homes, so the electricity figures are quite different than the figures for energy.

Household emissions

There are so many different ways that household emissions are described and divided up that it is almost impossible to identify an authoritative source. The table below is taken from the overview figures quoted above and divided across household activities using a range of sources.

Many government agencies apply the proportions used by the Australian government's Your Home calculator, which is based on the now disbanded Australian Greenhouse Office calculator built in 2008. In 2014, the CSIRO analysed 290 homes in detail and produced more specific numbers,

which explain energy use in different states over the months of the year. That has been used by a range of consultants in the environmental media to detail household energy.

The table below combines information from all these sources to assign the percentages of various parts of the household, and applies those percentages to the 2020 figures from DISER and the ABS. Each column displays a different way of dividing the figures that is in common use, and helps explain why so many different people make such wildly different claims.

	Wh/d each	% energy in home	% CO$_2$e in home	Wh/d electric	% domestic electricity	CO$_2$e kg/d	% Household emissions	% Carbon footprint
Cooling	1,042	9%	5%	1,041	14%	0.7	4%	1%
Heating	3,125	28%	41%	938	13%	5.9	31%	13%
Hot water	2,917	26%	35%	1167	16%	5.0	26%	11%
Appliances	2,917	26%	14%	2917	40%	1.9	10%	4%
Kitchen	625	6%	3%	625	9%	0.4	2%	1%
Lighting	521	5%	2%	521	7%	0.3	2%	1%
IN HOUSE	11,146	100%	100%	7,208	100%	14.2	75%	31%
Driving						4.7	25%	10%
FROM HOME						18.9	100%	41%
Food						14.5		31%
Waste						1.2		3%
Other						11.5		25%
Total per capita					16% emissions	46.1		100%
Household total	29,315			18,959		121.2		

These are national averages. Electricity use (and carbon footprint) varies widely from state to state. For example, heating in the southern states uses at least five times as much energy as cooling uses in the north. Heating houses is mostly provided by wood fires in Tasmania and by gas in Victoria. Around half of the hot water used in Australia is heated electrically, but the percentages of other fuels used vary widely.

Water

The Water Account released by the ABS in June 2020 covered the year 2017–2018.

In 2017–18, the total amount of water extracted from the environment was 70,300GL. This was a decrease of 6% from the previous year, primarily because most of the nation was in drought.

Industries extracting water include:

• Electricity and gas supply 53,000GL

• Agriculture 3,381GL

• Mining 1,108GL

• Manufacturing 297GL

The sewage and water supply authorities distributed 11,756GL. This is less than 14,828GL distributed in 2016–17 and much less than the 26,000GL used in many years between 2000 and 2009.

Sectors consuming distributed water include

• Agriculture: 7,327GL, 62%

• Household: 1,790GL, 15%

• Manufacturing: 235GL, 2%

• Electricity and gas supply: 146GL, 1%

• Mining: 102GL, 1%

Most calculations leave out the water self-extracted by electricity and gas supply as that is released back into the environment, and divide up the rest. By that method, the usage of water by each of these sectors is

• Agriculture 65%

• Household 10%

• Mining 7%

• Manufacturing 4%

• Energy supply 1%

These are the percentages used in calculating the contributions by these industries in the text of the book. The missing 13% is used in construction (concrete is included in manufacturing), municipal management (street cleaning, sewage treatment, etc) or lost in the system (including leaks).

The per capita use of water given in the accounts is 610kL/y or 1,671L/d. This is the total water footprint, including the water used by industry on behalf of each of us.

The per capita use of water in the household as presented in these most recent accounts is 199L/d or 73kL/y. Most government websites still use 97L/y or 100kL/y as the average Australian individual consumption. That is based on a 2014 report which combined ABS figures from 2009 and water agency figures from 2012. We use 200L/d as a round number for comparing the impact of particular tips.

The **Personal water target** refers to the per capita use of water in the household, because that is the number publicised during droughts. The total water footprint is used to consider the impact of food choices on the water footprint of an individual. See section Y.

Water use within the household varies considerably between jurisdictions. We have used figures provided by the Federal government's yourhome.gov.au to arrive at

- Garden 34%
- Shower 22%
- Toilet 18%
- Laundry 16%
- Kitchen 10%

These calculations are used to explain the impact of each tip and to inform the text.

Food

In addition to the large greenhouse gas and water footprint of agriculture, our food is processed, packaged, stored and transported before we begin cooking it at home. All stages of the food supply chain involve energy, water and manufactured inputs such as fertiliser, pesticides, packaging and preservatives.

The issues are complex and controversial. A NZ study showed that it was more energy and greenhouse gas efficient to grow food in NZ and transport it to Europe than grow and store it locally. A German study completely disagreed with that and the dispute came down to differences in the calculations about transport and impact of fertilisers and energy used in cold storage.

The research informing this book compared published Australian figures to global figures and then attempted to explain the differences. The primary challenges involve the water and carbon footprint of meat, cotton and rice. In these three cases, the sectors have worked with universities to provide rigorous research to back their claims, but the marketing spin they have put on them sometimes obscures the truth.

Those individual challenges have been identified in the relevant text and the resources are available in the bibliography published at ylyp.news.

Agriculture uses

- 51% of Australia's land
- 65% of the water extracted from the environment
- 20% of the emissions produced in Australia

65% of Australia's agricultural output is exported, mostly wheat, meat, wool, other grains and pulses.

90% of the fresh fruit and vegetables sold in Australia is grown here.

The relevant carbon and water footprint of common foods (grown, processed and retailed) is provided below:

Food 1kg grown processed & delivered	Carbon footprint kg CO_2e / kg food	Water footprint L water / kg food
Red meat	37.0	2,000
Rice	2.7	2,500
Apples	0.2	700
Tomatoes	3.0	25
Pulses	0.9	70

It is important to note that these figures are widely depending on the season and the region, and we have taken national averages, which may not be relevant to a particular individual's shopping habits.

On average, Australians eat 100kg of meat each year. Think about that. It is 10 individual servings of 200g. Most of us eat meat more than once a day, and often eat more than a recommended healthy serving when we do.

Transport

Globally, transport is responsible for 16% of emissions; in Australia it is 19%, according to National Greenhouse Gas Inventory. Road transport accounts for more than three quarters of this, aviation is one eighth and shipping slightly less, while 70% of the road transport emissions are personal car use.

The detailed transport figures are referred to in Chapter 5, *Garage* but are summarised here. These detailed figures come from state-based transport surveys such as the SEQ Transport Survey.

82% of all travel undertaken by Australians is by private car.

The emissions of driving a car depend on its size and fuel efficiency. Australia has notably poor fuel efficiency because of lack of regulation. On average we produce 200g CO_2e per km travelled.

In the city we drive 40km/d on average; in rural areas we drive double that distance. The 80% of us who drive ourselves to work travel 17km each way, those who do not work drive around 23km for shopping and recreation. A small number of us, 7%, use public transport and around 10% walk, ride or use some other form of active transport.

The production of a tonne of steel produces 1.8t of CO_2e and the average Australian car is responsible for at least 8t of CO_2e during its manufacture. A detailed analysis reported by Mike Berners-Lee in *The Guardian* in the UK indicates that manufacturing cars produces between 5 and 20t of CO_2e depending on its size. Published figures in Australia are much lower but are primarily based on steel use and transport by ship.

We keep our cars for 10 years and produce about 30t of CO_2e driving them around each year. All up, our cars are responsible for at least 10kg CO_2e per day. That is almost one quarter of our total personal carbon footprint.

Air transport consumes most of its fuel in take-off, meaning that long-distance flights are more fuel efficient than short haul ones in the same plane. The passenger to plane weight ratio and the altitude at which planes fly also effect the final calculation.

We have used the figure for air freight emissions of 750g of CO_2e per kg per 1,000km.

Although there is little discussion of passenger air travel in this book, the comparative figure would be 1,170g of CO_2e per kg per 1,000km. This assumes 100kg per passenger including baggage.

Textiles

The global and Australian carbon emissions and water use of textile growth and production are provided in Chapter 3 *Bedroom*.

PERSONAL CARBON TARGET

To help visualise the positive impact that a particular action will take on your contribution to climate change, this book employs an original infographic, the Personal carbon target.

The base of the target is your per capita share of the greenhouse gases emitted by consumption of goods and services in Australia. That is 16.96 tonnes of CO_2e per year or 46kg/d. You can examine the calculations behind that in the Ready Reckoner, above. That is commonly known as your **carbon footprint** (see the Glossary).

The per capita footprint of various countries is visualised in the introduction of the book on page 4.

The target

The idea of achieving a personal two-tonne target is based on the Paris agreement to

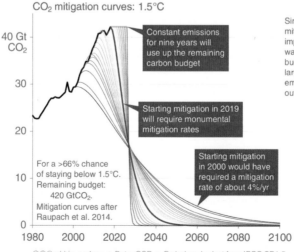

CO₂ mitigation curves: 1.5°C

Constant emissions for nine years will use up the remaining carbon budget

Starting mitigation in 2019 will require monumental mitigation rates

For a >66% chance of staying below 1.5°C. Remaining budget: 420 GtCO₂. Mitigation curves after Raupach et al. 2014.

Starting mitigation in 2000 would have required a mitigation rate of about 4%/yr

Since such steep mitigation is impossible, the only way to achieve this budget is with very large "negative" emissions: pulling CO₂ out of the atmosphere.

☺①②@robbie_andrew • Data: GCP • Emissions budget from IPCC SR1.5

keep global heating below two degrees. If our body temperature increases by two degrees we have a serious fever; any higher and we are in severe risk of death. Two degrees is now argued by many people as being unachievable, but all Federal government documents indicate a commitment to maintain this as the goal.

In 2014, the Australian Climate Change Authority indicated that a global target of 34Gt per year was the basis on which government policy should be formed, but up-to-date science using the same method indicates that this has now been reduced to 15Gt per year. We wasted six years emitting increased amounts of carbon, thereby increasing the sacrifices now required to meet the target.

With eight billion people on the planet that is a personal target of slightly less than two tonnes per year.

Clearly, we cannot do everything ourselves; we need governments to set energy policy and provide cheap efficient public transport, but it is important that we understand what our impact is in the overall context of limiting global heating. It is also important to understand why those most worried about climate chaos are calling for radical changes to energy policy and economic sacrifice, and those more worried about personal comfort advocate tolerating adaptation to larger temperature increases.

Making an impact

The impact of each tip is represented as a hole, shot in the Personal carbon target. The size of the hole represents the saving made if the average Australian in the 'typical'

Australian household as defined in the ready reckoner, were to follow the advice of the tip.

Replacing all your electricity consumption with power generated by solar photovoltaic cells installed on your roof, for example, would create a hole almost one sixth the size of the target. It eliminates nearly all the emissions from electricity use, which is over half of the emissions generated in the home, but that is only one third of the total household footprint. The panels, invertor and battery also add slightly to the footprint of the things you buy.

Some 'holes' will overlap. If I buy some rooftop solar and one energy-efficient electric heater at the same time, I will reduce my carbon footprint more than if I only did one tip, but not as much as I would think if I added together the maximum savings available from each tip. The 'holes' in the target overlap because some of the electricity savings from the heater involve renewable energy and some do not.

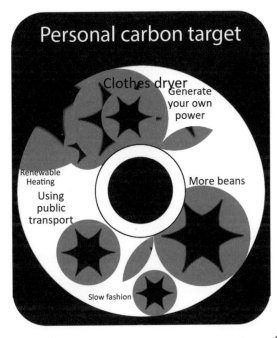

The typical or average household

When considering the impact that a tip would have on your life, it is important to think about the size of your carbon target compared to the average and the ways in which you differ from the typical Australian home. For example, if you already have rooftop photovoltaic panels, replacing your electric hot water service with a solar one is not going to have a great impact.

The location of the holes on the target is a visual reminder that only one third of the emissions represented by the target are emitted in the home; roughly another third is due to food and the final third due to all the other products. The impact of your food choices, for example, are all grouped together because those rips reduce the agricultural emissions released on your behalf and have very little impact on the household emissions.

The assumptions we make

Not only are the visualisations representative of the statistically typical home, they make assumptions about our behaviour.

The impact of Tip 1, An empty room does not need a light, assumes that we leave the lights on when we are not in the room about one sixth of the time (say one hour of the six hours we need the lights on). That is generous; we might behave worse than that, but we do not have comprehensive data on all Australian's light-switching habits and we do not want to overestimate the impact of any particular tip. Based on that assumption, turning them off every time we leave the room would save one sixth of the energy we use in lighting, therefore 0.16 (one sixth) x 0.06 (lighting as a fraction of electricity) x 0.23 (electricity as percentage of footprint) x 46kg/day or 120g per day.

Obviously we cannot detail the calculations behind every tip in this much detail, but the Ready Reckoner gives you the assumptions on which we base those calculations.

PERSONAL WATER TARGET

The concept of the Personal water target is very similar to that of the Personal carbon target, and the same warnings about averages and assumptions apply.

One thing that is radically different, though, is that the Personal water target represents the water used in the home because that is the figure widely promoted in the community and discussed in the media. For comparison purposes, and to examine the impact of food choices on your indirect consumption of water, we use the total water footprint, which has the Personal water target embedded in it, so that you can easily see the difference. The numbers used to calculate the total water footprint are explained in detail in the water section of the Ready Reckoner, section Σ of this chapter.

The key numbers for the Personal water target are 360 litres per day representing a large home with a swimming pool, well-watered lawns and no water restrictions applying; 200L/d which is the national average in the latest ABS Water Account; and 150L/d, which is a typical personal daily target during water restrictions.

These numbers compare to 100L/d, which is the target used in SEQ towns in early 2020 and 30L/d which is typical of the water allocated to each person per day on a sea-going yacht.

The tip in this book with the largest impact on your water usage is to process your greywater, but that is only meaningful if you use water in your garden. The typical Australian home uses one third (34%) of the 199L per day in the garden, a bit less than we use in the shower and the laundry. The impact of greywater is therefore given as 68L/d because that replaces the use of drinking water in the garden of a typical house. Even though the typical house could capture more greywater than that, it would not reduce overall water usage, though it would mean a greener than typical garden.

WORK-ENVIRONMENT-LIFE BALANCE (WELB)

The WELB combines the Personal carbon target and the Personal water target with four other indicators that show the impact it will have on your health and the health of the planet. The WELB is a web or radar diagram, used to represent balance and footprint in personal coaching and business strategy. The global and Australian footprints, compared on page 67 in Chapter 2 use a traditional approach where the size of the graph increases with the item being measured.

WORK ENVIRONMENT LIFE BALANCE

Time and money

The amount of time and money involved in carrying out any tip has been converted to hours per day and dollars per day. Because some tips will save time and money and others will require an investment of one or the other, the typical Australian household starts off in the middle of those axes. On the global axis, the amount of spare time in various countries as measured by UN and OECD surveys has been used.

Australians have two more spare hours each day than the global average, so the time axis is two hours long with the average Australian citizen 'resting' on zero and the amount of time taken each day to implement a tip shown as positive (green) or negative (red). A picnic might take four hours out of your day, but the benefits last for days, and you might only have a picnic once every two months. The impact of the picnic on your time budget has been given as eight minutes per day, which over one month equals four hours.

The average Australian wage was identified by the ABS as $89,128 per annum in May 2020 or $240/d. The global average is about $US10,000 ($AU1,429) or $40/d. We have six times the spending power of the global average.

Large investments in solar panels, cars or double glazing, for example, have been visualised by their initial cost over their lifetime minus the savings they provide over the same period. A $6,000 investment in solar panels with a guaranteed lifespan of 10 years represents an investment of $1.60 per day. An electric car that costs $15,000 more than its petrol-powered competitor represents an additional investment of $4.10 per day.

Body and soul

The measurement used to visualise the impact of behaving sustainability on the body and soul is based on a range of figures. The HILDA study, performed by Melbourne University and Roy Morgan Research for the Federal government, asks people how satisfied they are with life, and how connected they are with their neighbourhood.

On average, Australians score life satisfaction as 8 out of 10. There is some correlation with income, though the very rich are not any happier than the merely affluent.

On the other hand, Australians do not feel as connected with our community, giving a score of 7 out of 10. The literature indicates that connectedness correlates with mental health.

The Human Development Index collated by the United Nations Development Program combines income data with life expectancy and education to rank countries 'wellness'. That index gives Australia a rank of 6th of 198 countries measured and a score of 9.3 out of 10. By comparison China has a rank of 85/189 and a score of 7.5. Poorer African countries score 3.7 and similar.

The World Happiness Index, compiled by World Gallup Poll on behalf of the United Nations, gives similar results. Ideally, the cumulative impact of the tips would lead us toward the target in all areas of our life, what is likely though is that we will invest some time and money in reducing our carbon

footprint and get some benefit in our well-being as a result.

That is shown in the diagram here by the negative (red) area on the time and money axes and the green areas on the fire, water, body and soul axes.

As a result the WELB rates Australian's physical wellness as 9 out of 10 compared to a global average of 7 out of 10, and our mental wellness as 7 out of 10 compared to a global average of 5 out of 10.

Reading the WELB

To examine the impact of various tips or two compare two or more tips, we want to maintain the convention of the Personal carbon target and the Personal water target and show that smaller is better. For that reason, some of the axies have been reversed and so the average Australian footprint is a different shape.

The shape of the target is skewed out towards water because we have already restricted our daily usage significantly due to recent droughts. It is skewed in from carbon because we produce so much more greenhouse gas than we can afford.

Ideally, the cumulative impact of the tips would lead us toward the target in all areas of our life, what is likely though is that we will invest some time and money in reducing our carbon footprint significantly and getting some benefit in our well being as a result.

That is shown in the diagram here by the negative (red) area on the time and money axes and the green areas on the fire, water, body and soul axes.

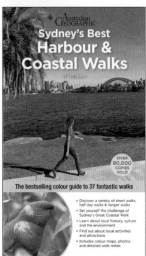

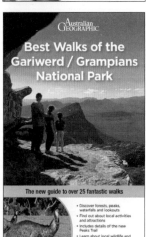

DISCOVER AUSTRALIA ON FOOT WITH AUSTRALIAN GEOGRAPHIC

Available from Australian Geographic and partner imprint Woodslane Press is a wide range of practical walking guides to cities and regions all over Australia.

- Sydney's Best Harbour & Coastal Walks
- Sydney's Best Bush Park & City Walks
- Great North Walk
- Blue Mountains Best Bushwalks
- Six Foot Track
- Best Walks of the Illawarra
- Best Walks of the Southern Highlands
- Best Walks of the Shoalhaven
- Canberra's Best Bush, Park & City Walks
- Walking & Cycling Canberra's Centenary Trail
- Melbourne's Best River, Bay and Lakeside Walks
- Best Walks East of Melbourne
- Best Walks of the Great Ocean Road

- Best Walks of the Gariwerd Grampians National Park
- Best Walks of Victoria's High Country
- Best River & Alpine Walks around Mt Kosciuszko
- Best Bush, Coast and Village Walks of South East Tasmania
- Brisbane's Best Bush, Bay & City Walks
- Best Village & Coastal Walks of the Sunshine Coast
- Best Walks around Cairns & the Tablelands
- Best Walks of the Red Centre
- Best Walks of the Top End
- Adelaide's Best Bush, Coast & City Walks
- Perth's Best Bush, Coast & City Walks

For more information go to:

woodslane.com.au/promotion/walkguides

australiangeographic.com.au